WAR WITH RUSSIA?

T0059485

Other Books by Stephen F. Cohen

The Great Purge Trial (Co-Editor)
Bukharin and the Bolshevik Revolution: A Political Biography
The Soviet Union Since Stalin (Co-Editor)
An End to Silence: Uncensored Opinion in the Soviet Union (Editor)
Rethinking the Soviet Experience: Politics and History Since 1917
Sovieticus: American Perceptions and Soviet Realities
Voices of Glasnost: Interviews With Gorbachev's Reformers
(With Katrina vanden Heuvel)
Failed Crusade: America and the Tragedy of Post-Communist Russia
Soviet Fates and Lost Alternatives: From Stalinism to the New Cold War
The Victims Return: Survivors of the Gulag After Stalin

WAR WITH RUSSIA?

FROM PUTIN & UKRAINE TO TRUMP & RUSSIAGATE

MEMORIAL EDITION

STEPHEN F. COHEN

HOT BOOKS
an imprint of Skyhorse Publishing, Inc.
New York, NY

Visit our website at www.hotbookspress.com.

10 9 8 7 6 5 4

Library of Congress Cataloging-in-Publication Data is available on file.

ISBN: 978-1-5107-5546-8
eBook: 978-1-5107-4582-7

Cover design by Brian Peterson

Printed in the United States of America

With loving gratitude to Katrina, who, while "not fully" agreeing with the contents and enduring some slings and arrows, made this book possible.

Table of Contents

PREFACE TO MEMORIAL EDITION

THOSE CLOSE TO STEPHEN COHEN KNEW he had a CD with a dozen versions of the song "My Way," from Billy Bragg to Frank Sinatra. It was natural, then, to title the 2021 book paying tribute to Steve's life and work, *His Way*.[1]

Steve's death inspired an outpouring of condolences and tributes in various fields and across numerous nations. A selection of these tributes is included in this memorial edition of *War With Russia?* Even two year later it's difficult to grasp both the full impact of losing such a committed American scholar as well as the scope of his contributions to history, teaching, and the course of US-Russia relations.

Steve's work often led friends and foes to address what set the historian and political analyst apart from others: his disagreement with the notion that the USSR's creation in 1917 was illegitimate; his discovery of the true history of Nikolai Bukharin; his influence on the architects of perestroika; and his theory that the Soviet Union was not doomed to end but could have been reformed instead.

Steve was a public intellectual, taking his often controversial, revisionist historical views of the Soviet Union, later Russia, to op-ed pages, the TV airwaves—and the columns in this collection. There was his view of New Economic Policy (NEP) as an alternative to Stalinism, his work chronicling the fates of dissidents who had returned from the gulag, and his unwavering support of the creation and development of the GULAG State Historical Museum. There was also Steve's passion for history's truths, his talent as an educator and lecturer, and his extraordinary friendship with former Soviet leader Mikhail Gorbachev. Later, he wrote critically of Boris Yeltsin, the

---

1 Katrina vanden Heuvel and Gennady Bordyugov, *His Way* (Moscow: AIRO-XXI, 2021).

looting of the Russian economy, the creation of rapacious oligarchs, and the de-democratization that began with Yeltsin—not Putin.

His primary academic field was the study of alternatives—options and consequences of decisions made at inflection points in history. His life, too, had choices and inflection points. In the spring of 1959, he had to decide between going on a trip to Pamplona or a tour of five cities in the Soviet Union, the sleeping giant just beginning to awaken and recover after decades of state terror, as he described it. Thirty years later, Steve was about to decline the chance to speak about alternatives in Soviet history at the 1989 May Day celebrations on Red Square, only to heed the urgings of his Russian friends and accept the invitation. "It was fate," he reflected in an interview for a Harriman Institute oral history project.

Steve was an independent thinker; the tiresome accusation that he was anyone's puppet was risible. He unwaveringly opposed several Cold wars, as a historian and a citizen. Many of the twists of his life were interconnected but not predetermined, and in the end were shaped by his determination. It took courage to denounce the Washington politicians who, impelled by triumphalism, expanded NATO eastward to Russia's borders, fomented anti-Russian hysteria in America, and demonized Vladimir Putin. It is painfully prescient today to read Steve's insights, analyses—and warnings. As we stand on the precipice of war with Russia, Steve's informed columns, assembled here in *War With Russia?* are especially relevant. His stances on Georgia, Ukraine, and Crimea led to baseless smears and public harassment. Steve was ostracized in academia and the media, yet he was prepared for these unexpected turns and stayed true to his path. Steve may not have seen his insights prevail, but his work and life offer a legacy of thought and integrity which I believe will withstand the test of time.

Katrina vanden Heuvel
February 2022

CONDOLENCES, TRIBUTES, AND APPRECIATION

Dear Katrina,

Please accept my sincere condolences on Steve's passing. He was one of the closest people to me in his views and understanding of the enormous events that occurred in the late 1980s in Russia and changed the world. Steve was a brilliant historian and a man of democratic convictions. He loved Russia, the Russian intelligentsia, and believed in our country's future. I always considered Steve and you my true friends. During perestroika and all the subsequent years, I felt your understanding and unwavering support. I thank you both. Dear Katrina, I feel deep sympathy for your grief, and I mourn together with you and Nika. Blessed memory for Steve.

I embrace you, Mikhail Gorbachev
19.09.2020

Mikhail Gorbachev general secretary of the Communist Party of the Soviet Union (1985–91) and president of the Soviet Union (1990–91).

Dear Katrina,

I was very sorry to learn yesterday of the death of Steve and wish to send you my sincere condolences on this sad loss. It was only a few weeks ago that I heard that Steve was gravely ill, and that came as a shock. He seemed so irrepressible and indestructible. Although the last time I saw both of you was, I'm fairly sure, at the 2015 ASEEES conference in Philadelphia in 2015, I always valued meeting Steve, whether in Moscow (as happened more than once) or every few years in the US. We didn't concur on everything. I am more critical of developments in the Russian political system during the Putin presidency, but I think that Steve was right in his vigorous criticism of the Yeltsin years. He was right also in noting the double standards that were applied when Russian foreign policy was condemned, and in showing the extent to which this was in reaction to Western disregard for Russian opinion and legitimate Russian interests in the post-perestroika years. Steve was likewise absolutely right to criticize American triumphalist accounts of the Cold War's ending. It would not have ended when it did, and in the peaceful and negotiated way it did, had any member of Chernenko's Politburo other than Mikhail Gorbachev succeeded the second last general secretary of the CPSU. As you know, I share your and Steve's high regard for Gorbachev and for his historic role in Russian and world politics. Steve was an important presence in Soviet and Russian historiography and as a public intellectual. His work had an influence not only in the West but in Russia, especially during the perestroika period with the translation of his Bukharin book. I know that his more recent books have also been published in Russian, but the time of greatest impact was in the second half of the 1980s. Those were years in which books and articles became major events in Russia, as people probed the limits of the new freedoms. Interest in ideas and in filling in the blank pages in the writing of Russian history has never been higher before or since. Steve was a stimulating scholar, an excellent writer, and a courageous controversialist. We always need people prepared to challenge the conventional wisdom. In the current political polarization in the United States, there is surely more conventional ignorance on the Trump and conservative side, but also too much conventional wisdom and unquestioned assumptions (including those which tend toward demonizing Russia) on the liberal side. Steve was in neither camp. I did not always agree with him, but I respected his refusal to bow to political or intellectual fashion.

With all good wishes, and with great sympathy at this difficult time,

Archie
September 19, 2020

Archie Brown is a British political scientist and historian. He is an emeritus professor of politics at the University of Oxford and an emeritus fellow at St. Anthony's College, Oxford, where he served as a professor of politics and director of St. Anthony's Russian and East European Centre. He is a Fellow of the British Academy.

The Man Who Knew Russia: A Tribute to Stephen F. Cohen
Bill Bradley

I knew Steve Cohen for over fifty years from my time with the New York Knicks (he loved basketball) to the US Senate (he loved politics) to business (it couldn't hold his attention). He was a public intellectual with core convictions informed by history. His magisterial biography of Nikolai Bukharin established his academic reputation. When I read it in the 1970s, it changed the way I thought about the origins of the Soviet Union. For Steve, ideas lived and language made a difference. He often marshaled his great clarity to challenge the status quo. Whether he was smuggling Solzhenitsyn novels into the Soviet Union in the 1970s, advising CBS News during the Gorbachev years, pleading with everyone to avoid a second Cold War or lecturing to a rapt class, he always expressed what he saw as the truth. Above all, he felt the Russian spirit, the pain of Russian history, and the irrepressible humanity of the Russian people.

As a US senator, I traveled often to Russia during the 1980s when Mikhail Gorbachev was in power. Steve saw Gorbachev as having potentially a seminal role in the history of the world, and he made no bones about it. With literally hundreds of Russian friends in the arts, journalism, academia, and government, Steve encouraged me to get to know the Russian people and the Russian land. So for six years between 1985 and 1992, I would travel the country from Moscow/St. Petersburg to Irkutsk with just one staff member and a friend of Steve's who worked for the US Information Agency and was a Ph.D. in Russian culture and language. We would often have meetings with Soviet officials in their offices and then we would go out and meet people in the streets or subways, at literary societies, and around Russian kitchen tables. On one of these trips, I asked a woman exiting the Tashkent subway what Perestroika and Glasnost meant to her. She paused before replying, "A new life for my children."

When I came back from those trips, I would have lunch with Secretary of State George Shultz and tell him what I had seen, heard, and felt, which he said was much different from those things that the CIA was telling him. Through many sources, Shultz recognized that Gorbachev was a special leader, convinced Reagan of it and the Cold War ended.

When Boris Yeltsin succeeded Gorbachev and the economy went into a freefall with inflation at 1,000 percent and a poverty rate of over 30 percent, Steve would say that Russia needed an FDR and instead got a Milton Friedman, leading to the rise of a kleptocracy.

Any good politician knows that when someone is down you call them up and tell them you're with them and that you know they'll get through the difficult times. The United States didn't do that with Russia. We sent free-market ideologues without any understanding of Russian history and with little appreciation for the emotional trauma and wounded pride that the end of the Soviet Union brought to Russia. When the Russian intelligentsia offered advice on how we could work together in the world we just kept on doing what Russians felt was contrary to their interests—NATO expansion, missile defense, Iraq, Kosovo, and Libya.

As we disregarded Russian fears and ignored the chance for a true partnership, Steve worried about the resumption of hostile relations between our two countries and possibly a new Cold War. He held out hope that America would come to its senses. That view increasingly was not popular among the American foreign policy establishment and the media. In fact, in Steve's last seven years, the *New York Times* rejected every op-ed he submitted. Some people even labeled him "Putin's apologist." Those comments hurt Steve deeply because he was first and always an American but one who could appreciate the legacy of Russian history and the opportunity that existed when tectonic plates shifted. Above all, he knew that it took courage and real leadership at the highest levels to create something new.

The relation between Steve and Gorbachev extended to their families. Gorbachev once told Steve that Steve's relationship with his wife Katrina reminded Gorbachev of the one he had had with his wife Raisa, who was his inseparable soulmate until she died in 1999. And when Steve's number two daughter, Nika, developed a consuming interest in both basketball and Russia, she honored her father's roots in Kentucky and his contribution to the world.

For those of us who knew and cared for him, we will carry with us the memory of a good man who tried to make a difference on a very large stage and who never let the slings and arrows of criticism slow him from calling it as he saw it.

Bill Bradley is a former member of the New York Knicks, a former US Senator, and a presidential candidate in 2000.

Published: The National Interest. 2020, October 9. https://nationalinte rest.org/ feature/man-who-knew-russia-tribute-stephen-f-cohen-170426

NATIONAL FIGURE
YANNI KOTSONIS

Steve was hired to NYU after his time at Princeton. He was a masterful lecturer who packed in 400 students each time he taught his survey of Soviet history, and he helped keep alive Soviet and Russian studies at a time when interest was falling. I admired that. For some of this time I was his chair in the Russian Department, and I worked with him regularly when we founded the Jordan Center and I became the director. I knew him socially.

He was a marvelous colleague, helpful to the Russian Department, to the Jordan Center, and to his colleagues. I can't recall a time when he turned us down. I want this to be known and appreciated. Steve, could you speak at a panel on Russian politics? Of course, he always replied with his gravelly voice, without caveat. Steve, can we arrange a larger public event on Russian politics? Yes, and he brought with him ambassadors and senators and consultants, unprompted. Steve, would you mind retiring so that we can hire a full-time historian of the USSR? Sure, but just make sure they use it for that purpose, otherwise I'll stay and keep the seat warm. I've got your back. I just need an office for my books. A few years later: Steve, about that office... No problem, when do you need me to vacate? Steve, we could use some funding for our MA students. How much? Steve, I have a donor who wants to meet you to seal the deal. Let's have Greek, you order, and make sure you bring your father. Steve, do you have a light? He always did.

He had that manner: he sounded brusque unless you were from New York, which he wasn't; he was proud to be "a boy from Kentucky." I guess he may have sounded abrupt or even abrasive. As I got to know him, I realized that he was sincere and well meaning. He had convictions and he argued them. Even in private conversation about third parties with whom he disagreed, he was not contemptuous. He disagreed. It was about ideas. In his famous exchanges with Richard Pipes, he managed to be polite to Richard Pipes.

He carried with him a permanent sense of beleaguerment, and it is true that there were long periods when he was beleaguered. In the 1970s and 1980s, he was an American leftist who thought he was facing a solid wall of conservative critics of the USSR. More recently, he was the rare public intellectual who did not discuss Russia in shrill, contemptuous, and categorical terms. This did not make him less outspoken in public; but he often sat a little to the side at a panel as if to emphasize that he was not part of the orthodoxy (though for a long time he was), hunched and inquiring shoulders asking if he was entitled to his opinions even as his voice carried on with his irrepressible confidence. In private he assumed the look of the enfant terrible, with a mischievous grin, assuming or insisting that his interlocutor agreed with him and was complicit, inviting you to join in a lonely but worthy cause. It made you want to go along for the ride.

He was a liberal to be sure, and he and his wife Katrina invested in basketball clubs in inner cities; Steve played basketball, too. It's his politics for which he was most known, renowned, and notorious. I first read his books, mainly his biography of Bukharin, as an undergraduate in Montreal in the 1980s, and I understood them as a voice of the left. He consolidated a view of the Bolshevik Party and of the USSR as heterogeneous and socially based; he paved the way for a generation of historians though he himself was not a historian. Not all socialism was Stalinism, and even Soviet socialism was not always Stalinism. In hindsight I realize that Steve's texts were radically liberal, an American understanding of the left, more about pluralism and egalitarianism than about class as such.

Then came the 1990s—around when I got to know him—and the social cataclysm of privatization, the declining international standing of the Russian Federation, and finally the international isolation of Russia after 2012 and the obsessive identification of one country with one person, Putin. Somehow conversations about Russia evolved around Putin and civil rights—fair enough—but hardly at all around the tens of millions rendered poor and insecure and who made Putin possible. I think we all dealt with it in different ways; by the mid-2010s many of us went quiet, and I avoided Facebook at all costs.

Not so Steve. Steve had flourished in a different era, and he was something of a national figure with his regular appearances on the CBS *Evening News* with Dan Rather, something of the national interpreter of things Soviet and then Russian. He had an excellent mind, and he was a master of rhetoric. He could speak compellingly to an audience of colleagues and intelligibly to a TV audience at 6:30 p.m. Over time US media attention on Russia declined. And while many of us went quiet, Steve persisted and sought that national audience just about anywhere he could find it. By the 2010s, the problem was not simply that media attention had declined; any new attention was vapid and simplistic. It was hard to have a conversation about Russia without centering it on Putin; from 2016, Russia was only about election interference. Steve insisted that this was a large country, still geopolitically important, and we would ignore or misunderstand it at our peril. There had to be more to it than what we read in the *Times* or the *New Yorker*, which is a narrative of Putin vs the intelligentsia who knew certain journalists—not wrong, but shockingly narrow. Narcissism comes in many forms.

By 2014 or so he was very much a lone voice, in the academy and in the media, and the invitations were fewer. In Russia he was a star, because he was one of the few remaining American public intellectuals who did not make a career of trashing Russia or reducing Russia to one man and his critics; even Russian critics of the regime found in him a voice. He argued, and I think he was right, that we had adopted a new orthodoxy, to the effect that Russia/Putin was inexcusable (fine) but also not in need of serious explanation (not at all fine); and to even explain it in any other terms was retrograde. This was a pity, because whatever one might think of his opinions, he was intelligent. We needed a debate or, as he would have put it, there can't be just one line. I was very pleased to offer him a forum at the Jordan Center. I wish more institutions had done the same: it's better to have the argument than dismiss with a guffaw. Even as Steve's opinions became more singular relative to the academy and the media, my successors Joshua Tucker and Anne Lounsbery insisted that he be given a place to speak—quite brave and correct, it seems to me, especially given that they disagreed.

By that time, in ways that are complicated, Steve had become more of the voice of Russia's image internationally than of the left. Or it was a certain kind of American left. The common criticism of Steve was that he was identifying with Russia as it is now constituted, forced to defend what he might otherwise not have defended. There's a bigger story here about the American left in relation to Russia, I think, and Steve was a part of it. Should Russia be measured by the standards of a progressive (in which case, опять двойка), or did it suffice that a country, any country, had the capacity to act as a check on the US globally (Steve believed that Russia had that capacity). It's a conversation we did not have, and I regret that.

If you knew him, he was a dear.

Yanni Kotsonis is Professor of History and Professor of Russian and Slavic Studies at NYU.
Published: 2020, September 21 www.jordanrussiacenter.org/news/stephen-cohen-1938-2020-professor-emeritus-nyu-russian-and-slavic-studies

STEPHEN COHEN OBITUARY
JONATHAN STEELE

US historian who argued that the Soviet Union could have been reformed and need not have ended when it did.

The scholar of Russian history and politics Stephen Cohen, who has died aged 81 of lung cancer, challenged the orthodox western analysis of the Soviet Union and post-Soviet affairs. In his magisterial book *Soviet Fates and Lost Alternatives* (2009), he demolished the claim that Leninism led inevitably to totalitarian dictatorship under Stalin and that the Soviet system of one-party rule and state ownership of property could never be reformed.

He cited three periods when developments could have gone differently from what actually happened: in the late 1920s, when debates within the Politburo came to a head over the New Economic Policy (NEP), which allowed for private enterprise and ownership of land and property; in the early 60s, when Nikita Khrushchev launched key political reforms; and in 1990 and 1991, after Mikhail Gorbachev introduced a mixed economy and social democratic solutions based on political pluralism in place of the Communist party's monopoly of power.

With his sense of humour, gravelly voice and iconoclastic arguments, Cohen entranced generations of students from his academic perch at Princeton University for the three decades from 1968, in which he rose to be professor of politics and Russian studies, and then at New York University (1998–2011).

He wrote a column in *The Nation*, under the byline Sovieticus from 1982 to 1987 and in recent years hosted a weekly radio broadcast on Russian-American relations, which he feared were leading to a new cold war. He blamed Bill Clinton and policymakers in Washington for failing to include Russia in a new European order after the Soviet Union came to an end and for expanding Nato eastwards in a spirit of "we won" triumphalism. George W. Bush and Barack Obama compounded the failure by siting US anti-ballistic missile systems on Russia's borders.

During the Soviet period Cohen was unusual among western specialists on Russia in having friends among dissidents as well as reformist intellectuals in the Moscow thinktanks. His book *The Victims Return* was based on interviews with dozens of survivors of Stalin's labour camps about their problems in returning to freedom.

Amid the new freedoms permitted by Gorbachev after 1985, Cohen and his wife, Katrina vanden Heuvel, the publisher and editor of *The Nation*, made frequent long trips to Moscow and got to know the new Soviet leader personally. At one of the last May Day celebrations in Red Square, Gorbachev invited them both to stand beside the Lenin mausoleum to watch the parade. On Cohen's death the former Soviet president sent Vanden Heuvel a tribute about her husband, saying: "He was one of the closest people to me in his views and understanding of the enormous events that occurred in the late 80s in Russia and changed the world. Steve was a brilliant historian and a man of democratic convictions. He loved Russia, the Russian intelligentsia and believed in our country's future."

A Russian version of Cohen's 1973 biography of Nikolai Bukharin, a brilliant young Bolshevik who championed the NEP in the 20s, was later published in Moscow and had a wide readership amid new interest in Bukharin's liberalising ideas. Gorbachev told Cohen he had learned much from the book.

Discussion of the NEP was banned in the Soviet Union after Stalin changed course and embarked on the forced collectivization of agriculture. Bukharin was arrested and shot after long interrogations and a show trial in Moscow.

During his 70s researches, Cohen had tracked down and met Bukharin's widow, Anna Larina, and they became friends. She appointed Cohen as proxy to examine the archives for her husband's papers.

Born in Indianapolis, Stephen was the older of two children of Marvin Cohen and his wife, Ruth (nee Frand). His father owned a jewellery shop and a golf course in Hollywood. Stephen went to school in Owensboro, Kentucky, and then to Pine Crest school, Fort Lauderdale, Florida, which he left in 1956.

As an undergraduate at Indiana University, he went to Britain on a study-abroad scheme and then on a 30-day trip to the Soviet Union. Intrigued by what he saw, he abandoned plans to become a professional golfer and took up Russian studies. He earned a bachelor's degree in economics and public policy (1960) and a master's in Russian studies (1962). He went onto Columbia University and gained a PhD in 1969 with a dissertation on Bukharin's economic thinking.

In 1962 he married an opera singer, Lynn Blair, but the marriage ended in divorce. He and Katrina married in 1988.

It was Cohen's early work on Bukharin that led him to the themes that became central to his preoccupations: was the Soviet Union reformable and why did it come to an end? He did not agree with the consensus among western analysts who, with the advantage of hindsight since 1991, claimed that the Soviet Union was doomed to die. He took particular issue with the view that the Soviet Union had come into existence in an illegitimate way in 1917 and had committed so many crimes that it could never become a democracy.

Cohen called himself a "boy from Kentucky" who had accepted segregation until adulthood. He suggested that the gap between the Soviet Union's professed ideals and Soviet reality was comparable to the long US history of tolerating slavery and discrimination while professing democracy. If the US could change, so could the Soviet Union.

Cohen challenged other arguments. To those who said the Soviet system was unreformable because the communist ruling class would never permit changes that threatened its power, Cohen pointed out that Gorbachev's main reforms, the introduction of contested elections and the abolition of the party's monopoly of power, were ratified in the politburo, central committee, and two-party congresses.

To those who argued that the Soviet system was swept away by a popular revolution from below, Cohen replied that there was no such anti-Soviet movement. The evidence from public opinion surveys up to 1991 was that many Soviet citizens continued to oppose free-market capitalism and to support basic features of the Soviet system, such as public ownership of large industries.

As for the fate of the multi-national federation, Cohen argued that as late as November 1991, during negotiations with Gorbachev, Boris Yeltsin, the Russian president, was expressing support for a new kind of union. Three weeks later he invited the presidents of Ukraine and Belarus to join him in declaring the Soviet Union dead. So it was destroyed by personal ambition in a coup d'etat. It did not implode or fall apart.

Cohen's last book, *War With Russia?*, published last year, was a collection of articles and broadcasts from the previous five years during the time when US-Russian relations descended into name-calling. He described himself as an "American patriot" who wanted to see a partnership between the US and Russia to tackle common threats, such as international terrorism.

He passionately opposed what he felt was blind anti-Russian hysteria and the demonization of Vladimir Putin. "In the three cases widely given as examples of Putin's 'aggression' the evidence points to US-led instigation," he wrote. The proxy US-Russian war in Georgia in 2008 was started by the US-backed Georgian president who had been encouraged to aspire to NATO membership. The crisis and war in Ukraine resulted from Washington's long-standing effort to bring that country into NATO despite Ukraine's shared civilization with Russia.

Putin's intervention in Syria was done on a valid premise: to defeat the Islamic State group after Obama refused to join Russia in an anti-Isis alliance.

Cohen was often denounced as "Putin's Number One American apologist." Yanni Kotsonis, a colleague at New York University, summed up Cohen's life differently: "He was one of the few remaining American public intellectuals who did not make a career of trashing Russia or reducing Russia to one man and his critics."

Cohen is survived by Katrina, his children, Andrew, and Alexandra, from his first marriage, and Nicola from his second; four grandchildren, and a sister, Judith.

Jonathan Steele is a British journalist, columnist, and writer. He has worked for the Guardian since 1965.

Published: Guardian. 2020. October 13: https://www.theguardian.com/education/2020/oct/13/stephen-cohen-obituary

STEPHEN COHEN HAS DIED. REMEMBER HIS URGENT WARNINGS AGAINST THE NEW COLD WAR
CAITLIN JOHNSTONE

Stephen F Cohen, the renowned American scholar on Russia and leading authority on US-Russian relations, has died of lung cancer at the age of 81.

As one of the precious few western voices of sanity on the subject of Russia while everyone else has been frantically flushing their brains down the toilet, this is a real loss. I myself have cited Cohen's expert analysis many times in my own work, and his perspective has played a formative role in my understanding of what's really going on with the monolithic cross-partisan manufacturing of consent for increased western aggressions against Moscow.

In a world that is increasingly confusing and awash with propaganda, Cohen's death is a blow to humanity's desperate quest for clarity and understanding.

I don't know how long Cohen had cancer. I don't know how long he was aware that he might not have much time left on this earth. What I do know is he spent much of his energy in his final years urgently trying to warn the world about the rapidly escalating danger of nuclear war, which in our strange new reality he saw as in many ways completely unprecedented.

The last of the many books Cohen authored was 2019's *War With Russia?*, detailing his ideas on how the complex multi-front nature of the post-2016 cold war escalations against Moscow combines with Russiagate and other factors to make it in some ways more dangerous even than the most dangerous point of the previous cold war.

"We're in a new cold war with Russia that is much more dangerous than the preceding cold war for various reasons," Cohen told *The Young Turks* in 2017. "One is that there are at least three cold war fronts that are fraught with hot war: that would be Ukraine, that would be the Baltic Black Sea region where NATO is undertaking an unprecedented military buildup on Russia's border, and of course in Syria, where American and Russian aircraft are flying in the same airspace. And I would add to those three cold war fronts what is now called Russiagate, because the accusation that Trump needs to be impeached because he's somehow a Russian agent so distorts and cripples the possibility of the White House making Russia policy that I think it's a cold war front."

Cohen repeatedly points to the most likely cause of a future nuclear war: not one that is planned but one which erupts intense, complex situations where anything could happen in the chaos and confusion as a result of misfire, miscommunication or technical malfunction, as nearly happened many times during the last cold war.

"I think this is the most dangerous moment in American-Russian relations, at least since the Cuban missile crisis," Cohen told *Democracy Now!* in 2017. "And arguably, it's more dangerous, because it's more complex. Therefore, we—and then, meanwhile, we have in Washington these—and, in my judgment, factless accusations that Trump has somehow been compromised by the Kremlin. So, at this worst moment in American-Russian relations, we have an American president who's being politically crippled by the worst imaginable—it's unprecedented. Let's stop and think. No American president has ever been accused, essentially, of treason. This is what we're talking about here, or that his associates have committed treason."

"Imagine, for example, John Kennedy during the Cuban missile crisis," Cohen added. "Imagine if Kennedy had been accused of being a secret Soviet Kremlin agent. He would have been crippled. And the only way he could have proved he wasn't was to have launched a war against the Soviet Union. And at that time, the option was nuclear war."

"A recurring theme of my recently published book *War With Russia?* is that the new Cold War is more dangerous, more fraught with hot war, than the one we survived," Cohen wrote last year. "Histories of the 40-year US-Soviet Cold War tell us that both sides came to understand their mutual responsibility for the conflict, a recognition that created political space for the constant peacekeeping negotiations, including nuclear arms control agreements, often known as détente. But as I also chronicle in the book, today's American Cold Warriors blame only Russia, specifically 'Putin's Russia,' leaving no room or incentive for rethinking any US policy toward post-Soviet Russia since 1991."

"Finally, there continues to be no effective, organized American opposition to the new Cold War," Cohen added. "This too is a major theme of my book and another reason why this Cold War is more dangerous than was its predecessor. In the 1970s and 1980s, advocates of détente were well-organized, well-funded, and well-represented, from grassroots politics and universities to think tanks, mainstream media, Congress, the State Department, and even the White House. Today there is no such opposition anywhere."

"A major factor is, of course, 'Russiagate'," Cohen continued. "As evidenced in the sources I cite above, much of the extreme American Cold War advocacy we witness today is a mindless response to President Trump's pledge to find ways to 'cooperate with Russia' and to the still-unproven allegations generated by it. Certainly, the Democratic Party is not an opposition party in regard to the new Cold War."

"Détente with Russia has always been a fiercely opposed, crisis-ridden policy pursuit, but one manifestly in the interests of the United States and the world," Cohen wrote in another essay last year. "No American president can achieve it without substantial bipartisan support at home, which Trump manifestly lacks. What kind of catastrophe will it take—in Ukraine, the Baltic region, Syria, or somewhere on Russia's electric grid—to shock US Democrats and others out of what has been called, not unreasonably, their Trump Derangement Syndrome, particularly in the realm of American national security? Meanwhile, the Bulletin of Atomic Scientists has recently reset its Doomsday Clock to two minutes before midnight."

And now Stephen Cohen is dead, and that clock is inching ever closer to midnight. The Russiagate psyop that he predicted would pressure Trump to advance dangerous cold war escalations with no opposition from the supposed opposition party has indeed done exactly that with nary a peep of criticism from either partisan faction of the political/media class. Cohen has for years been correctly predicting this chilling scenario which now threatens the life of every organism on earth, even while his own life was nearing its end.

And now the complex cold war escalations he kept urgently warning us about have become even more complex with the addition of nuclear-armed China to the multiple fronts the US-centralized empire has been plate-spinning its brinkmanship upon, and it is clear from the ramping up of anti-China propaganda since last year that we are being prepped for those aggressions to continue to increase.

We should heed the dire warnings that Cohen spent his last breaths issuing. We should demand a walk-back of these insane imperialist aggressions which benefit nobody and call for détente with Russia and China. We should begin creating an opposition to this world-threatening flirtation with Armageddon before it is too late. Every life on this planet may well depend on our doing so.

Stephen Cohen is dead, and we are marching toward the death of everything. God help us all.

Caitlin Johnstone is a reader-supported independent journalist from Melbourne, Australia. Her political writings can be found on Medium and on her Facebook page, facebook.com/CaitlinAJohnstone.

Published: 2020. September 19. https://caityjohnstone.medium.com/stephen-cohen-has-died-remember-his-urgent-warnings-against-the-new-cold-war-cf6d4c844dd

To My Readers

THIS BOOK IS UNLIKE OTHERS I have published. Above all, it evolved during the years since 2014 when US-Russian relations were becoming more dangerous than they had ever been—and then made even worse by the allegations known as Russiagate. How this happened and what these unprecedented realities mean are ongoing themes in the pages that follow.

War With Russia? is also different in another respect. Over the years, I have written several kinds of books for other scholars and general readers—biography, narrative and interpretive political history, collections of essays and columns. The contents of this volume, however, were not originally intended to be a book. Nor were the words initially written. They began as radio broadcasts.

In 2014, the host of *The John Batchelor Show*, a popular nation-wide news program based at WABC AM in New York City, offered me a weekly segment on Tuesdays at 10 pm for one hour—about 40 minutes of discussion apart from commercial breaks. I had previously known John, a novelist and historian, and considered him to be one of the most erudite, intellectual, and, despite his formal role as a "conservative," ecumenical hosts in American talk radio. I accepted.

There was an equally important consideration. I had been arguing for years—very much against the American political-media grain—that a new US-Russian Cold War was unfolding, driven primarily by politics in Washington, not in Moscow. For this perspective, I had been largely excluded from influential print, broadcast, and cable outlets where I had previously been welcomed.

Virtually alone among major US media figures, John Batchelor—whose show has some 2.7 million listeners a week across the United States as well as 5 million downloaded podcasts a month here and abroad—evidently agreed with my general perspective, or at least thought it important enough to follow. "The New US-Russian Cold War" became, and remains, the rubric of our broadcasts, though subjects sometimes range more widely.

Our procedure changed over the years. Initially, John and I broadcast live, but due to our schedules began taping the night's discussion around 7 pm, when we already had the US and Russian "news" of the day. From the beginning, the podcast was posted the next day on the website (TheNation.com) of *The Nation* magazine, where I had been a contributor for many years. In 2014-2015, because I was writing articles for the magazine, the podcast was accompanied by only a brief paragraph listing the topics of the broadcast. Beginning in January 2016, as the new Cold War grew more perilous, I began writing longer commentaries expanding on each of my contributions to the Batchelor program—I did so very quickly overnight, sometimes with little regard for literary polish—and posting them with the podcast.

Inadvertently, I became a weekly web columnist, resuming an experiment in scholarly journalism I had undertaken in the 1980s in a monthly column, "Sovieticus," for *The Nation*. Then and now again, I wanted to provide essential historical context missing in news reports and analysis. Most of the weekly broadcasts and my commentaries—John and I skipped a few weeks due to holidays or scheduling problems on my part—were done in New York City, but some where I occasionally found myself on Tuesdays, from my hometown in Kentucky to Moscow.

Part I of this book is composed of four abridged articles I wrote for *The Nation* in 2014 and 2015. All of the articles in the Prologue and sections II, III, and IV are selected from almost 150 of my web "columns." Except for the Prologue, written in late 2018, they appear in chronological order as an analytical narrative of ongoing events. The date under each title is the day it was posted at TheNation.com. The commentaries appear here largely as posted, though for the book I polished the language somewhat, added some clarifying information, and combined a few related commentaries into one or two.

I also made some deletions in order to avoid unnecessary repetition. But repetition of large themes and ongoing subjects became unavoidable, indeed necessary, for the purpose of my weekly commentaries—and of this book: to make accessible to general readers an alternative, dissenting narrative of what I think are among the most fateful developments of our time. Whether I have succeeded or not is for readers to judge.

Quite a few writers in mainstream publications disliked what I was writing. Their agitated responses were noted in a November 24, 2017 feature article about me in *The Chronicle Review*, the magazine supplement of The Chronicle of Higher Education. It was subtitled "The Most Controversial Russia Expert in America." My scholarly work—my biography of Nikolai Bukharin and essays collected in *Rethinking the Soviet Experience* and *Soviet Fates and Lost Alternatives*, for example—has always been controversial because it has been what scholars term "revisionist"—reconsiderations, based on new research and perspectives, of prevailing interpretations of Soviet and post-Soviet Russian history.

But the "controversy" surrounding me since 2014, mostly in reaction to the contents of this book, has been different—inspired by usually vacuous, defamatory assaults on me as "Putin's No. 1 American Apologist," "Best Friend," and the like. I never respond specifically to these slurs because they offer no truly substantive criticism of my arguments, only ad hominem attacks. Instead, I argue, as readers will see in the first section, that I am a patriot of American national security, that the orthodox policies my assailants promote are gravely endangering our security, and that therefore we—I and others they assail—are patriotic heretics. Here too readers can judge.

I should add that emails and letters I received over the years from listeners and readers lauding my commentaries, for which I remain grateful, far out-numbered the public slurs. But slurring any Americans who think differently about US policy toward Russia has silenced too many skeptics and contributed to another theme of this book—a new and more dangerous Cold War without any real public debate in our mainstream politics or media.

Part of the animus against me seems to be due to my criticism of mainstream media malpractice in covering Russia, yet another recurring subject in the pages that follow. As I explained in a previous book, *Failed Crusade: America and the Tragedy of Post-Communist Russia* (2000), readers should not mistake my media criticism for ivy-tower resentment or contempt.

On the contrary, I have long combined my vocation as a university scholar with my own contributions to mainstream journalism. So much that in the late 1970s, while I was a tenured Princeton professor, the *New York Times* offered me a position as one of its correspondents in Moscow. (I declined for family reasons and because I sensed that big changes in the Soviet Union were still some years away.) Moreover, my subsequent *Nation* "Sovieticus" column was frequently reprinted in influential newspapers. And from the late 1980s, I was for many years a prominent on-air consultant for CBS News.

In short, no professional or personal antipathies underlie my criticism of mainstream media, only my conviction that violations of their own professional standards in reporting and commenting on Russia and relations between Washington and Moscow have contributed to this new and more dangerous Cold War. Hence my weekly efforts, and now in this book, to offer readers an alternative narrative and explanation of how it came about.

***

All writers have help along the way, I perhaps more than many due to the wide range of my weekly subjects. Three people regularly helped me with information and, equally important, critical feedback: James Carden, Lev Golinkin, and Pietro Shakarian. My research assistant, Mariya Salier, provided expertise, both technical and substantive, well beyond that of the usual assistant. David Johnson's daily email digest, *Johnson's Russia List*, which includes non-mainstream articles and other materials, has been invaluable, as it is for anyone occupied with Russia. Also valuable is the website of the American Committee for East-West Accord (eastwestaccord.com), of which I am a board member, edited by James Carden.

Farther away, my longtime friend Dmitri Muratov, chief editor of Russia's most important independent newspaper, *Novaya Gazeta*, made my views accessible to readers in that country by translating and publishing a number of the articles in this book. (Reactions, not surprisingly, were mixed but nonetheless valuable.)

At *The Nation*, Ricky D'Ambrose, an innovative filmmaker in his other life, played an indispensable role every Wednesday by shepherding each weekly commentary from my computer to the website and in the process by making important editorial improvements.

And at the end, despite my missed deadlines, Tony Lyons, Oren Eades, and the team at Skyhorse Publishing turned my manuscript into this book with remarkable speed and skill.

I am very grateful to all of these people. And, of course, to John Batchelor, who gave me a national platform and made my evidently distinctive voice widely recognized from shops and restaurants to airports and a hospital operating room.

But the book would not have been possible in any way without the support of my wife, Katrina vanden Heuvel, who is Editor and Publisher of *The Nation*. I owe her much more than gratitude. My commentaries put her in an unenviable position. That she did not "fully agree" or "only partially agreed" with many of them was customary in our thirty-year marriage. That some members of *The Nation* community were outraged by not a few of my commentaries, and made their "concerns" known privately and publicly, put a special burden on Katrina.

So did other public attacks that named her as my accomplice, even though Katrina has a long editorial history of printing a range of views on controversial subjects, including Russia. And even though she has her own very well-informed views on matters related to Russia frequently expressed not only in *The Nation* but also in her weekly *Washington Post* web column. In the age of widely professed feminism, it puzzles me why my critics so often associate Katrina with my views in virtually hyphenated ways.

Whatever the explanation, readers will understand why I owe my wife much more than gratitude. Whatever her own opinions, no matter the external pressures, Katrina posted every commentary I wrote.

All that said, I must emphasize, especially in these toxic times, an important caveat. Anything ill-informed or otherwise unwise in this book is entirely of my own doing.

SFC
October 2018

Prologue

The Putin Specter—Who He Is Not

"Putin is an evil man, and he is intent on evil deeds."
—Senator John McCain[1]

"[Putin] was a KGB agent. By definition, he doesn't have a soul."
"If this sounds familiar, it's what Hitler did back in the 1930s."
—2016 Democratic Presidential Nominee Hillary Clinton[2,3]

THE SPECTER OF AN EVIL-DOING VLADIMIR PUTIN HAS loomed over and undermined US thinking about Russia for at least a decade. Inescapably, it is therefore a theme that runs through this book. Henry Kissinger deserves credit for having warned, perhaps alone among prominent American political figures, against this badly distorted image of Russia's leader since 2000: "The demonization of Vladimir Putin is not a policy. It is an alibi for not having one."[4]

But Kissinger was also wrong. Washington has made many policies strongly influenced by the demonizing of Putin—a personal vilification far exceeding any ever applied to Soviet Russia's latter-day Communist leaders. Those policies spread from growing complaints in the early 2000s to US-Russian proxy wars in Georgia, Ukraine, Syria, and eventually even at home, in Russiagate allegations. Indeed, policy-makers adopted an earlier formulation by the late Senator John McCain as an integral part of a new and more dangerous Cold War: "Putin [is] an unreconstructed Russian imperialist and

K.G.B. apparatchik. . . . His world is a brutish, cynical place. . . . We must prevent the darkness of Mr. Putin's world from befalling more of humanity."[5]

Mainstream media outlets have played a major prosecutorial role in the demonization. Far from atypically, the *Washington Post's* editorial page editor wrote, "Putin likes to make the bodies bounce. . . . The rule-by-fear is Soviet, but this time there is no ideology—only a noxious mixture of personal aggrandizement, xenophobia, homophobia and primitive anti-Americanism."[6] Esteemed publications and writers now routinely degrade themselves by competing to denigrate "the flabbily muscled form" of the "small gray ghoul named Vladimir Putin."[7,8] There are hundreds of such examples, if not more, over many years. Vilifying Russia's leader has become a canon in the orthodox US narrative of the new Cold War.

As with all institutions, the demonization of Putin has its own history. When he first appeared on the world scene as Boris Yeltsin's anointed successor, in 1999–2000, Putin was welcomed by leading representatives of the US political-media establishment. The *New York Times'* chief Moscow correspondent and other verifiers reported that Russia's new leader had an "emotional commitment to building a strong democracy." Two years later, President George W. Bush lauded his summit with Putin and "the beginning of a very constructive relationship."[9]

But the Putin-friendly narrative soon gave away to unrelenting Putin-bashing. In 2004, *Times* columnist Nicholas Kristof inadvertently explained why, at least partially. Kristof complained bitterly of having been "suckered by Mr. Putin. He is not a sober version of Boris Yeltsin." By 2006, a *Wall Street Journal* editor, expressing the establishment's revised opinion, declared it "time we start thinking of Vladimir Putin's Russia as an enemy of the United States."[10,11] The rest, as they say, is history.

Who has Putin really been during his many years in power? We may have to leave this large, complex question to future historians, when materials for full biographical study—memoirs, archive documents, and others—are available. Even so, it may surprise readers to know that Russia's own historians, policy intellectuals, and journalists already argue publicly and differ considerably as to the "pluses and minuses" of Putin's leadership. (My own evaluation is somewhere in the middle.)

In America and elsewhere in the West, however, only purported "minuses" reckon in the extreme vilifying, or anti-cult, of Putin. Many are substantially uninformed, based on highly selective or unverified sources, and motivated by political grievances, including those of several Yeltsin-era oligarchs and their agents in the West.

By identifying and examining, however briefly, the primary "minuses" that underpin the demonization of Putin, we can understand at least who he is not:

• Putin is not the man who, after coming to power in 2000, "de-democratized" a Russian democracy established by President Boris Yeltsin in the 1990s and restored a system akin to Soviet "totalitarianism." Democratization began and developed in Soviet Russia under the last Soviet leader, Mikhail Gorbachev, in the years from 1987 to 1991.

Yeltsin repeatedly dealt that historic Russian experiment grievous, possibly fatal, blows. Among his other acts, by using tanks, in October 1993, to destroy Russia's freely elected parliament and with it the entire constitutional order that had made Yeltsin president. By waging two bloody wars against the tiny breakaway province of Chechnya. By enabling a small group of Kremlin-connected oligarchs to plunder Russia's richest assets and abet the plunging of some two-thirds of its people into poverty and misery, including the once-large and professionalized Soviet middle classes. By rigging his own reelection in 1996. And by enacting a "super-presidential" constitution, at the expense of the legislature and judiciary but to his successor's benefit. Putin may have furthered the de-democratization of the Yeltsin 1990s, but he did not initiate it.

• Nor did Putin then make himself a Tsar or Soviet-like "autocrat," which means a despot with absolute power to turn his will into policy. The last Kremlin leader with that kind of power was Stalin, who died in 1953, and with him his 20-year mass terror. Due to the increasing bureaucratic routinization of the political-administrative system, each successive Soviet leader had less personal power than his predecessor. Putin may have more, but if he really is a "cold-blooded, ruthless" autocrat—"the worst dictator on the planet"[12]—tens of thousands of protesters would not have repeatedly appeared in Moscow streets, sometimes officially sanctioned. Or their protests (and selective arrests) been shown on state television.

Political scientists generally agree that Putin has been a "soft authoritarian" leader governing a system that has authoritarian and democratic components inherited from the past. They disagree as to how to specify, define, and balance these elements, but most would also generally agree with a brief Facebook post, on September 7, 2018, by the eminent diplomat-scholar Jack Matlock: "Putin . . . is not the absolute dictator some have pictured him. His power seems to be based on balancing various patronage networks, some of which are still criminal. (In the 1990s, most were, and nobody was controlling them.) Therefore he cannot admit publicly that [criminal acts]

happened without his approval since this would indicate that he is not completely in charge."

• Putin is not a Kremlin leader who "reveres Stalin" and whose "Russia
is a gangster shadow of Stalin's Soviet Union."[13,14] These assertions are so
far-fetched and uninformed about Stalin's terror-ridden regime, Putin, and
Russia today, they barely warrant comment. Stalin's Russia was often as close
to unfreedom as imaginable. In today's Russia, apart from varying political liberties, most citizens are freer to live, study, work, write, speak, and
travel than they have ever been. (When vocational demonizers like David
Kramer allege an "appalling human rights situation in Putin's Russia,"[15] they
should be asked: compared to when in Russian history, or elsewhere in the
world today?)

Putin clearly understands that millions of Russians have and often express
pro-Stalin sentiments. Nonetheless, his role in these still-ongoing controversies over the despot's historical reputation has been, in one unprecedented way, that of an anti-Stalinist leader. Briefly illustrated, if Putin reveres
the memory of Stalin, why did his personal support finally make possible two
memorials (the excellent State Museum of the History of the Gulag and the
highly evocative "Wall of Grief") to the tyrant's millions of victims, both
in central Moscow? The latter memorial monument was first proposed by
then-Kremlin leader Nikita Khrushchev, in 1961. It was not built under any
of his successors—until Putin, in 2017.

• Nor did Putin create post–Soviet Russia's "kleptocratic economic system," with its oligarchic and other widespread corruption. This too took
shape under Yeltsin during the Kremlin's shock-therapy "privatization"
schemes of the 1990s, when the "swindlers and thieves" still denounced by
today's opposition actually emerged.

Putin has adopted a number of "anti-corruption" policies over the years.
How successful they have been is the subject of legitimate debate. As are
how much power he has had to rein in fully both Yeltsin's oligarchs and his
own, and how sincere he has been. But branding Putin "a kleptocrat"[16] also
lacks context and is little more than barely informed demonizing.

A recent scholarly book finds, for example, that while they may be "corrupt," Putin "and the liberal technocratic economic team on which he relies
have also skillfully managed Russia's economic fortunes."[17] A former IMF
director goes further, concluding that Putin's current economic team does
not "tolerate corruption" and that "Russia now ranks 35th out of 190 in the
World Bank's Doing Business ratings. It was at 124 in 2010."[18]

Viewed in human terms, when Putin came to power in 2000, some 75

percent of Russians were living in poverty. Most had lost even modest legacies of the Soviet era—their life savings; medical and other social benefits;
real wages; pensions; occupations; and for men life expectancy, which had
fallen well below the age of 60. In only a few years, the "kleptocrat" Putin had
mobilized enough wealth to undo and reverse those human catastrophes and
put billions of dollars in rainy-day funds that buffered the nation in different
hard times ahead. We judge this historic achievement as we might, but it is
why many Russians still call Putin "Vladimir the Savior."

• Which brings us to the most sinister allegation against him: Putin,
trained as "a KGB thug," regularly orders the killing of inconvenient journalists and personal enemies, like a "mafia state boss." This should be the easiest
demonizing axiom to dismiss because there is no actual evidence, or barely
any logic, to support it. And yet, it is ubiquitous. *Times* editorial writers and
columnists—and far from them alone—characterize Putin as a "thug" and
his policies as "thuggery" so often—sometimes doubling down on "autocratic
thug"[19]—that the practice may be specified in some internal manual. Little
wonder so many politicians also routinely practice it, as did US Senator Ben
Sasse: "We should tell the American people and tell the world that we know
that Vladimir Putin is a thug. He's a former KGB agent who's a murderer."[20]

Few, if any, modern-day world leaders have been so slurred, or so regularly.
Nor does Sasse actually "know" any of this. He and the others imbibe it from
reams of influential media accounts that fully indict Putin while burying a
nullifying "but" regarding actual evidence. Thus another *Times* columnist: "I
realize that this evidence is only circumstantial and well short of proof. But
it's one of many suspicious patterns."[21] This, too, is a journalistic "pattern"
when Putin is involved.

Leaving aside other world leaders with minor or major previous careers in
intelligences services, Putin's years as a KGB intelligence officer in then–East
Germany were clearly formative. Many years later, at age 67, he still spoke of
them with pride. Whatever else that experience contributed, it made Putin a
Europeanized Russian, a fluent German speaker, and a political leader with a
remarkable, demonstrated capacity for retaining and coolly analyzing a very
wide range of information. (Read or watch a few of his long interviews.) Not
a bad leadership trait in very fraught times.

Moreover, no serious biographer would treat only one period in a subject's
long public career as definitive, as Putin demonizers do. Why not instead the
period after he left the KGB in 1991, when he served as deputy to the mayor
of St. Petersburg, then considered one of the two or three most democratic
leaders in Russia? Or the years immediately following in Moscow, where he

saw first-hand the full extent of Yeltsin-era corruption? Or his subsequent years, while still relatively young, as president?

As for being a "murderer" of journalists and other "enemies," the list has grown to scores of Russians who died, at home or abroad, by foul or natural causes—all reflexively attributed to Putin. Our hallowed tradition puts the burden of proof on the accusers. Putin's accusers have produced none, only assumptions, innuendoes, and mistranslated statements by Putin about the fate of "traitors." The two cases that firmly established this defamatory practice were those of the investigative journalist Anna Politkovskaya, who was shot to death in Moscow in 2006; and Alexander Litvinenko, a shadowy one-time KGB defector with ties to aggrieved Yeltsin-era oligarchs, who died of radiation poisoning in London, also in 2006.

Not a shred of actual proof points to Putin in either case. The editor of Politkovskaya's paper, the devoutly independent *Novaya Gazeta*, still believes her assassination was ordered by Chechen officials, whose human-rights abuses she was investigating. Regarding Litvinenko, despite frenzied media claims and a kangaroo-like "hearing" suggesting that Putin was "probably" responsible, there is still no conclusive proof even as to whether Litvinenko's poisoning was intentional or accidental. The same paucity of evidence applies to many subsequent cases, notably the shooting of the opposition politician Boris Nemtsov, "in [distant] view of the Kremlin," in 2015.

About Russian journalists, there is, however, a significant overlooked statistic. According to the American Committee to Protect Journalists, as of 2012, 77 had been murdered—41 during the Yeltsin years, 36 under Putin. By 2018, the total was 82—41 under Yeltsin, the same under Putin. This strongly suggests that the still–partially corrupt post-Soviet economic system, not Yeltsin or Putin personally, led to the killing of so many journalists after 1991, most of them investigative reporters. The former wife of one journalist thought to have been poisoned concludes as much: "Many Western analysts place the responsibility for these crimes on Putin. But the cause is more likely the system of mutual responsibility and the culture of impunity that began to form before Putin, in the late 1990s."[22]

• More recently, there is yet another allegation: Putin is a fascist and white supremacist. The accusation is made mostly, it seems, by people wishing to deflect attention from the role being played by neo-Nazis in US-backed Ukraine. Putin no doubt regards it as a blood slur, and even on the surface it is, to be exceedingly charitable, entirely uninformed. How else to explain Senator Ron Wyden's solemn warnings, at a hearing on November 1, 2017, about "the current fascist leadership of Russia"? A young scholar recently dismantled a senior Yale professor's nearly inexplicable propounding of this thesis.[23] My own approach is compatible, though different.

Whatever Putin's failings, the fascist allegation is absurd. Nothing in his statements over nearly 20 years in power are akin to fascism, whose core belief is a cult of blood based on the asserted superiority of one ethnicity over all others. As head of a vast multi-ethnic state—embracing scores of diverse groups with a broad range of skin colors—such utterances or related acts by Putin would be inconceivable, if not political suicide. This is why he endlessly appeals for harmony in "our entire multi-ethnic nation" with its "multi-ethnic culture," as he did once again in his re-inauguration speech in 2018.[24]

Russia has, of course, fascist-white supremacist thinkers and activists, though many have been imprisoned. But a mass fascist movement is scarcely feasible in a country where so many millions died in the war against Nazi Germany, a war that directly affected Putin and clearly left a formative mark on him. Though he was born after the war, his mother and father barely survived near-fatal wounds and disease, his older brother died in the long German siege of Leningrad, and several of his uncles perished. Only people who never endured such an experience, or are unable to imagine it, can conjure up a fascist Putin.

There is another, easily understood, indicative fact. Not a trace of anti-Semitism is evident in Putin. Little noted here but widely reported both in Russia and in Israel, life for Russian Jews is better under Putin than it has ever been in that country's long history.[25]

• Finally, at least for now, there is the ramifying demonization allegation that, as a foreign-policy leader, Putin has been exceedingly "aggressive" abroad and his behavior has been the sole cause of the new cold war.[26] At best, this is an "in-the-eye-of-the-beholder" assertion, and half-blind. At worst, it justifies what even a German foreign minister characterized as the West's "war-mongering" against Russia.[27]

In the three cases widely given as examples of Putin's "aggression," the evidence, long cited by myself and others, points to US-led instigations, primarily in the process of expanding the NATO military alliance since the late 1990s from Germany to Russia's borders today. The proxy US-Russian war in Georgia in 2008 was initiated by the US-backed president of that country, who had been encouraged to aspire to NATO membership. The 2014 crisis and subsequent proxy war in Ukraine resulted from the longstanding effort to bring that country, despite large regions' shared civilization with Russia, into NATO. And Putin's 2015 military intervention in Syria was done on a valid premise: either it would be Syrian President Bashar al-Assad in Damascus or the terrorist Islamic State—and on President Barack Obama's refusal to join Russia in an anti-ISIS alliance. As a result of this history, Putin is often seen in Russia as a belatedly reactive leader abroad, as a not sufficiently "aggressive" one.

Embedded in the "aggressive Putin" axiom are two others. One is that Putin is a neo-Soviet leader who seeks to restore the Soviet Union at the expense of Russia's neighbors. He is obsessively misquoted as having said, in 2005, "The collapse of the Soviet Union was the greatest geopolitical catastrophe of the twentieth century," apparently ranking it above two World Wars. What he actually said was "a major geopolitical catastrophe of the twentieth century," as it was for most Russians.

Though often critical of the Soviet system and its two formative leaders, Lenin and Stalin, Putin, like most of his generation, naturally remains in part a Soviet person. But what he said in 2010 reflects his real perspective and that of very many other Russians: "Anyone who does not regret the break-up of the Soviet Union has no heart. Anyone who wants its rebirth in its previous form has no head."[28,29]

The other fallacious sub-axiom is that Putin has always been "anti-Western," specifically "anti-American," has "always viewed the United States" with "smoldering suspicions."—so much that eventually he set into motion a "Plot Against America."[30,31] A simple reading of his years in power tells us otherwise. A Westernized Russian, Putin came to the presidency in 2000 in the still prevailing tradition of Gorbachev and Yeltsin—in hope of a "strategic friendship and partnership" with the United States.

How else to explain Putin's abundant assistant to US forces fighting in Afghanistan after 9/11 and continued facilitation of supplying American and NATO troops there? Or his backing of harsh sanctions against Iran's nuclear ambitions and refusal to sell Tehran a highly effective air-defense system? Or the information his intelligence services shared with Washington that if heeded could have prevented the Boston Marathon bombings in April 2012?

Or, until he finally concluded that Russia would never be treated as an equal and that NATO had encroached too close, Putin was a full partner in the US-European clubs of major world leaders? Indeed, as late as May 2018, contrary to Russiagate allegations, he still hoped, as he had from the beginning, to rebuild Russia partly through economic partnerships with the West: "To attract capital from friendly companies and countries, we need good relations with Europe and with the whole world, including the United States."[32]

Given all that has happened during the past nearly two decades—particularly what Putin and other Russian leaders perceive to have happened—it would be remarkable if his views of the West, especially America, had not changed. As he remarked in 2018, "We all change."[33] A few years earlier, Putin remarkably admitted that initially he had "illusions" about foreign policy, without specifying which. Perhaps he meant this, spoken at the end of 2017: "Our most serious mistake in relations with the West is that we trusted you too much. And your mistake is that you took that trust as weakness and abused it."[34]

If my refutation of the axioms of Putin demonization is valid, where does that leave us? Certainly, not with an apologia for Putin, but with the question, "Who is Putin?" Russians like to say, "let history judge," but given the perils of the new Cold War, we cannot wait. We can begin at least with a few historical truths. In 2000, a young and little-experienced man became the leader of a vast state that had precipitously disintegrated, or "collapsed," twice in the twentieth century—in 1917 and again in 1991—with disastrous consequences for its people. And in both instances it had lost its "sovereignty" and thus its security in fundamental ways.

These have been recurring themes in Putin's words and deeds. They are where to begin an understanding. No one can doubt that he is already the most consequential "statesman" of the twenty-first century, though the word is rarely, if ever, applied to him in the United States. And what does "consequential" mean? Even without the pseudo-minuses spelled out above, a balanced evaluation will include valid ones.

For example, at home, was it necessary to so strengthen and expand the Kremlin's "vertical" throughout the rest of the country in order to pull Russia back together? Should not the historic experiment with democracy have been given equal priority? Abroad, were there alternatives to annexing Crimea, even given the perceived threats? And did Putin's leadership really do nothing to reawaken fears in small East European countries victimized for centuries by Russia? These are only a few questions that might yield minuses alongside Putin's deserved pluses.

Whatever the approach, whoever undertakes a balanced evaluation should do so, to paraphrase Spinoza, not in order to demonize, not to mock, not to hate, but to understand.

Part I

The New Cold War Erupts

2014–2015

Patriotic Heresy vs. Cold War

August 27, 2014

(Adapted from a talk given in Washington, DC, on June 16, 2014.)

W E MEET TODAY DURING THE WORST and potentially most dangerous American-Russian confrontation in many decades, probably since the 1962 Cuban Missile Crisis. The Ukrainian civil war, precipitated by the unlawful change of government in Kiev in February, is already growing into a proxy US-Russian war. The seemingly unthinkable is becoming imaginable: an actual war between US-led NATO and post-Soviet Russia.

Certainly, we are already in a new Cold War that Western sanctions will only deepen, institutionalize, and prolong—one potentially more dangerous than its 40-year predecessor, which the world barely survived.

We—opponents of the US policies that have contributed so woefully to the current crisis—are few in number, without influential supporters, and unorganized. I am old enough to know our position was very different in the 1970s and 1980s, when we struggled for what was then called détente. We were a minority, but a substantial minority with allies in high places, including in Congress and the State Department. Our views were solicited by mainstream newspapers, television, and radio. In addition to grassroots support, we had our own well-funded lobbying organization in Washington, the American Committee for East-West Accord, whose board included corporate CEOs, political figures, prominent academics, and statesmen of the stature of George Kennan.

We have none of that today. We have no access to the Obama administration, virtually none to Congress, now a bipartisan bastion of Cold War politics, and very little to the mainstream media. We have access to important alternative media, but they are not considered authoritative, or essential, inside the Beltway. In my long lifetime, I do not recall such a failure of American democratic discourse in any comparable time of crisis.

I want to speak generally about this dire situation—almost certainly a fateful turning point in world affairs—as a participant in what little mainstream media debate has been permitted but also as a longtime scholarly historian of Russia and of US-Russian relations and informed observer who believes there is still a way out of this terrible crisis.

Regarding my episodic participation in the very limited mainstream media discussion, I will speak in a more personal way than I usually do. From the outset, I saw my role as twofold.

Recalling the American adage "There are two sides to every story," I sought to explain Moscow's view of the Ukrainian crisis, which is almost entirely missing in US mainstream coverage. What, for example, did Putin mean when he said Western policy-makers were "trying to drive us into some kind of corner," "have lied to us many times" and "have crossed the line" in Ukraine? Second, having argued since the 1990s, in my books and *Nation* articles, that Washington's bipartisan Russia policies could lead to a new Cold War and to just such a crisis, I wanted to bring my longstanding analysis to bear on today's confrontation over Ukraine.

As a result, I have been repeatedly assailed—even in purportedly liberal publications—as Putin's No. 1 American "apologist," "useful idiot," "dupe," "best friend," and, perhaps a new low in immature invective, "toady." I expected to be criticized, as I was during nearly twenty years as a CBS News commentator, but not in such personal and scurrilous ways. (Something has changed in our political culture, perhaps related to the Internet, but I think more generally.)

Until now, I have not replied to any of these defamatory attacks. I do so today because I now think they are directed at many of us in this room and indeed at anyone critical of Washington's Russia policies, not just me. Re-reading the attacks, I have come to the following conclusions:

None of these character assassins present any factual refutations of anything I have written or said. They indulge instead in ad hominem slurs based on distortions and on the general premise that any American who seeks to understand Moscow's perspectives is a "Putin apologist" and thus unpatriotic. Such a premise only abets the possibility of war.

Some of these writers, or people who stand behind them, are longtime proponents of the twenty-year US policies that have led to the Ukrainian crisis. By defaming us, they seek to obscure their complicity in the unfolding disaster and their unwillingness to rethink it. Failure to rethink dooms us to the worst outcome.

Equally important, these kinds of neo-McCarthyites are trying to stifle democratic debate by stigmatizing us in ways that make our views unwelcome on mainstream television and radio broadcasts and op-ed pages—and to policy-makers. They are largely succeeding.

Let us be clear. This means that we, not the people on the left and the right who defame us, are the true American democrats and the real patriots of US national security. We do not seek to ostracize or silence the new cold warriors, but to engage them in public debate. And we, not they, understand that current US policy may have catastrophic consequences for international and American security.

The perils and costs of another prolonged Cold War will afflict our children and grandchildren. If nothing else, this reckless policy, couched even at high levels in a ritualistic demonizing of Putin, is already costing Washington an essential partner in the Kremlin in vital areas of US security—from Iran, Syria, and Afghanistan to efforts to counter nuclear proliferation and international terrorism.

But we ourselves are partially to blame for the one-sided, or nonexistent, public debate. As I said, we are not organized. Too often, we do not publicly defend each other. . . . And often we do not speak boldly enough. (We should not worry, for example, as do too many silent critics, if our arguments sometimes coincide with what Moscow is saying. Doing so results in self-censorship.)

Some people who privately share our concerns—in Congress, the media, universities, and think tanks—do not speak out at all. For whatever reason—concern about being stigmatized, about their career, personal disposition—they are silent. But in our democracy, where the cost of dissent is relatively low, silence is no longer a patriotic option.

We should, however, exempt young people from this imperative. They have more to lose. A few have sought my guidance, and I always advise, "Even petty penalties for dissent in regard to Russia could adversely affect your career. At this stage of life, your first obligation is to your family and thus to your future prospects. Your time to fight lies ahead." Not all of them heed my advice.

Finally, in connection with our struggle for a wiser American policy, I have come to another conclusion. Most of us were taught that moderation in thought and speech is always the best principle. But in a fateful crisis such as the one now confronting us, moderation for its own sake is no virtue. It becomes conformism, and conformism becomes complicity.

I recall this issue being discussed long ago in a very different context—by Soviet-era dissidents when I lived among them in Moscow in the 1970s and 1980s. . . . A few people have called us "American dissidents," but the analogy is imperfect: my Soviet friends had far fewer possibilities for dissent than we have and risked much worse consequences.

Nonetheless, the analogy is instructive. Soviet dissidents were protesting an entrenched orthodoxy of dogmas, vested interests, and ossified policy-making, which is why they were denounced as heretics by Soviet authorities and media. Since the 1990s, beginning with the Clinton administration, exceedingly unwise notions about post-Soviet Russia and the political correctness of US policy have congealed into a bipartisan American orthodoxy. The natural, historical response to orthodoxy is heresy. So let us be patriotic heretics, regardless of personal consequences, in the hope that many others will join us, as has often happened in history.

I turn now, in my capacity as a historian, to that orthodoxy. The late Senator Daniel Patrick Moynihan famously said: "Everyone is entitled to his own opinions, but not to his own facts." The US establishment's new Cold War orthodoxy rests almost entirely on fallacious opinions. Five of these fallacies are particularly important today.

Fallacy No. 1: Ever since the end of the Soviet Union in 1991, Washington has treated post-Communist Russia generously as a desired friend and partner, making every effort to help it become a democratic, prosperous member of the Western system of international security. Unwilling or unable, Russia rejected this American altruism, emphatically under Putin.

Fact: Beginning in the 1990s with the Clinton administration, every American president and Congress has treated post-Soviet Russia as a defeated nation with inferior legitimate rights at home and abroad. This triumphalist, winner-take-all approach has been spearheaded by the expansion of NATO—accompanied by non-reciprocal negotiations and now missile defense—into Russia's traditional zones of national security, while excluding Moscow from Europe's security system. Early on, Ukraine and, to a lesser extent, Georgia were Washington's "great prize."

Fallacy No. 2: There exists a "Ukrainian people" who yearn to escape centuries of Russian influence and join the West.

Fact: Ukraine is a country long divided by ethnic, linguistic, religious, cultural, economic, and political differences—particularly its western and eastern regions, but not only those. When the current crisis began in late 2013, Ukraine was one state, but it was not a single people or a united nation. Some of these divisions were made worse after 1991 by a corrupt elite, but most of them had developed over centuries.

Fallacy No. 3: In November 2013, the European Union, backed by Washington, offered Ukrainian President Viktor Yanukovych a benign association with European democracy and prosperity. Yanukovych was prepared to sign the agreement, but Putin bullied and bribed him into rejecting it. Thus began Kiev's Maidan protests and all that has since followed.

Fact: The EU proposal was a reckless provocation compelling the democratically elected president of a deeply divided country to choose between Russia and the West. So too was the EU's rejection of Putin's counterproposal for a Russian-European-American plan to save Ukraine from financial collapse. On its own, the EU proposal was not economically feasible. Offering little financial assistance, it required the Ukrainian government to enact harsh austerity measures and would have sharply curtailed its longstanding and essential economic relations with Russia. Nor was the EU proposal entirely benign. It included protocols requiring Ukraine to adhere to Europe's "military and security" policies—which meant in effect, without mentioning the alliance, NATO. Again, it was not Putin's alleged "aggression" that initiated today's crisis but instead a kind of velvet aggression by Brussels and Washington to bring all of Ukraine into the West, including (in fine print) into NATO.

Fallacy No. 4: Today's civil war in Ukraine was caused by Putin's aggressive response to the peaceful Maidan protests against Yanukovych's decision.

Fact: In February 2014, the radicalized Maidan protests, strongly influenced by extreme nationalist and even semi-fascist street forces, turned violent. Hoping for a peaceful resolution, European foreign ministers brokered a compromise between Maidan's parliamentary representatives and Yanukovych. It would have left him as president, with less power, of a coalition reconciliation government until early elections in December. Within hours, violent street fighters aborted the agreement. Europe's leaders and Washington did not defend their own diplomatic accord. Yanukovych fled to Russia. Minority parliamentary parties representing Maidan and, predominantly, western Ukraine—among them Svoboda, an ultranationalist movement previously anathematized by the European Parliament as incompatible with European values—formed a new government. Washington and Brussels endorsed the coup and have supported the outcome ever since. Everything that followed, from Russia's annexation of Crimea and the spread of rebellion in southeastern Ukraine to the civil war and Kiev's "anti-terrorist operation," was triggered by the February coup. Putin's actions were mostly reactive.

Fallacy No. 5: The only way out of the crisis is for Putin to end his "aggression" and call off his agents in southeastern Ukraine.

Fact: The underlying causes of the crisis are Ukraine's own internal divisions, not primarily Putin's actions. The essential factor escalating the crisis has been Kiev's "anti-terrorist" military campaign against its own citizens, mainly in Luhansk and Donetsk. Putin influences and no doubt aids the Donbass "self-defenders." Considering the pressure on him in Moscow, he is likely to continue to do so, perhaps even more directly, but he does not fully control them. If Kiev's assault ends, Putin probably can compel the rebels to negotiate. But only the Obama administration can compel Kiev to stop, and it has not done so.

In short, twenty years of US policy have led to this fateful American-Russian confrontation. Putin may have contributed to it along the way, but his role during his fourteen years in power has been almost entirely reactive—a complaint frequently directed against him by more hardline forces in Moscow.

* * *

In politics as in history, there are always alternatives. The Ukrainian crisis could have at least three different outcomes. The civil war escalates and widens, drawing in Russian and possibly NATO military forces. This would be the worst outcome: a kind of latter-day Cuban Missile Crisis. In the second outcome, today's de facto partitioning of Ukraine becomes institutionalized in the form of two Ukrainian states—one allied with the West, the other with Russia. This would not be the best outcome, but neither would it be the worst.

The best outcome would be the preservation of a united Ukraine. It will require good-faith negotiations between representatives of all of Ukraine's regions, including leaders of the rebellious southeast, probably under the auspices of Washington, Moscow, the European Union, and eventually the UN. Putin and his foreign minister, Sergei Lavrov, have proposed this for months. Ukraine's tragedy continues to grow. Thousands of innocent people have already been killed or wounded.

Alas, there is no wise leadership in Washington. President Barack Obama has vanished as a statesman in the Ukrainian crisis. Secretary of State John Kerry speaks publicly more like a secretary of war than as our top diplomat.

The Senate is preparing even more bellicose legislation. The establishment media rely uncritically on Kiev's propaganda and cheerlead for its policies. American television rarely, if ever, shows Kiev's military assaults on Luhansk, Donetsk, or other Ukrainian rebel cities, thereby arousing no public qualms or opposition.

And so we patriotic heretics remain mostly alone and often defamed. The most encouraging perspective I can offer is to remind you that positive change in history frequently begins as heresy. Or to quote the personal testimony of Mikhail Gorbachev, who said of his struggle for change in the late 1980s inside the even more rigidly orthodox Soviet nomenklatura: "Everything new in philosophy begins as heresy and in politics as the opinion of a minority." As for patriotism, here is Woodrow Wilson: "The most patriotic man is sometimes the man who goes in the direction he thinks right even when he sees half of the world against him."

Distorting Russia

February 12, 2014

THE DEGRADATION OF MAINSTREAM AMERICAN PRESS coverage of Russia, a country still vital to US national security, has been under way for many years. If the recent tsunami of shamefully unprofessional and politically inflammatory articles in leading newspapers and magazines—most recently about the Sochi Olympics, Ukraine, and, as usual, Russian President Vladimir Putin—is an indication, this media malpractice is now pervasive and the new norm.

There are notable exceptions, but a general pattern has developed. Even in the venerable *New York Times* and *Washington Post*, news reports, editorials, and commentaries no longer adhere rigorously to traditional journalistic standards, often failing to provide essential facts and context; make a clear distinction between reporting and analysis; require at least two different political or "expert" views on major developments; or publish opposing opinions on their op-ed pages. As a result, American media on Russia today are less objective, less balanced, more conformist, and scarcely less ideological than when they covered Soviet Russia during the preceding Cold War.

The history of this degradation is also clear. It began in the early 1990s, following the end of the Soviet Union, when the US media adopted Washington's narrative that almost everything President Boris Yeltsin did was a "transition from communism to democracy" and thus in America's best interests. This included Yeltsin's economic "shock therapy" and oligarchic looting of essential state assets, which destroyed tens of millions of Russian lives; armed destruction of a popularly elected Parliament and imposition of a "presidential" Constitution, which dealt a crippling blow to democratization and now empowers Putin; brutal war in Chechnya, which gave rise to terrorists in Russia's North Caucasus; rigging of his own reelection in 1996; and leaving behind in 1999, his approval ratings in single digits, a disintegrating country laden with weapons of mass destruction. Indeed, most American journalists still give the impression that Yeltsin was an ideal Russian leader.

Since the early 2000s, the media have followed a different leader-centric narrative, also consistent with US policy, that devalues multifaceted analysis for a relentless demonization of Putin, with little regard for facts. If Russia under Yeltsin was presented as having entirely legitimate politics and national interests, we are now made to believe that Putin's Russia has none at all, at home or abroad—even on its own borders, as in Ukraine.

Russia today has serious problems and many repugnant Kremlin policies. But anyone relying on mainstream American media will not find there any of their origins or influences in Yeltsin's Russia or in provocative US policies since the 1990s—only in the "autocrat" Putin who, however authoritarian, in reality lacks such power. Nor is he credited with stabilizing a disintegrating nuclear-armed country, assisting US security pursuits from Afghanistan and Syria to Iran, or even with granting amnesty, in December, to more than 1,000 jailed prisoners, including mothers of young children.

Not surprisingly, in January *The Wall Street Journal* featured the widely discredited former president of Georgia, Mikheil Saakashvili, branding Putin's government as one of "deceit, violence and cynicism," and the Kremlin as the "nerve center of the troubles that bedevil the West." But wanton Putin-bashing is also the dominant narrative in centrist, liberal, and progressive media, from the *Post*, *Times*, and *The New Republic* to CNN, MSNBC, and HBO's *Real Time with Bill Maher*, where Howard Dean, not previously known for his Russia expertise, recently declared, to Maher's and his panel's great approval, "Vladimir Putin is a thug."

American media therefore eagerly await Putin's downfall—due to his "failing economy" (some of its indicators are better than US ones), the valor of street protesters and other right-minded oppositionists (whose policies are rarely examined), the defection of his electorate (his approval ratings remain around 65 percent), or some welcomed "cataclysm." Evidently believing, as does the *Times*, for example, that democrats and a "much better future" will succeed Putin (not zealous ultranationalists growing in the streets and corridors of power), US commentators remain indifferent to what the hoped-for "destabilization of his regime" might mean in the world's largest nuclear country.

* * *

For weeks, this toxic coverage has focused on the Sochi Olympics and the deepening crisis in Ukraine. Even before the Games began, the *Times* declared the newly built complex a "Soviet-style dystopia" and warned in a headline, "Terrorism and Tension, Not Sports and Joy." On opening day, the paper found space for three anti-Putin articles and a lead editorial, a feat rivaled by the *Post*. Facts hardly mattered. Virtually every US report insisted that a record $51 billion "squandered" by Putin on the Sochi Games proved the funds were "corrupt." But as Ben Aris of *Business New Europe* pointed out, as much as $44 billion may have been spent "to develop the infrastructure of the entire region," investment "the entire country needs."

Overall pre-Sochi coverage was even worse, exploiting the threat of terrorism so licentiously it seemed pornographic. The *Post*, long known among critical-minded Russia-watchers as Pravda on the Potomac, exemplified the media ethos. A sports columnist and an editorial page editor turned the Olympics into "a contest of wills" between the despised Putin's "thugocracy" and terrorist "insurgents." The "two warring parties" were so equated readers might have wondered which to cheer for. If nothing else, American journalists gave terrorists an early victory, tainting "Putin's Games" and frightening away many foreign spectators, including some relatives of the athletes.

The Sochi Games will soon pass, triumphantly or tragically, but the potentially fateful Ukrainian crisis will not. A new Cold War divide between West and East may now be unfolding, not in distant Berlin but in the heart of Russia's historical civilization. The result could be a permanent confrontation fraught with instability and the threat of a hot war far worse than the proxy one in Georgia in 2008. These dangers have been all but ignored in highly selective, partisan, and inflammatory US media accounts that portray the European Union's "Partnership" proposal benignly as Ukraine's chance for democracy, prosperity, and escape from Russia thwarted only by a "bullying" Putin and his "cronies" in Kiev.

Perhaps the largest untruth promoted by most US media is the claim that "Ukraine's future integration into Europe" is "yearned for throughout the country." Every informed observer knows—from Ukraine's history, geography, languages, religions, culture, recent politics, and opinion surveys—that the country is deeply divided as to whether it should join Europe or remain close politically and economically to Russia. There is not one Ukraine or one "Ukrainian people" but at least two, generally situated in its Western and Eastern regions.

Such factual distortions point to two flagrant omissions. . . . The now exceedingly dangerous confrontation between the two Ukraines was not "ignited," as the *Times* claims, by President Viktor Yanukovych's duplicitous negotiating—or by Putin—but, as I pointed out, by the EU's reckless ultimatum, in November 2013, that the democratically elected president of a profoundly divided country choose between Europe and Russia. Putin's proposal instead for a tripartite EU-Ukraine-Russia trade arrangement, rarely if ever reported, was flatly rejected by US and EU officials.

But the most crucial media omission is Moscow's reasonable conviction that the struggle for Ukraine is yet another chapter in the West's ongoing, US-led march toward post-Soviet Russia, which began in the late 1990s with NATO's eastward expansion and continued with US-funded NGO political activities inside Russia, a US-NATO military outpost in Georgia, and missile-defense installations near Russia. Whether this longstanding Washington-Brussels policy is wise or reckless, it—not Putin's December 2013 financial offer to save Ukraine's collapsing economy—is deceitful. The EU's "civilizational" proposal, for example, includes "security policy" provisions, almost never reported, that would apparently subordinate Ukraine to NATO.

Any doubts about the Obama administration's real intentions in Ukraine should have been dispelled by the recently revealed taped conversation between a top State Department official, Victoria Nuland, and the US ambassador in Kiev. The media predictably focused on the source of the "leak" and on Nuland's verbal "gaffe"—"Fuck the EU." But the essential revelation was that high-level US officials were plotting to "midwife" a new, anti-Russian Ukrainian government by ousting or neutralizing Yanukovych, the democratically elected president—that is, a coup.

Americans are left with a new edition of an old question. Has Washington's twenty-year winner-take-all approach to post-Soviet Russia shaped today's degraded news coverage, or is official policy shaped by the coverage? Did Senator John McCain stand in Kiev alongside the well-known leader of an extreme nationalist party because he was ill-informed by the media, or have the media deleted this part of the story because of McCain's folly? Whatever the explanation, as Russian intellectuals say when faced with two bad alternatives, "Both are worst."

Why Cold War Again?

April 2, 2014

THE EAST-WEST CONFRONTATION OVER UKRAINE, WHICH led to Moscow's annexation of Crimea but long predated it, is potentially the worst international crisis in more than fifty years—and the most fateful. A negotiated resolution is possible, but time is running out.

A new Cold War divide is already descending in Europe—not in Berlin but on Russia's borders. Worse may follow. If NATO forces move toward Poland's border with Ukraine, as is being called for in Washington and Europe, Moscow may send its forces into eastern Ukraine. The result would be a danger of war comparable to the Cuban Missile Crisis of 1962.

Even if the outcome is a non-military "isolation of Russia," today's Western mantra, the consequences will be dire. Moscow will not bow but will turn, politically and economically, to the East, as it has done before, above all to fuller alliance with China. The United States will risk losing an essential partner in vital areas of its own national security, from Iran, Syria, and Afghanistan to threats of a new arms race, nuclear proliferation, and more terrorism. And—no small matter—prospects for a resumption of Russia's democratization will be greatly diminished for at least a generation.

Why did this happen, nearly twenty-three years after the end of Soviet Communism, when both Washington and Moscow proclaimed a new era of "friendship and strategic partnership"? The answer given by the Obama administration, and overwhelmingly by the US political-media establishment, is that Russian President Putin is solely to blame. According to this assertion, his "autocratic" rule at home and "neo-Soviet imperialist" policies abroad eviscerated the partnership established in the 1990s by Presidents Bill Clinton and Boris Yeltsin. This fundamental premise underpins the American mainstream narrative of two decades of US-Russian relations, and now the Ukrainian crisis.

But there is an alternative explanation, one more in accord with the facts. Beginning with the Clinton administration, and supported by every subsequent Republican and Democratic president and Congress, the US-led West has unrelentingly moved its military, political, and economic power ever closer to post-Soviet Russia. Spearheaded by NATO's eastward expansion, already encamped in the former Soviet Baltic republics on Russia's border—now augmented by missile defense installations in neighboring states—this bipartisan, winner-take-all approach has come in various forms.

They include US-funded "democracy promotion" NGOs more deeply involved in Russia's internal politics than foreign ones are permitted to be in our country; the 1999 bombing of Moscow's Slav ally Serbia, forcibly detaching its historic province of Kosovo; a US military outpost in former Soviet Georgia (along with Ukraine, one of Putin's previously declared "red lines"), contributing to the brief proxy war in 2008; and, throughout, one-sided negotiations, called "selective cooperation," which took concessions from the Kremlin without meaningful White House reciprocity, and followed by broken American promises.

All of this has unfolded, sincerely for some proponents, in the name of "democracy" and "sovereign choice" for the many countries involved, but the underlying geopolitical agenda has been clear. During the first East-West conflict over Ukraine, occasioned by its 2004 "Orange Revolution," an influential GOP columnist, Charles Krauthammer, acknowledged, "This is about Russia first, democracy only second.... The West wants to finish the job begun with the fall of the Berlin Wall and continue Europe's march to the east.... The great prize is Ukraine." The late Richard Holbrooke, an aspiring Democratic secretary of state, concurred, hoping even then for Ukraine's "final break with Moscow" and to "accelerate" Kiev's membership in NATO.

That Russia's political elite has long had this same menacing view of US intentions makes it no less true—or any less consequential. Formally announcing the annexation of Crimea on March 18, 2014, Putin vented Moscow's longstanding resentments. Several of his assertions were untrue and alarming, but others were reasonable, or at least understandable, not "delusional." Referring to Western, primarily American, policy-makers since the 1990s, he complained bitterly that they were "trying to drive us into some kind of corner," "have lied to us many times," and in Ukraine "have crossed the line." Putin warned, "Everything has its limits."

The Détente Imperative and Parity Principle

April 14, 2015

(Adapted from a talk given in Washington, DC, on March 26, 2015.)

WHEN I SPOKE AT THIS FORUM nine months ago, in June 2014, I warned that the Ukrainian crisis was the worst US-Russian confrontation in many decades. It had already plunged us into a new (or renewed) Cold War potentially even more perilous than its forty-year US-Soviet predecessor. . . . I also warned that we might soon be closer to actual war with Russia than we had been since the 1962 Cuban Missile Crisis.

Today, the crisis is even worse. The new Cold War has been deepened and institutionalized by transforming what began, in February 2014, as essentially a Ukrainian civil war into a US/NATO-Russian proxy war; by a torrent of inflammatory misinformation out of Washington, Moscow, Kiev, and Brussels; and by Western economic sanctions that are compelling Russia to retreat politically, as it did in the late 1940s, from the West.

Still worse, both sides are again aggressively deploying their conventional and nuclear weapons and probing the other's defenses in the air and at sea. Diplomacy between Washington and Moscow is being displaced by resurgent militarized thinking, while cooperative relationships nurtured over many decades, from trade, education, and science to arms control are being shredded. And yet, despite this fateful crisis and its growing dangers, there is still no mainstream debate about, still less any effective political opposition to, the US policies that have contributed to it.

Indeed, the current best hope to avert a larger war is being assailed by political forces, especially in Washington and in US-backed Kiev, that seem to want a military showdown with Russia's unreasonably vilified president, Vladimir Putin. In February, German Chancellor Angela Merkel and French President Francois Hollande brokered in Minsk a military and political agreement with Putin and Ukrainian President Petro Poroshenko that, if implemented, would end the Ukrainian civil war.

Powerful enemies of the Minsk accord—again, both in Washington and Kiev—are denouncing it as appeasement of Putin while demanding that President Obama send $3 billion of weapons to Kiev. Such a step would escalate the war in Ukraine, sabotage the ceasefire and political negotiations agreed upon in Minsk, and possibly provoke a Russian military response with unpredictable consequences. While Europe is splitting over the crisis, and with it perhaps the vaunted transatlantic alliance, the recklessness in Washington is fully bipartisan, urged on by four all-but-unanimous votes in Congress.

* * *

A new Washington-Moscow détente is the only way to avert another prolonged and even more dangerous Cold War. For this, we must relearn a fundamental lesson from the history of the 40-year US-Soviet Cold War and how it ended, a history largely forgotten, distorted, or unknown to many younger Americans. Simply recalled, détente, as an idea and a policy, meant expanding elements of cooperation in US-Soviet relations while diminishing areas of dangerous conflict, particularly, though not only, in the existential realm of the nuclear arms race. In this regard, détente had a long, always embattled, often defeated, but ultimately victorious history.

Leaving aside the first détente of 1933, when Washington officially recognized Soviet Russia after fifteen years of diplomatic non-recognition (the first Cold War), latter-day détente began in the mid-1950s under President Dwight Eisenhower and Soviet leader Nikita Khrushchev. It was soon disrupted by Cold War forces and events on both sides.

The pattern continued for thirty years: under President John Kennedy and Khrushchev, after the Cuban Missile Crisis; under President Lyndon

Johnson and Soviet leader Leonid Brezhnev, in the growing shadow of Vietnam; under President Richard Nixon and Brezhnev in the 1970s; and briefly under Presidents Gerald Ford and Jimmy Carter, also with Brezhnev. Each time, détente was gravely undermined, intentionally and unintentionally, and abandoned as Washington policy, though not by its determined American proponents. (Having been among them in the 1970s and 1980s, I can testify on their behalf.)

Then, in 1985, the seemingly most Cold War president ever, Ronald Reagan, began with Soviet leader Mikhail Gorbachev a renewed détente so far-reaching that both men, as well as Reagan's successor, President George H.W. Bush, believed they had ended the Cold War. How did détente, despite three decades of repeated defeats and political defamation, remain a vital and ultimately triumphant (as it seemed at the time to most observers) American policy?

Above all, because Washington gradually acknowledged that Soviet Russia was a co-equal great power with comparable legitimate national interests in world affairs. This recognition was given a conceptual basis and a name: "parity."

It is true that "parity" began as a grudging recognition of the US-Soviet nuclear capacity for "mutually assured destruction" and that, due to their different systems (and "isms") at home, the parity principle (as I termed it in 1981 in a *New York Times* op-ed) did not mean moral equivalence. It is also true that powerful American political forces never accepted the principle and relentlessly assailed it. Even so, the principle existed—like sex in Victorian England, acknowledged only obliquely in public but amply practiced—as reflected in the commonplace expression "the two superpowers," without the modifier "nuclear."

Most important, every US president returned to it, from Eisenhower to Reagan. Thus, Jack F. Matlock Jr., a leading diplomatic participant in and historian of the Reagan-Gorbachev-Bush détente, tells us that for Reagan, "détente was based on several logical principles," the first being "the countries would deal with each other as equals."

Three elements of US-Soviet parity were especially important. First, both sides had recognized spheres of influence, "red lines" that should not be directly challenged. This understanding was occasionally tested, even violated, as in Cuba in 1962, but it prevailed. Second, neither side should interfere excessively, apart from the mutual propaganda war, in the other's internal politics. This too was tested—particularly in regard to Soviet Jewish emigration and political dissidents—but generally negotiated and observed.

And third, Washington and Moscow had a shared responsibility for peace and mutual security in Europe, even while competing economically and militarily in what was called the Third World. This assumption was also tested by serious crises, but they did not negate the underlying parity principle.

Those tenets of parity prevented a US-Soviet hot war during the long Cold War. They were the basis of détente's great diplomatic successes, from symbolic bilateral leadership summits, arms control agreements, and the 1975 Helsinki Accords on European security, based on sovereign equality, to many other forms of cooperation now being discarded. And in 1985-1989, they made possible what both sides declared to be the end of the Cold War.

* * *

We are in a new Cold War with Russia today, and specifically over the Ukrainian confrontation, largely because Washington nullified the parity principle. Indeed, we know when, why, and how this happened.

The three leaders who negotiated an end to the US-Soviet Cold War said repeatedly at the time, in 1988-90, that they did so "without any losers." Both sides, they assured each other, were "winners." But when the Soviet Union itself ended nearly two years later, in December 1991, Washington conflated the two historic events, leading the first President Bush to change his mind and declare, in his 1992 State of the Union address, "By the grace of God, America won the Cold War."

Bush added that there was now "one sole and pre-eminent power, the United States of America." This dual rejection of parity and assertion of America's pre-eminence in international relations became, and remains, a virtually sacred US policy-making axiom, one embodied in the formulation by President Bill Clinton's secretary of state, Madeleine Albright, that "America is the world's indispensable nation." It was echoed in President Obama's 2014 address to West Point cadets: "The United States is and remains the one indispensable nation."

This official American triumphalist narrative is what we have told ourselves and taught our children for nearly twenty-five years. Rarely is it challenged by leading American politicians or commentators. It is a bipartisan orthodoxy that has led to many US foreign policy disasters, not least in regard to Russia.

For more than two decades, Washington has perceived post-Soviet Russia as a defeated and thus lesser nation, presumably analogous to Germany and Japan after World War II, and therefore as a state without legitimate rights and interests comparable to America's, either abroad or at home, even in its own region. Anti-parity thinking has shaped every major Washington policy toward Moscow, from the disastrous crusade to remake Russia in America's image in the 1990s, ongoing expansion of NATO to Russia's borders, non-reciprocal negotiations known as "selective cooperation," double-standard conduct abroad, and broken promises to persistent "democracy-promotion" intrusions into Russia's domestic politics.

Two exceedingly dangerous examples are directly related to the Ukrainian crisis. For years, US leaders have repeatedly asserted that Russia is not entitled to any "sphere of influence," even on its own borders, while at the same time enlarging the US sphere of influence, spearheaded by NATO, to those borders—by an estimated 400,000 square miles, probably the largest such "sphere" inflation ever in peacetime. Along the way, the US political-media establishment has vilified Putin personally in ways it never demonized Soviet Communist leaders, at least after Stalin, creating the impression of another orientation antithetical to parity—the delegitimization of Russia's government.

Moscow has repeatedly protested this US sphere creep, loudly after it resulted in a previous proxy war in another former Soviet republic, Georgia, in 2008, but to deaf or defiant ears in Washington. Inexorably, it seems, Washington's anti-parity principle led to today's Ukrainian crisis. Moscow reacted as it would have under any established national leader, and as any well-informed observer knew it would.

Unless the idea of détente is fully rehabilitated, and with it the essential parity principle, the new Cold War will include a growing risk of actual war with nuclear Russia. Time may not be on our side, but reason is.

Part II

US Follies and Media Malpractices
2016

Secret Diplomacy On Ukraine

January 20

DIPLOMATIC ACTIVITY BY WASHINGTON, PARIS, GERMANY, MOSCOW, and Kiev since early January, largely unreported in the American media, may be the last, best chance to end the Ukrainian crisis. Russian President Vladimir Putin appointed two trusted and experienced associates as his personal representatives to Kiev and to the anti-Kiev rebels in Donbass. A few days later, on January 13, President Barack Obama placed a call to Putin, the man he had vowed to "isolate" in international affairs, with Ukraine a priority of their discussion. Two days later, a leading American and Russian opponent of negotiations, Victoria Nuland and Vyacheslav Surkov, met privately in a remote Russian enclave. On January 18–19, representatives of German Chancellor Angela Merkel and French President Francois Hollande met with Ukrainian President Petro Poroshenko in Kiev.

At issue were two essential elements of the Minsk Accords, drafted by Merkel and Hollande and ratified by Putin and Poroshenko but resisted for many months by Poroshenko: constitutional legislation in Kiev granting the rebel regions a significant degree of home rule; and the legitimacy of forthcoming elections in those regions. All sides reported significant progress, though Poroshenko said he lacked sufficient votes in the Ukrainian Parliament, a tacit admission he fears the possibility of a violent backlash by armed ultranationalist forces.

Dire problems at home have compelled all of these leaders to undertake the intense negotiations, problems ranging from Europe and Syria to Russia's economic woes, as well as their own political standing at home. In this context, the US media-political narrative is wrong about what Putin wants in

Ukraine: not a permanently destabilized country, as is incessantly reported, but a peaceful neighbor that does not threaten Russia's vital economic or security interests—or permanently divide millions of inter-married Russian-Ukrainian families.

These negotiations face many obstacles—in particular, powerful opposition in Washington and NATO. But the secret diplomacy represents a possible turning point, a fork in the road, one that will test the qualities of the leaders involved and could shape their historical reputations, first and foremost those of Presidents Obama and Putin.

The Obama Administration Escalates Military Confrontation With Russia

February 3

THE PENTAGON HAS ANNOUNCED IT WILL quickly quadruple the positioning of US-NATO heavy weapons and troops near Russia's western borders. The result will be to further militarize the new Cold War, making it more confrontational and more likely to lead to actual war.

The move is unprecedented in modern times. Except for Nazi Germany's invasion of the Soviet Union during World War II, Western military power has never been positioned so close to Russia, thereby making the new Cold War even more dangerous than was the preceding one.

Russia will certainly react, probably by moving more of its own heavy weapons, including new missiles, to its Western borders, possibly along with tactical nuclear weapons. This should remind us that a new and more dangerous US-Russian nuclear arms race has also been under way for several years. The Obama administration's decision can only intensify it. The decision will have other woeful consequences, undermining ongoing negotiations by Secretary of

State John Kerry and Russian Foreign Minister Sergei Lavrov for cooperation on the Ukrainian and Syrian crises and further dividing Europe, which is far from united on Washington's increasingly hawkish approach to Moscow.

We can only despair that these ongoing developments have barely been reported in the US media and publicly debated not at all, not even by current American presidential candidates or raised by moderators of their "debates." Never before has such a dire international situation been so ignored in a US presidential campaign. The reason may be that everything which has happened since the Ukrainian crisis erupted in 2014 has been blamed solely on the "aggression" of Russian President Putin—a highly questionable assertion but an orthodox media narrative.

Another Turning Point in the New Cold War

February 24

UKRAINE REMAINS THE POLITICAL EPICENTER OF the new Cold War, but Syria is where it may become a hot war. The Syrian ceasefire agreement—brokered by Secretary of State Kerry and his Russian counterpart Lavrov, and emphatically endorsed by Russian President Putin but less so by President Obama—offers hope on several levels, from the suffering Syrian people to those of us who want a US–Russian coalition against the Islamic State and its terrorist accomplices, and thus the possibility of diminishing the new Cold War.

The actual chances of a successful ceasefire are slim, due partly to the number of combatants and lack of a monitoring mechanism, but mainly to powerful forces opposed to the ceasefire both in Washington and Moscow. American opposition is already clear from statements by leading politicians, from Secretary of Defense Ashton Carter's clear dissatisfaction with Kerry's negotiations with Moscow and from anti-ceasefire reports and editorials in the establishment media.

At the same time, Putin's unusual personal ten-minute announcement of the ceasefire on Russian television suggests that some of his own military-security advisers are opposed to the agreement, for understandable reasons. They want to pursue Moscow's military success in Syria achieved since it intervened in September 2015. The ceasefire is now Putin's own diplomatic policy, leaving him vulnerable to the commitment of President Obama, who has previously violated agreements with the Kremlin, most recently and consequentially by disregarding his pledge not to pursue regime change in Libya.

In Ukraine, President Poroshenko continues to demonstrate that he is less a national leader than a compliant representative of domestic and foreign political forces. Having again promised Germany and France that he would implement the Minsk Accords for ending Ukraine's civil war, which they designed, he promptly reneged, bowing to Ukrainian ultra-right movements that threaten to remove him. And having called for the ouster of his exceedingly unpopular Prime Minister Arseny Yatsenyuk—"our guy," as the US State Department termed him in 2014 and still views him—Poroshenko then instructed members of his party to vote against the parliamentary motion, leaving Yatsenyuk in office, at least for now.

With Washington, and Vice President Joseph Biden in particular, widely seen to be behind this duplicity, Poroshenko increasingly resembles a pro-consul of a faraway great power. At the same time, on the second anniversary of the violent Maidan protests that brought to power the current US–backed government, the State Department hailed the "glories" of what is now becoming a failed Ukrainian state and ruined country.

The Obama Administration Attacks Its Own Syrian Ceasefire

March 2

THE US-RUSSIAN-BROKERED CEASEFIRE IN SYRIA PRESENTS an opportunity to deal a major blow to the Islamic State, greatly diminish the Syrian civil war, and generate cooperation between Washington and Moscow elsewhere, including in Ukraine. The agreement is, however, under fierce attack on many fronts. US "allies" Turkey and Saudi Arabia are threatening to disregard the ceasefire provisions by launching their own war in Syria. In Washington, Secretary of Defense Carter and his top generals informed the White House and Congress that Secretary of State Kerry's agreement with Moscow is a "ruse," and that Putin's Russia remains the "No. 1 existential threat" to the United States—charges amply echoed in the American mainstream press.

Much is at stake. The "Plan B" proposed by Carter apparently means a larger US military intervention in Syria to create an anti-Russian, anti-Assad "safe zone" that would in effect partition the country. Viewed more broadly, this would continue the partitioning of political territories that began with the end of the Soviet Union and Yugoslavia in the 1990s and now looms over Syria, Ukraine, and possibly even the European Union.

Moreover, though today's severe international crises get scant attention in the ongoing US presidential campaigns, candidate Hillary Clinton has a potentially large and highly vulnerable stake in the Syrian crisis. As documented by a two-part *New York Times* investigation, then-Secretary of State Clinton played the leading role in the White House's decision to topple Libyan leader Moammar Gaddafi in 2011. That folly led to a terrorist-ridden failed state and growing bastion of the Islamic State. Clinton's campaign statements suggest that she does not support Kerry's initiatives but instead a replication of the Libyan operation in order to remove Syrian President Assad—a version, it seems, of Carter's "Plan B."

Meanwhile, there is the familiar (and meaningless) accusation that Putin has "weaponized information," including about Syria. A critical-minded reader should ask whether US mainstream information is any more reliable than Russia's.

Was Putin's Syria Withdrawal Really a "Surprise"?

March 16

WHY HAVE PURPORTED US EXPERTS BEEN repeatedly surprised by what President Vladimir Putin does and does not do? Clearly, they do not read or listen to him.

When Putin began the air campaign in Syria in the fall of 2015, he announced that it had two purposes. To bolster the crumbling Syrian Army so it could fight terrorist groups on the ground and prevent the Islamic State from taking Damascus. And thereby to bring about peace negotiations among anti-terrorist forces. Putin said he hoped to achieve this in a few months.

In short, mission, in Putin's words, now "generally accomplished," though you would not know it from American media reports. US policy- makers and pundits seem to believe their own anti-Putin propaganda, which for years has so demonized him that they cannot imagine he seeks anything other than military conquest and empire building. Nor can they concede that Russia has legitimate national security interests in Syria.

They similarly do not understand what Putin hopes to achieve: a de-militarization of the new Cold War. In particular, if the end of Russia's Syrian bombing campaign abets peace negotiations under way in Geneva or anywhere else, the diplomatic process could spread to Ukraine, another militarized conflict between Washington and Moscow.

Also unnoticed, Putin's decision to withdraw militarily from Syria, even though only partially, exposes him to political risks at home, where he is, we need to recall, considerably less than an absolute dictator. Hard-liners in the Russian political-security establishment—de facto allies of Washington's own war party—are already asking why he stalled the achieved Russian-Syrian military advantage instead of taking Aleppo, pressing on toward the Syrian-Turkish border, and inflicting more damage on ISIS. Why, they ask, would Putin again seek compromise with the Obama administration, which has repeatedly "betrayed" him, most recently in Libya in 2011 and by its anti-Russian coup in Kiev in 2014? And why, they also ask, if Washington perceives the Syrian withdrawal as "weakness" on Putin's part, will the United States not escalate its "aggression" in Ukraine?

All this comes as Russia's economic hardships have enabled Putin's political opponents at home, the large Communist Party in particular, to try to mount a new challenge to his leadership. But the gravest threat to his clear preference for diplomacy over war is less his domestic critics than the Obama administration, which seems not to have decided which it prefers.

Trump vs. Triumphalism

March 23

WHATEVER ELSE ONE MAY THINK ABOUT Donald Trump as a presidential candidate, his foreign policy views expressed, however elliptically, in a *Washington Post* interview this week should be welcomed. They challenge the bipartisan neocon/liberal interventionist principles and practices that have guided Washington policy-making since the 1990s—with disastrous results.

That policy-making has involved the premise that the United States is the sole, indispensable superpower with a right to intervene wherever it so decides by military means and political regime changes. In the process, Washington has used select NATO members ("coalitions of the willing") as its own United Nations and rule-maker. In recent years, from Iraq and Libya to Ukraine and Syria, the results have been international instability, wars (unilateral, proxy, and civil), growing terrorism, failed "nation building," mounting refugee crises, and a new Cold War with Russia.

Trump seems to propose instead diplomacy ("deals") toward forming partnerships, including with Russia; rethinking NATO's mission; urging Europe to take political and financial responsibility for its own crises, as in Ukraine; and perhaps diminishing America's military footprint in the world. In effect, a less missionary and militarized American national-security policy.

Trump may be calling on an older Republican foreign policy tradition. In any event, he appears to be advocating two realist perspectives. The world is no longer unipolar, pivoting around Washington; and the United States must share and balance power with other great powers, from Europe to Russia and China.

The orthodox bipartisan establishment, Republicans and Democrats alike, have reacted to Trump's proposals as though he is the foreign policy anti-Christ, leveling all-out assaults on his remarks. It is possible that this confrontation might lead, if the mainstream media do their job, to the public debate over US foreign policy that has been missing for twenty years, certainly during the 2016 presidential campaign.

A Fragile Mini-Détente In Syria

March 30

BY REGAINING CONTROL OF PALMYRA, A major and ancient city, the Syrian army and its ground allies, backed by Russian air power, have dealt ISIS its most important military defeat. The victory belies the US political-media establishment's allegations that President Putin's six-month military intervention was a sinister move designed to thwart the West's fight against terrorism. Instead, it has gravely wounded the Islamic State, whose agents were behind recent terrorist assaults on Paris and Brussels.

This comes in the context of fledgling US–Russian cooperation in Syria, a kind of mini-détente brokered by Secretary of State Kerry and Russian Foreign Minister Lavrov. Not surprisingly, these positive developments are being assailed by the US policy-media war party, which has redoubled its vilification of Putin. Preposterously, for example, he is accused of "weaponizing the migration crisis" in Europe, even though the crisis began long before Russia's intervention in Syria. (If the intervention continues to be successful, it might eventually diminish the number of immigrants fleeing that war-torn, terror-ridden country.)

Putin is clearly behind Lavrov's initiatives, even meeting with Kerry several times. Obama's position, however, remains unclear. And neither he nor the US commander of NATO congratulated or otherwise applauded the Russian-Syrian victory in Palmyra, while Obama again went out of his way to insult Putin personally (twice).

With White House backing, the Kerry-Lavrov mini-détente might extend to the political epicenter of the new Cold War, Ukraine. Instead, Washington is seeking to make the US-born Natalie Jaresko prime minister of Ukraine, putting an American face on the ongoing Western colonization of the Kiev government. Jaresko is also the candidate of the US-controlled IMF, on which Kiev is financially dependent but whose demands for austerity measures and "privatization" of state enterprises will almost certainly further diminish the government's popular support, abet the rise of ultra-right-wing forces, and worsen Kiev's conflict with Russia.

Donald Trump has emerged as the only American presidential candidate to challenge the bipartisan policies that contributed so greatly to this new Cold War. Predictably, the US national security establishment has reacted to Trump with a version of the preceding Cold War's red-baiting. Thus, Hillary Clinton charged that Trump's less militarized proposals would be like "Christmas in the Kremlin." The mainstream media have taken the same approach to Trump, thereby continuing to deprive America of the foreign policy debate it urgently needs.

"Information War" vs. Embryonic Détente

April 6

THE KREMLIN IS CHARGING THAT A spate of Western news allegations against President Putin are designed to disrupt US-Russian relations at a critical point. The allegations include not only the Panama Papers investigation of Kremlin offshore investments but also apartments purchased for Putin's daughters, his "suspected" involvement in the Washington death of a former top Russian official, and even a rumored romance between the Russian president and Rupert Murdoch's ex-wife.

Whether or not this is an organized "information war" is unclear, but similar anti-Kremlin "news" appeared regularly during the preceding 40-year Cold War when relations seemed headed toward détente. This is such a moment in the new Cold War, as negotiations between Secretary of State Kerry and Russian Foreign Minister Lavrov suddenly seem promising, especially in regard to the Syrian ceasefire and possibly even Ukraine.

Why, then, in the aftermath of the Syrian-Russian victory over the Islamic State at Palmyra and elsewhere, are "moderate oppositionists" backed by the United States, Saudi Arabia, and Turkey violating the ceasefire agreement by attacking Syrian forces? And why the sudden spate of news reports, apparently inspired by the Obama administration, about Putin's alleged personal "corruption?" They can only be intended to present him as an unfit US ally in Syria or anywhere else.

But the Panama Papers did more political damage to Petro Poroshenko, president of the Washington-backed government in Kiev. They revealed that he had personally established offshore accounts and, still worse, while his Ukrainian army was suffering a humiliating defeat at the hands of the Russian-backed rebels in Eastern Ukraine in August 2014. (Unlike Putin, Poroshenko and his offshore accounts were named in the investigation.)

With the Kiev government already in deep political and economic crisis, this is a further blow to Poroshenko's standing with the Ukrainian elite and people. There are already calls for his impeachment. How will the Obama administration deal with this latest crisis of its "Ukrainian project," as it is sometimes derisively termed, which has all but wrecked Washington's relations with Moscow?

Among the current American presidential candidates, only Donald Trump continues to say anything meaningful and critical about US bipartisan foreign policy. In effect, he has asked five fundamental (and dissenting) questions. Should the United States always be the world's leader and policeman? What is NATO's proper mission today, 25 years after the end of the Soviet Union and when international terrorism is the main threat to the West? Why does Washington repeatedly pursue a policy of regime change—in Iraq, Libya, Ukraine, and now in Damascus, even though it always ends in "disaster"? Why is the United States treating Putin's Russia as an enemy and not as a security partner? And should US nuclear-weapons doctrine adopt a no–first use pledge?

Trump's foreign policy questions are fundamental and urgent. Instead of engaging them, his opponents (including President Obama) and the mainstream media dismiss them as ignorant and dangerous. Some of his outraged critics are even branding him "the Kremlin's Candidate"—thereby anathematizing alternative views and continuing to shut off the debate our country so urgently needs.

The Crisis of the US "Ukrainian Project"

April 13

UKRAINE REMAINS THE POLITICAL EPICENTER OF a new Cold War that prevents Washington and Moscow from cooperating on issues of vital national security, most recently mounting threats of terrorism, potentially nuclear terrorism, in Europe and, soon no doubt, elsewhere.

Petro Poroshenko, president of the US-backed Kiev government, has suffered a recent succession of political blows, including right-wing and "liberal" threats to overthrow him; an inability to appoint a new prime minister; a Dutch referendum vote against giving his government the European Union partnership he wants; the Panama Papers revelations about his personal offshore accounts; and more. The US political-media establishment blames Poroshenko's problems on Ukraine's rampant financial corruption and on the "aggression" of Russian President Putin, but the underlying cause is the real political history of Poroshenko's "Maidan Revolution" regime.

As the second anniversary of Ukraine's civil war (and US-Russian proxy war) approaches, we need to recall some of the disgraceful episodes of the proclaimed "Revolution of Dignity." That history includes the following episodes:

• The violent overthrow of Ukraine's constitutionally elected president, Viktor Yanukovych, in February 2014.

• Kiev's refusal to seriously investigate the "Maidan snipers," whose killings precipitated Yanukovych's ouster, assassins who now seem to have been not his agents, as initially alleged, but those of right-wing Maidan forces.

• The new government's similar refusal to prosecute extreme nationalists behind the subsequent massacre of pro-Russian protesters in Odessa shortly later in 2014.

• And the new Maidan government's unwillingness to negotiate with suddenly disenfranchised regions of Eastern Ukraine, which had largely voted for Yanukovych, and instead to launch an "anti-terrorist" military assault on them.

• Even Poroshenko's subsequent election as president was questionably democratic, opposition regions and parties having been effectively banned.

All this was done, and not done, officially in the name of "European values" and in order to "join Europe," and with the full support of the West, particularly the Obama administration. Two years later, the Ukrainian civil war has taken nearly 10,000 lives, created perhaps 2 million refugees, empowered armed quasi-fascist forces that threaten to overthrow Poroshenko, and left the country in near economic and social ruin.

The Dutch referendum was not the first sign that the European Union is wearying of the disaster it helped to create. Two of its top officials had already stated that Kiev actually had no chance of joining the European Union for "20 to 25 years." More and more Europeans are asking why their leaders forced Kiev in 2013 to choose between the EU and its traditional trading partner, Russia, instead of embracing Putin's proposal for a three-way economic arrangement that would have included Russia.

In Cold-War Washington and its media, the question as to why the Obama administration also imposed the choice on Ukraine is not even raised. There is only more blaming of "Putin's Russia" for a tragedy that continues to unfold. For a truer understanding, look back to its origins.

Is War With Russia Possible?

May 4

URING THE PAST TWO WEEKS, THE Obama administration appears to have been undermining cooperation with Moscow on three new Cold War fronts.

It has refused to accept President Putin's compelling argument that the Syrian army and its allies are the only "boots on the ground" fighting the Islamic State effectively, currently around the pivotal city of Aleppo. Instead, Washington and its compliant media are condemning the Syrian-Russian military campaign against "moderate" anti-Assad fighters in the area, many of them actually also jihadists. At risk are the Geneva peace negotiations brokered by Secretary of State Kerry and Russian Foreign Minister Lavrov.

Regarding the confrontation over Ukraine, where Kiev's political and economic crisis grows ever worse, the best hope for ending that civil and proxy war, the Minsk Accords, was virtually sabotaged at the UN, where US Ambassador Samantha Power claimed the accords require Russia returning Crimea to Ukraine. In fact, Crimea is not even mentioned in the Minsk agreement.

And in Europe, where opinion mounts favoring an end to the economic sanctions against Russia—as evidenced by the Dutch referendum against admitting Ukraine to the European Union and by the French Parliament's vote in favor of ending the sanctions—the Obama administration (not only Ambassador Power but President Obama himself) is lobbying hard against such a step when the issue comes up for a vote this summer.

Meanwhile, US-led NATO continues to increase its land, sea, and air build-up on or near Russia's borders. Not surprisingly, Moscow responds by sending its planes to inspect a US warship sailing not far from Russia's military-naval base at Kaliningrad. Preposterously, having for two decades steadily moved NATO's military presence from Berlin to Russia's borders, and now escalating it, Washington and Brussels accuse Moscow of "provocations against NATO." But who is "provoking"—"aggressing" against—whom? The NATO buildup can only stir in Russians memories of the Nazi

German invasion in 1941, the last time such hostile military forces mobilized on the country's frontier. Some 27.5 million Soviet citizens died in the aftermath.

Though not reported in the US media, an influential faction in Kremlin politics has long insisted, mostly but not always behind closed doors, that the US-led West is preparing an actual hot war against Russia, and that Putin has not prepared the country adequately at home or abroad. During the past two weeks, this conflict over policy has erupted in public with three prominent members of the Russian elite charging, sometimes implicitly but also explicitly, that Putin has supported his "fifth column" government headed by Prime Minister Dmitri Medvedev. Critics are not seeking to remove Putin; there is no alternative to him and his public approval ratings, exceeding 80 percent, are too high.

But they do want the Medvedev government replaced and their own policies adopted. Those policies include a Soviet-style mobilization of the economy for war and more proactive military policies abroad, especially in Ukraine. In this context, we should ask whether US and NATO policy-makers are sleepwalking toward war with Russia or whether they actively seek it.

Stalin Resurgent, Again

June 1

IN ANOTHER EXAMPLE OF UNINFORMED COVERAGE of Russia, American media are misrepresenting the current upsurge of pro-Stalin sentiments as unique to the Putin era. In public opinion surveys, nearly 60 percent of Russians asked now view the despot as a positive figure in their country's history.

Having studied and written about the Stalin era and its legacy for many decades, most recently in my book *The Victims Return*, I have often explained that Russia has been deeply divided over Stalin's historical role ever since his death in 1953, 63 years ago.

Looking back, Russians see two towering mountains, each informed by contested history. On one side, a mountain of Stalin's achievements in the form of industrialization and modernization in the 1930s, however draconian, that prepared the county, they insist, for the great victory over Nazi Germany in 1941–1945. And on the other, a mountain of human victims resulting from Stalin's brutal forced collectivization of the peasantry and Great Terror with its Gulag of torture prisons, mass executions, and often murderous forced labor camps, both of which killed millions of people.

Russian and Western historians, with access since the 1990s to long closed archives, are still trying to strike a scholarly balance, but for ordinary Russians the balance is more directly affected by their perceptions of their own well-being at home and of Russia's national security. Positive views of Stalin do not mean they want a new Stalin in the Kremlin or a recapitulation of Stalinism, but that the despot is for many a historical, and still relevant, symbol of a strong state, law and order, and national security.

These conflicts over Stalin's reputation began publicly long ago, in the 1950s under Soviet leader Nikita Khrushchev, who assailed the personal cult created by Stalin. They continued under Leonid Brezhnev when the disputes were muffled by tightened censorship. They burst fully into the open during Gorbachev's attempted anti-Stalinist reformation known as glasnost and perestroika in the late 1980s and during the Yeltsin 1990s, when economic and social hard times afflicted most Russian citizens and caused Stalin's popular ratings to surge again. And, of course, they continue under Putin.

There are three American media misrepresentations regarding the most recent resurgence of pro-Stalin sentiments. Under Putin, the Stalinist past is not again being censored. Anti-Stalinist historians, journalists, filmmakers, TV producers, and others continue to present their work to the public. Today, the horrors of the Stalin era are widely known in Russia. Second, nothing remotely akin to historical Stalinism is present or unfolding in Russia today, contrary to assertions by several leading US newspapers.

And third, Putin, who has had to try politically to straddle and unite profoundly conflicting eras in Russian history—Tsarist, Soviet, and post-Soviet—is not himself, in words or deeds, a Stalinist. To the contrary, due to his personal support there is now in Moscow a large, modern State Museum of the History of the Gulag and currently under construction a national monument memorializing Stalin's victims, first called for by Khrushchev in 1961, but never even begun under any of Putin's predecessors. (For perspective, note that in Washington there is still no national monument dedicated to the victims of American slavery.)

Nor is Stalin merely an historical issue in Russia. Intensified moments during the preceding Cold War always inflated pro-Stalin sentiments in Soviet Russia. This is happening again today in response to NATO's perceived military encirclement of Russia, from the Baltics to Ukraine and Georgia, and in response to the Western sanctions that have contributed to economic hardships for many Russians. How this will affect Putin's leadership and own popular support (still well above 80 percent) remains to be seen. But it is worth noting that the Russian Communist Party, the second largest in the country and itself somewhat divided over the Stalinist past, has decided to put Stalin's image on its campaign materials for the forthcoming parliamentary elections in September.

Has Washington Gone Rogue?

June 22

WHAT IS THE MEANING OF THE recent escalation of Washington's anti-Russian behavior? Consider only its growing NATO military buildup on Russia's western borders, refusal to cooperate with Moscow against the Islamic State in Syria, and the Obama administration's unwillingness to compel the US-backed government in Kiev to implement a negotiated settlement of the Ukrainian civil war. Is an undeclared US war against Russia already underway? Given that many US allies are unhappy with these developments, has Washington gone "rogue"? And does the recent spate of US warfare "information" reflect this reality?

Undoubtably, there is some alarming evidence. NATO's "exercises" on Russia's borders on land, sea, and in the air are becoming permanent. The Obama administration refuses to separate its "moderate oppositionists" in

Syria from anti-Assad fighters who are affiliated with terrorist groups, despite having promised to do so. There is the unprecedented public demand by 51 State Department "diplomats" that Obama launch air strikes against Assad's Syrian army, which is allied with Moscow, even if it might mean "military confrontation with Russia." And we have the questionable allegation that the Kremlin hacked files of the Democratic National Committee followed by a NATO statement that hacking a member state might now be regarded as war against the entire military alliance, requiring military retaliation.

Some of Washington's European and other allies clearly are unhappy with these developments, even opposed to them. The German Foreign Minister, for example, denounced NATO's ongoing buildup as "war-mongering." Several major European countries, which (unlike the United States) are suffering the reciprocal costs of economic sanctions on Russia are expressing discontent with them. There is the relative success of Russia's international economic conference in St. Petersburg last week, hosted by President Putin personally, whom the Obama administration continues to try to "isolate." There is even a growing political and security relationship between Israeli Prime Minister Benjamin Netanyahu and the Russian president.

Whether or not Washington's behavior constitutes undeclared war, Putin warned, at the international conference, that if such US conduct continues it will mean "war." As a result, Moscow is preparing for the worst, bringing the two nuclear superpowers closer to their worst confrontation since the 1962 Cuban Missile Crisis.

Some American pundits think warlike steps by Washington will benefit Hillary Clinton in the presidential election. She has long and clearly associated herself with hardline US policies toward Russia, but the question is larger. Even though a presidential election is supposed to feature the best aspects of American democracy, including full public discussion of foreign policy, the mainstream media have largely deleted these vital questions from their election coverage. Given full coverage, including of Donald Trump's foreign-policy views, which are significantly unlike those of Clinton, especially regarding Russia, we might learn two important things. Would Trump's less hawkish positions appeal to American voters? And will those voters see through and reject establishment media cheerleading for, in effect, Washington's rogue-like flirting with war with Russia?

Blaming Brexit on Putin and Voters

June 29

For years, I and others have pointed to the gradual disintegration of what Washington calls "the post–Cold War world order," even though Russia, the world's largest territorial country, was excluded by the expansion of NATO and the (in effect) US-led European Union. And even though multiple crises of this US-led "order"—from economic inequality and Europe's refugee crisis to the Ukrainian civil war—were abetted by Washington's own policies. Brexit is the most recent manifestation of this ongoing historic process.

But instead of reconsidering Western policies, the US political-media establishment is blaming Brexit on Putin for "ruthlessly playing a weak hand," as did a *New York Times* editorial on June 26, and on "imbecilic" British voters, as did *Times* columnist Roger Cohen on June 28. In fact, Putin took a determinedly neutral stand on Brexit throughout, partly because Moscow, unlike Washington, is hesitant to meddle so directly in elections in distant countries. But also because the Kremlin was—and remains—unsure as to whether Brexit might be on balance a "plus or minus" for Russia.

Judging by the debate still under way in Russian media, Moscow worries Brexit will be a "minus" due to adverse economic consequences for Russia. In addition, the Kremlin worries that with the UK soon to be outside the EU, the United States and its traditionally Russophobic British partner will now increase NATO "aggression" against Russia, as indeed a *Washington Post* editorial urged on June 27. Therefore, contrary to the legion of American cold warriors, Brexit evoked no "celebration in the Kremlin," only wait-and-see concern.

The denigration of British voters, who mostly voted their working and lower-middle class economic and social interests, as they saw them, is perhaps even more shameful. It reveals Western elite attitudes toward democracy and "imbecilic" citizens. Not surprisingly, the UK establishment, with US encouragement, is desperately seeking a way to reverse the Brexit referendum, much as the Republican establishment is trying to deprive Donald Trump of the presidential nomination he won democratically in the primaries.

This is not the first time ruling elites have shown their contempt for democratic process. Twenty-five years ago, in 1991, the Soviet nomenklatura, in pursuit of state property, disregarded a national referendum that by a much larger majority than in the Brexit case favored preserving the Soviet Union.

There's also some irony here. During the week that Brexit furthered the disintegration of the EU, Putin was further integrating Russia's economy and security with China and with the multinational Shanghai Cooperation Organization, which may soon include India and Pakistan. Considering the size of those economies and of their populace, who is being "isolated"—Putin or the American president who announced his determination "to isolate" him?

Considering the largely negative US role in world affairs since the end of the Soviet Union, not the least of which is its new Cold War against Russia, it may be time for an American Exit (Amexit) from Washington's ceaseless quest for international hegemony.

The Imperative of a US-Russian Alliance vs. Terrorism

July 6

PRESIDENT OBAMA'S GENERALS HAVE REPEATEDLY INSISTED that Russia under Vladimir Putin is the "number-one existential threat" in the world today. This is a virtually impeachable misconception of national security.

The evidence cited is mostly bogus—for example, that Putin is planning a military takeover of the three small Baltic states, perhaps also Poland, and that he seeks to break up the European Union. In reality, Putin needs a stable and prosperous EU as an essential Russian trading partner. And he wants security guarantees for Russia, instead of NATO's ongoing buildup, from the Baltics to the Black Sea, which will be ratified and made permanent at NATO's Warsaw summit on July 6-7. Any actual Russian threats today are primarily of the West's own making—reactions to US-led policies in recent years.

The real "number-one" threat, from the Middle East and Europe to the American homeland, is international terrorism. Today's terrorist organizations are a new phenomenon, no longer loners or tiny groups with a gun or a bomb, but a highly organized menace with state-like funding, armies, technology, modern communications, and a capacity to recruit adherents. Still worse, they are in search of radioactive materials to enrich their already highly destructive explosives, which could make areas they strike uninhabitable for many years. Imagine the consequences if the planes of 9/11 had had such materials aboard.

Russia—because of decades fighting terrorism at home and abroad and its geopolitical location both in the West and in the Islamic world—is America's essential partner in the struggle against this new terrorism. Moscow has experience, intelligence, and other assets that Washington and its current allies lack. It should be enough to remember that Moscow informed Washington about the Boston Marathon bombers months before they struck, but the warning was disregarded.

And yet, Washington has steadfastly excluded a willing Kremlin from its own ineffectual and often counter-productive "war against terrorism," refusing systematic cooperation with Moscow. For their part, mainstream media "analyses" about what to do, after each new terrorist act, rarely if ever even mention a role for Russia. This despite the considerable damage inflicted on the Islamic State in Syria by Putin's air campaign allied with Syrian Army and Iranian "boots on the ground"—an achievement only denigrated, when noted at all, by the US political-media establishment. It does so partly because of its Cold War against Russia, reflected in NATO's provocative build-up on Russia's Western borders, and because of Washington's self-defeating obsession with overthrowing Syrian President Assad.

There may be, however, a positive development. According to sources close to Obama, the president now wants at least a partial rapprochement with Russia before leaving office as part of his presidential legacy, beginning in Syria. Related reports were published by the *Washington Post*, though only to express strong opposition, inspired, it seems, by Secretary of Defense Ashton Carter, to any kind of détente with Putin.

American Cold Warriors understand that cooperation in Syria could spread to resolving the Ukrainian crisis and other US-Russian conflicts—that is, to ending or at least winding down the new Cold War. For his part, Putin recently made several public statements expressing his readiness for large-scale cooperation with Obama—"We do not hold grudges," he remarked—and in particular for a "broad anti-terrorism front."

The same sources also report that in this regard Obama is virtually alone in high-level Washington circles, even among his own White House security advisers. If so, there is yet another irony: Obama, who once vowed to "isolate" Putin—probably the world's busiest international statesman in recent months—may now find himself isolated in his own administration.

The Friends and Foes of Détente

July 20

IN RECENT WEEKS, THERE HAS BEEN a behind-the-scenes diplomacy on behalf of full US-Russian military cooperation against the Islamic State in Syria. With Secretary of State Kerry's visit to Moscow last week, the proposal became public. Understanding that a mini-détente in Syria could spread to US-Russian conflicts elsewhere—particularly to the NATO buildup on Russia's border, the conflict over Ukraine, and nuclear-weapons policies—political forces in the American establishment escalated their opposition. They further demonized Putin, charging Obama with "appeasement," and threatened to ban Russia from the upcoming Olympic games in Rio de Janeiro.

The failed coup in Turkey may be an important factor in this struggle, though as with the failed coup against Soviet leader Mikhail Gorbachev 25 years ago, in August 1991, we may not learn the full story for some time. Nonetheless, Turkish President Recep Tayyip Erdoğan, increasingly alienated from the EU and fellow members of NATO, is likely now to resume his previously close relationship with Moscow. If so, he may end his obstruction of the proposed alliance against the Islamic State in Syria.

At the same time, Obama's formal condemnation of the coup has unnerved the US-backed government in Kiev, which came to power in 2014 by overthrowing a president who had also been popularly elected. In response, there is some evidence that Ukraine's current president, Petro Poroshenko, is escalating his military attacks on rebel Donbass, presumably to revive his fading political support in the West.

Meanwhile, at the Republican National Convention in Cleveland, Trump representatives rejected an attempt by cold warriors to write into the party platform a promise to increased US military aid to Kiev—Obama has long refused to do so despite considerable public and private pressure—reinforcing earlier statements by Trump that he, unlike Hillary Clinton, is pro-détente. In response, cold warriors confirmed that there is indeed a new Cold War by echoing an ugly feature of the preceding one—McCarthyism. They accused the Trump campaign of being in cahoots with Putin, even having received money from Moscow.

I have argued for more than 10 years that Washington policy was leading to a renewed Cold War with Moscow. The return of Cold-War Olympic politics and McCarthy-like slurs should eliminate any doubt about the nature of today's US-Russian relations and the vital importance of a new détente.

Neo-McCarthyism

July 27

Having entered academic Russian studies in the 1960s, I recall that even then the field was still afflicted by remnants of the self-censorship bred by the McCarthyism of the 1940s and 1950s. Cold War brings with it this kind of limitation on free speech, so I am not surprised that it may be happening again as a result of the new Cold War with "Putin's Russia." This time, however, it is coming significantly from longstanding liberals who purported to protect us against such civil liberties abuses.

Many liberals and their publications have recently branded Donald Trump as Putin's "puppet" (Franklin Foer), "de facto agent" (Jeffrey Goldberg),

"Kremlin client" (Timothy Snyder). *New York Times* columnist Paul Krugman spells out the implication that Trump "would, in office, actually follow a pro-Putin foreign policy, at the expense of America's allies and her own self-interest." These disgraceful allegations are based on little more than a mistranslation of a casual remark Putin made about Trump, Trump's elliptical suggestions that he may favor détente with Moscow, his tacit endorsement of Obama's refusal to escalate the military conflict in Ukraine, and Russian business relations of Trump's "associates" of the kind eagerly sought since the late 1980s by many American corporations, from ExxonMobil to MacDonald's.

This is, of course, an ominous recapitulation of McCarthy's accusations, which seriously damaged American democracy and ruined many lives. Still worse, this Kremlin-baiting of Trump is coming from the Clinton campaign, which most of the liberals involved support, as reflected in a page-one *Times* story headlined "A Trump-Putin Alliance." Clinton apparently intends to run against Trump-Putin. If so, the new Cold War can only become more dangerous, especially if she wins and if this neo- McCarthyite tactic reflects her hawkish views on "Putin's Russia."

Perhaps not unrelated, Obama's proposal for a US-Russian alliance against the Islamic State in Syria, with its potential for easing the conflict in Ukraine and NATO's buildup on Russia's borders, is now being openly opposed by Secretary of Defense Carter. As a result, it seems, the original proposal to Putin was withdrawn for one that would compel Moscow to accept the longstanding US policy of removing Syrian President Assad. Not surprisingly, it was rejected by Putin, though Secretary of State Kerry has resumed negotiations with his Russian counterpart Lavrov. Where the silent President Obama stands on this vital issue—as Russian and Syrian forces stand ready to take the crucial city of Aleppo, long held by jihadists—is unclear.

Cold-War Casualties From Kiev to the New York Times

August 17

T HE PRECEDING 40-YEAR COLD WAR WAS accompanied by intense high-level factional politics for and against US-Soviet Cold War relations. Sometimes the politics played out behind the scenes, sometimes openly, if obliquely, in the media. It is happening again, perhaps more dangerously and disgracefully.

Last week's still somewhat mysterious episode in Crimea was an important example. Russian President Putin declared that Kiev had sent agents with terrorist intent to (now) Russia's Crimean peninsula. They were captured and one or more Russian security agents killed. Putin said the episode showed that Kiev had no real interest in the Minsk peace talks and that he would no longer participate in them, the other participants being the leaders of Germany, France, and Ukraine. Kiev said the episode was a Russian provocation signaling Putin's intent to launch a large-scale "invasion" of Ukraine.

As must always be asked when a crime is committed, who had a motive? Putin had none that are apparent. Kiev, on the other hand, is in a deepening economic, social, and political crisis and losing its Western support, especially in Europe. It is fully possible that Kiev staged the episode to rally that flagging support by (yet again) pointing to Putin's impending "aggression." Washington seemed to support Kiev's version, raising the question as to whether a faction in the Obama administration was also involved, especially since Europe, particularly Germany, openly doubted Kiev's version. If Putin is serious about quitting the Minsk negotiations, a larger war is now the only way to resolve the Ukrainian civil and proxy war—a way apparently favored by some factions in Washington, Kiev, and possibly in Moscow.

Factional politics were even clearer regarding Syria, where President Obama had proposed military cooperation with Russia against the Islamic State—in effect, finally accepting Putin's longstanding proposal—along with important agreements that would reduce the danger of nuclear war. The *Wall Street Journal* and the *Washington Post* had reported strong factional opposition to both of Obama's initiatives—in effect, a kind of détente with Russia.

Both initiatives have been halted, whether temporarily or permanently is unclear. We may soon know because Putin needs a decision by Obama now, as the crucial battle for Aleppo intensifies. Under his own pressure at home, Putin seems resolved to end the Islamic State's occupation of Syria, Aleppo being a strategic site, without or with US cooperation, which he would prefer to have.

Meanwhile, the *New York Times* continues to make its own factional contributions to the new Cold War, and to Hillary Clinton's presidential campaign, at the expense of its own journalistic standards. Consider its recent article about Paul Manafort, in effect Donald Trump's campaign manager. It alleges that Manafort committed pro-Russian and corrupt dealings on behalf of Ukraine's now deposed President Viktor Yanukovych when Manafort served him as a well-paid political adviser. The *Times* has already printed a number of neo-McCarthyite articles against Trump and his associates, labeling them Putin's "agents."

The Manafort article is another telling example. It violates several journalistic standards. Its source for Manafort's financial corruption in Ukraine came from Kiev's "Anti-Corruption Committee," which even the IMF regards as an oxymoron and a reason the funding organization has not released billions of dollars pledged to Kiev. Even if Manafort was corrupt, The *Times* must have known the questionable nature of the source when it received the "documents," but readers were not told.

More important politically, when working to rebrand Yanukovych as a presidential candidate after his earlier electoral defeat, Manafort was hardly "pro-Russian." Putin profoundly distrusted and personally disliked Yanukoyvch at that time.

One reason was fundamental. Manafort urged Yanukovych, in order to broaden his appeal from his electoral base in southeast Ukraine, to strike a pro-Western economic arrangement with the European Union instead of with Putin's Eurasian Economic Union. Yanukovych tried to do so and almost succeeded. (The last-minute collapse of EU negotiations detonated the Ukrainian crisis in November 2013.) Assuming the *Times* knew this well-known history—admittedly an assumption when it involves *Times* coverage of Russia—this too it did not tell its readers.

The paper's expose of Manafort was also highly selective. However financially corrupt he may have been, Manafort did no more politically in Ukraine, indeed considerably less, than had other well-paid American electoral advisers in other countries. All we need do, though the *Times* did not, is recall the 1996 reelection campaign of then Russian President Boris Yeltsin.

So desperate was the Clinton administration to save the failing but compliant Yeltsin from his Communist Party opponent, it arranged for American election operatives to encamp in Moscow to help manage his campaign. (The administration also arranged for billions of IMF dollars to be sent to enable Yeltsin to pay pensions, wages, and other arrears, some of which was stolen by Yeltsin's associates and diverted to a New York bank.) So large was the role of the American "advisers" in Yeltsin's (purported) victory that *Time* magazine bannered it, "Yanks to The Rescue," on its July 15, 1996 cover and ShowTime made a feature film, "Spinning Boris," about their heroic exploits as late as 2003. No one asked, as we should, whether any Americans should be so intimately involved in any foreign elections.

Finally, the revelation that Manafort had financial dealings with Russian "oligarchs" is ludicrous—and also highly selective. Which of the scores of American corporations doing business in Russia and neighboring countries, from ExxonMobil to McDonald's and Ford, have not, given Russia's oligarchic economic system?

The degradation of the *Times*—in effect, announced on its front page last week in a declaration that it would suspend its own journalistic standards in covering Trump and his presidential campaign—is especially lamentable. In the past, the *Times* set standards for aspiring young journalists. Judging by the growing number of young "journalists" who assail critics of US policy toward Russia as Kremlin "apologists," "stooges," and "useful idiots," rather than actually study the issues and report disagreements even-handedly, the *Times* is no longer an exemplar. Unprofessional, unbalanced journalism remains another casualty of this new Cold War.

More Lost Opportunities

September 7

THREE SIGNIFICANT BUT LITTLE-NOTED DEVELOPMENTS OCCURRED at the G20 meeting in China last week.

Following a private meeting with Russian President Putin, President

Obama retreated from their agreement for joint military action against the Islamic State in Syria. Obama blamed a lack of trust in Putin, but clearly he had capitulated to powerful opposition in Washington to any rapprochement with Moscow. Obama said talks would continue, but yet another lack of resolve on his part was more likely to reinforce Putin's lack of trust in the American president and make it harder for him to sell any such agreement to his own political elite in Moscow.

At the same time, Obama also withdrew his own proposals that would have made nuclear war considerably less likely. They entailed a mutual US-Russian declaration of a doctrine of no-first-use of nuclear weapons; and taking nuclear warheads off high-alert, giving both sides more than the current 14 minutes or so to determine whether or not the other had actually launched a nuclear attack and to decide whether or not to retaliate. Obama was said to have been persuaded by Strangelovian arguments by advisers that such a wise decision, long called for by experts, would undermine US national security.

And in Kiev, President Poroshenko unilaterally reversed the order of steps spelled out in the Minsk Accords to end the Ukrainian civil and proxy war. He declared that returning control of the Eastern border with Russia to Kiev had to be the first step of implementation, not the final step as spelled in the Minsk agreements. In effect, Poroshenko's announcement betrayed German Chancellor Merkel and French President Hollande, who had brokered the Minsk agreements.

Unless Poroshenko relents, he has ended the only existing option for negotiating an end to the Ukrainian conflict. It is hard to imagine that Poroshenko took this step without the permission of the Obama administration, particularly of Vice President Joseph Biden, who has been in charge of the "Ukrainian project" at least since 2014.

There was other largely unreported news at the G20 meeting. Two years ago, Obama declared his intention to "isolate" Putin in world affairs. At the G20 meeting, the Russian president was the most sought-after leader by other world leaders. Obama, on the other hand, seemed marginalized apart from the formal ceremonies. Whether this was because he is a "lame duck" president or is no longer taken seriously as a foreign-policy leader, or both, is a matter of interpretation.

Unlike in the American political-media establishment, there was little evidence at the G20 meeting of the demonization of Putin, which has been a central feature of US policy toward Russia for several years. In this regard, America under Obama hardly seems to be the "leader of the free world."

Despite their pro-forma stances, other countries, including European ones, may continue to drift away from Washington in their actual relations with Russia.

As for the current US presidential campaign, there was little evidence at the G20 meeting that other capitals took seriously Washington charges (all without actual evidence) that Putin's Kremlin was trying to disrupt or decide the outcome of the election. In Europe, for example, a full debate is under way about relations with Russia, while in the US establishment anyone who proposes better relations, particularly Donald Trump, is subjected to neo-McCarthyite charges of being a "Kremlin client" or "Putin puppet."

Undeterred, Trump renewed his call for what once meant "détente," arguing that it would be better to have "friendly" relations with Russia, even a partnership, than today's exceedingly hostile relationship. In effect, Trump has become the pro-détente candidate in the 2016 presidential election, a position previously also taken by other Republican presidents—Eisenhower, Nixon, and Reagan. The pro–Cold War party's refusal to engage Trump on these vital issues, instead of Kremlin-baiting him, continues to be detrimental to US national security and to American democracy.

Another Endangered Chance to Diminish the New Cold War

September 14

TWO POSSIBLE DIPLOMATIC BREAKTHROUGHS, INVOLVING SYRIA and Ukraine, might end or substantially reduce the US-Russian proxy wars in those countries and thus the new Cold War itself.

Representing their respective bosses, Presidents Obama and Putin, Secretary of State Kerry and Foreign Minister Lavrov have announced a plan that, if implemented in the next seven days, would lead to joint US-Russian operations against the terrorist organizations ISIS and Al-Nusra in Syria. If so, the result could be an American-Russian military alliance, the first since World War II, that might end both the war in Syria and the dangerous escalation of the new Cold War elsewhere.

The nearly simultaneous announcements of a unilateral cease fire by Donbass rebels and of a willingness to move on home-rule legislation for Donbass by Ukrainian President Poroshenko, which he has previously refused to do, strongly suggested that this possible diplomatic breakthrough, in effect implementing the Minsk peace accords, was timed to coincide with the one regarding Syria. Given the vital role of Syria and Ukraine in the Cold War, this two-front détente diplomacy represents a fateful opportunity, to be seized or lost as were previous ones.

But opposition to the Obama-Putin Syrian diplomacy is fierce, especially in Washington. It is openly expressed by Department of Defense Secretary Carter and faithfully echoed in leading media, particularly the *Washington Post*, the *New York Times*, and MSNBC. The primary tactic is to further vilify Putin as an unworthy American partner in any regard—an approach driven by years of Putin-phobia and now by an awareness that cooperation in Syria would mark Russia's full return as a great power on the world stage.

Much now depends on whether or not Obama will fight for his own anti–Cold War diplomacy, as President Reagan did in the 1980s but as Obama repeatedly has failed to do. His foreign-policy legacy is at stake, as are international relations.

Opposition to a diplomatic breakthrough in Ukraine is also fierce and potentially dangerous for Poroshenko. Heavily armed ultra-right Ukrainian forces continue to threaten to overthrow him if he yields to European pressure to grant more home rule to rebel Donbass. Under pressure from France, Germany, and possibly the White House, Poroshenko may now think he has no choice, or he may be playing for time, as some observers think. Either way, the Ukrainian conflict is at a turning point, for better or worse, as is the one in Syria.

Unavoidably, these developments are spilling over into the American presidential campaign. However ironically, Donald Trump has, in his own way, like Obama, called for US-Russian military cooperation in Syria. Certainly, his position in this regard is considerably closer to that of President Obama (no matter what the latter unwisely continues to say publicly about Putin) than is that of Hillary Clinton, who thus far has maintained her considerably more hawkish positions both on Russia and Syria.

A full debate on these fateful issues is long overdue in American politics, especially in a presidential electoral year. The mainstream media has all but banned it with neo-McCarthyite allegations against Trump. Will the mainstream media now play their obligatory role or continue to promote the new Cold War?

Who's Making US Foreign Policy?

September 21

THE PRECEDING 40-YEAR COLD WAR WITNESSED many instances of high-level attempts to sabotage détente policies of US and Soviet leaders. It is happening again in the new Cold War, as evidenced when American war planes unexpectedly attacked Syrian Army forces.

The attack blatantly violated preconditions of the Obama-Putin plan for a US-Russian alliance against terrorist forces in Syria. Considering that US military intelligence knew the area very well and that the Department of Defense, headed by Ashton Carter, had openly expressed opposition to the Obama-Putin plan, the attack was almost certainly not "accidental," as DOD claims and as American media similarly reports.

If the attack was intentional, we are reminded of the power of the American war party, which is based not only in DOD but in segments of the intelligence agencies, State Department, Congress, and in the mainstream media, notably the *Washington Post*. Judging by Ambassador Samantha Power's tirade against Russia at the UN, not even Obama's own team fully supports his overtures to Moscow, undertaken in part perhaps to enhance his desultory foreign policy legacy.

Why is the war party so adamantly opposed to any cooperation with Russia anywhere in the world when it is manifestly in US interests, as in Syria? Several considerations play a role. Among them, only Russian President Putin, of major foreign leaders, has politically opposed the neocon/liberal interventionist aspiration for a US-dominated "world order." Hence the incessant demonizing of Putin.

Still more, Russia's return as an international great power, 25 years after the end of the Soviet Union, contradicts and offends the ideological premises of this aspiration. Another but little-noted example is Moscow's recent plan to mediate the decades-long Israeli-Palestinian conflict, a diplomatic initiative based on increasingly warm relations between Putin's government and Israel. Any cooperation with Moscow would therefore validate the "resurgent Russia" phenomenon so resented by the American war party.

One way American cold warriors challenge Russia's role in world affairs today is to denigrate its elections, as though they are mere replicas of Soviet-era charades. Several little-noted results of the September Russian parliamentary (Duma) elections are therefore worth emphasizing.

The elections were relatively "free and fair." (As everywhere, such judgments should be in the context of a country's own history, not our own.) This said while understanding that going back to the "democratic" Yeltsin years, the Kremlin has regularly redistributed some 5 to 10 percent of the votes to its own party or to other parties it wishes to play a minority role in the Duma.

This time those votes seem to have been taken from the only real nationwide opposition party, the Communist Party, which probably received closer to 20 percent of the votes than the just over 13 percent registered, and given to the Kremlin party and to a minority party. (The latter, unlike the Communists, habitually votes for the Kremlin's economic and social legislation.) Contrary to most preelection polling, the Kremlin party got 54 percent, a "constitutional majority," as it is called, suggesting that the Putin leadership may be planning major policy changes at home.

One other result should be emphasized. The several "liberal," pro-Western parties, without any help or harm by the Kremlin, garnered a total of barely 4 percent of the vote. This may be the most authentic result of the election: there is no longer any electoral base for such politics in Russia.

Most American commentators blame the outcome on Putin's repression, but a much larger factor has been US Cold War policies, which are deeply resented by a large majority of Russians. Indeed, a number of independent Russian commentators concluded that the electoral results were a reaffirmation of popular support for Putin and against US-led assaults on his leadership and reputation.

Slouching Toward War?

October 6

THE OBAMA ADMINISTRATION HAS TERMINATED MONTHS-LONG negotiations with Moscow for a joint US-Russian campaign against jihad terrorist forces in Syria. Cooperation in Syria would have been the first major episode of détente in the new Cold War, indeed the first US-Russian military alliance since World War II. Its spirit might have spread to the dangerous conflicts in Ukraine and on Russia's border with Eastern Europe, where NATO continues to build up its forces.

The Syrian agreement was sabotaged not by Russia, as is alleged in Washington and by the mainstream media, but by American enemies of détente, first and foremost in the Department of Defense. DOD's opposition was so intense that one of its spokesmen told the press it might disobey an Obama presidential order to share intelligence with Moscow, as called for by the agreement.

It was a flagrant threat to disregard the US constitution. A *New York Times* editorial not only failed to protest the threat but appeared to endorse it. Other major media seemed not even to notice the possibility of a constitutional crisis, another indication of how badly the new Cold War, and the demonization of Russian President Putin, has degraded the US political-media establishment.

The consequences of thwarted diplomacy in Syria are already evident. American politicians and media are calling for military action against Russian-Syrian forces, in particular, imposition of a "no-fly zone," which would almost certainly lead to war with Russia. Others call for more economic sanctions against Russia, perhaps to ward off growing West European attitudes favoring an end to existing sanctions.

In any event, developments in Syria have now deepened the new Cold War in words and deeds. This is the case in Moscow as well. Putin, who has long pursued negotiations with the West over the objections of his own hardliners, now seems resolved to destroy the jihadist forces encamped in Aleppo without the American partner he had hoped for. Meanwhile, talk of war also fills Russian media, and the Putin government has just begun a highly unusual nation-wide "civil defense" exercise to prepare the country for that eventuality.

In short, the collapse of diplomacy in Syria has fully remilitarized US-Russian relations and brought the countries closer to war than at any time since the Cuban Missile Crisis. Unlike during the preceding Cold War, none of this is being discussed critically in establishment American media. The *New York Times* and the *Washington Post*, for example, publish articles and editorials, one after the other, declaring Putin to be an "outlaw" and "rogue" leader unfit to be an American partner on any front. In the mainstream, no one proposes or is permitted to propose any rethinking of US policies that may have contributed to this dire situation.

No one asks, for example, if the Kremlin might be right in insisting that the overthrow of the Assad government, the primary US goal, would only strengthen terrorist forces in Syria, whose defeat is Moscow's primary objective. In this connection, Moscow charges that détente in Syria failed in large part because Washington and its allies continue to arm and coddle, directly or indirectly, Syrian terrorists and their "moderate" anti-Assad abettors.

This factor, for which there is considerable evidence, also is not explored or discussed in the US media, even in a presidential election year. Instead, CBS News' *60 Minutes*, which, like the *Times*, was once a gold standard of professional American journalism, recently broadcast a nuclear warmongering segment giddily marveling that the United States would soon have more "usable" nuclear weapons to deploy against Russia.

Again, where was the publicly silent President Obama while his proposed détente was being killed by members of his own administration? Russians and West Europeans are also asking this question.

Washington Warmongers,
Moscow Prepares

October 12

WE SHOULD BE "SHOCKED" LESS BY Donald Trump's sexual antics or by Hillary Clinton's misdeeds as secretary of state than by the entire US political-media establishment's indifference to Washington's drift toward war with Russia.

Since the breakdown of the Obama-Putin agreement to cooperate militarily against terrorists in Syria—a failure for which the Obama administration is primarily responsible—Washington has escalated its warfare rhetoric against the Kremlin and particularly Russian President Putin. The man with whom the Obama administration proposed to partner with in Syria only two weeks ago is now denounced as a "war criminal" for Russia's fight against terrorists in Aleppo, which was to be "liberated" by the now aborted US-Russian military alliance. The ever-bellicose *Washington Post* was more specific, publishing a leaked account of how Putin might be arrested outside of Russia and put on trial.

But the first victim might have been Secretary of State Kerry, who negotiated and advocated the proposed alliance and who now must level "war crimes" accusations against Russia, dealing a considerable blow to his own reputation. Putting another nail in the coffin of its jettisoned cooperation with the Kremlin, the White House also officially accused the Putin leadership of trying to undermine the American electoral system through systematic hacking, though it presented no real evidence.

Meanwhile, mainstream media continue to base their coverage of US national security in this regard on unrelenting vilification of Putin, not on actual US interests. Any talk of partnership with Russia, though still advocated by Donald Trump, is being widely traduced as "insanity," as, for example, by MSNBC's unabashedly Russophobic Rachel Maddow.

Moscow is reacting in kind to Washington's words and deeds. The reaction includes unusually harsh speeches by Putin and Foreign Minister Lavrov (formerly Kerry's partner); an unusual nationwide civil-defense exercise; a proposal to give military officials control over regional political leaders in the event of war; and a beefing up of Russian ground-to-air missile defense systems in Syria. While Lavrov spoke of an American policy driven by "aggressive Russophobia," Putin said normal relations could be restored only by Washington reversing all of its Cold War policies in recent years, from NATO expansion to Russia's borders to economic sanctions. Though clearly Putin did not mean this literally, it seems to have been his most expansive condition to date.

For those of us with historical memory, there is a precedent for a way out in dark times in US-Russian relations. Only a generation ago, in the mid- and late 1980s, President Ronald Reagan decided to meet halfway in very fraught times repeatedly with Soviet leader Mikhail Gorbachev. A breakthrough as achieved by Reagan and Gorbachev is urgently needed, but no such leader seems likely to occupy the White House any time soon, unless it might be Trump.

Did the White House Declare War on Russia?

October 19

A STATEMENT BY VICE PRESIDENT JOSEPH BIDEN on NBC's *Meet the Press* on October 16, pre- released on October 14, stunned Moscow, though it was scarcely noted in the American media. In response to a question about alleged Kremlin hacking of Democratic Party headquarters in order to disrupt the presidential election and throw it to Donald Trump, Biden said the Obama administration was preparing to send Putin a harsh "message," presumably in the form of some kind of cyber-attack.

The Kremlin spokesman and several leading Russian commentators characterized Biden's announcement as a virtual "American declaration of war on Russia" and as the first ever in history. At this potentially explosive stage in the new Cold War, Biden's statement, which must have been approved by the White House, could scarcely have been more dangerous or reckless.

Biden was reacting, of course, to official US charges of Kremlin political hacking. No actual evidence for this allegation has yet been produced, only suppositions or, as Glenn Greenwald has pointed out, "unproven assertions." While the political-media establishment has uncritically stated the allegation as fact, a MIT expert, Professor Theodore Postol, has written there is "no technical way that the US intelligence community could know who did the hacking if it was done by sophisticated nation-state actors." Instead, the charges, leveled daily by the Clinton campaign as part of its neo-McCarthyite Kremlin-baiting of Trump, are mostly political. We should ask why some US intelligence officials have permitted themselves to be used for this unprofessional purpose.

Still more, the warlike context includes a stunning reversal of the American political-media establishment's narrative of the ongoing battle for the Syrian city of Aleppo. Only a few weeks ago, as I pointed out, President Obama had agreed with Putin on a joint US-Russian military campaign against "terrorists" in Aleppo. That agreement collapsed primarily due to an attack by US warplanes on Syrian forces. Russia and its Syrian allies continued their air assault on east Aleppo but now, according to Washington and its mainstream media, against anti-Assad "rebels."

Where have the jihad terrorists gone? They have been deleted from the US narrative, which now accuses Russia of "war crimes" in Aleppo for the same military campaign in which Washington was to have been a full partner. Equally obscured is that west Aleppo, largely controlled by Assad's forces, is also being assaulted—by "rebels"—and children are dying there as well.

And why is there no US government or media concern about the children who will almost certainly die in the American-backed campaign to recapture Mosul, in Iraq? Here too the stenographic American media has gone from the fog of cold war to falsification.

Trump Could End the New Cold War

November 16

W ILL, OR CAN, A PRESIDENT TRUMP enact a policy of détente—replac-
ing elements of conflict with elements of cooperation—in US relations with Russia? As we saw earlier, détente had a long 20th-century history.
Indeed, its major episodes were initiated by Republican presidents, from
Eisenhower and Nixon to, most spectacularly, Reagan in 1985.

The history of détente teaches that at least four prerequisites are required:
a determined American president who is willing to fight for the policy against
fierce mainstream political opposition, including in his own party; a leader
who can rally some public support by prominent figures who did not support
his presidential candidacy; a president with like-minded appointees at his
side; and A White House occupant who has a pro-détente partner in the
Kremlin, as Reagan had with Soviet leader Gorbachev.

Whether or not he knows the history of détente, Trump seems determined. During his primary and presidential campaigns, he alone repeatedly
called for cooperation with Moscow for the sake of US national security and
refused to indulge in today's fact-free vilification of Russian President Putin.
Trump also seems little impressed by the bipartisan foreign-policy establishment, even contemptuous of its record during the preceding two decades.
The establishment's certain opposition is unlikely to deter him.

Less clear is whether or not many of Trump's previous opponents in
either party will support détente or whether he will have in his inner circle
of appointees—particularly a secretary of state and ambassador to Moscow—
who will wisely advise and assist him in this vital pursuit, as Reagan had. As
for a partner in the Kremlin, Putin is clearly ready for détente. He has said
and demonstrated as much many times, contrary to commentary about him
in the American media.

In many respects, as we have seen, the new Cold War is more dangerous than was the preceding 40-year Cold War. Three of its current fronts—
Ukraine, the Baltic region, and Syria—are ever more fraught with the possibility of hot war. Détente succeeds, however, when mutual national interests
are agreed upon and negotiated.

The Ukrainian civil and proxy war has become a disaster for Washington,

Moscow, and for the Ukrainian people themselves. Ending it is therefore a common interest, but perhaps the most difficult to negotiate. NATO's ongoing buildup up in the Baltic region and in Poland, and Russia's counter-buildup on its Western borders, are fraught with accidental or intentional war. Avoiding war, as Reagan and Gorbachev agreed, is an existential common interest.

If Trump is determined, he has the power to end the buildup and even reverse it, though the new eastern-most members of NATO will loudly protest. On the other hand, despite claims to the contrary, Russia represents no military threat to these countries, as wise Trump advisers will assure him. Agreement on Syria should be the easiest. Both Trump and Putin have insisted that the real threat there is not Syrian President Assad but the Islamic State and other terrorists. The first major step of a new détente might well be the US-Russian military alliance against terrorist forces that even President Obama once proposed but abandoned.

There are, of course, other new Cold War conflicts, large and smaller ones. Some could be easily and quickly negotiated in order to build elite and popular support for détente in the US. This could begin with the "banomania" both sides have enacted since 2014. For example, Putin could end the ban on American adoptions of Russian orphans, which wrecked the hopes of scores of American families and Russian children. Such a good-will step would give détente a human face and soften opposition in the US.

The largest ban is, of course, US and European economic sanctions on Russia, which Putin wants ended. A more complex issue, this is likely to come to the fore only if or when détente progresses. On the other hand, a number of European countries, which have suffered economically from Russia's counter-sanctions, also want them ended. Trump will not be without allies if he moves in this direction.

There are other considerations. History shows that successful, stable détente requires the give-and-take of diplomacy, something not practiced by the White House with Russia for several years. The standard version of why Obama's détente ("reset") failed, to take an often-cited example, is untrue. Putin did not wreck it. The Obama administration took Moscow's major concessions while making almost none of its own. In this regard, Trump's businessman model of negotiations may be an asset. Businessmen understand that a mutual interest (profit) is gained only when both sides make concessions.

There is also a larger question. As I explained previously, détente rests on what was formerly called "parity," in particular recognition that both sides have legitimate national interests. For many years, due largely to the demonization of Putin, the American political-media establishment has implied that Russia has no legitimate national interests of its own conception, not even on its borders. Trump seems to think otherwise, but as with many of his other elliptical statements, time will tell.

And there is this. Reagan and Gorbachev began with nuclear and other military issues. Trump and Putin might do so as well—for example, by agreeing to take nuclear warheads off high-alert and adopting a mutual doctrine of no-first-use of nuclear weapons, which Obama also briefly proposed but also abandoned. Given current toxic relations between the two countries, however, more political steps may be needed first.

Whether or not Trump vigorously pursues détente with Russia may tell us more about his presidency generally if only because an American president usually has more freedom of action in foreign affairs than in other policy realms. And no issue is now more important than the state of US-Russian relations.

The Friends and Foes of Détente, II

November 23

ANTI-DÉTENTE OPPOSITION HAS QUICKLY EXPRESSED ITSELF in response to President-elect Trump's still elliptical indications that he may seek a strategic partner in Russian President Putin. The opposition is led in the Senate by the usual Cold-War bipartisan axis that includes John McCain, Lindsay Graham, and Benjamin Cardin, and in the print media by the *New York Times* and the *Washington Post*. Their thinking and goals are expressed by one of their stenographers, *Post* columnist Josh Rogin. He warns readers that détente is both impermissible and unattainable because of Putin's "long-term strategy to undermine the stability and confidence of liberal Western democracies."

There is, of course, no evidence that this is Putin's goal. The allegation merely recapitulates existential language of the preceding 40-year Cold War, as though the Soviet Union never ended. Rogin concludes by assuring readers that these American foes of détente are readying a campaign, here and abroad, to "stop the next Russian reset [the term Obama used for détente] before it even begins." If Trump is determined to reduce or even end the new Cold War, another historic struggle over détente has thus begun.

There is, however, a new important factor. Europe is playing a larger and more active role in this Cold War than it did in the preceding one, and there the friends and foes of détente are more evenly divided. Socially, politically, and electorally, a growing number of European countries are increasingly opposed to confronting and trying to isolate Russia. For economic reasons, they are also eager to end the economic sanctions imposed on Moscow by the West.

Non-anti-Russia governments (not necessarily "pro-Russian" ones) have recently come to power in Moldova and Bulgaria. More are possible within a year or so in Austria, Italy, and elsewhere, even in Germany. The Netherlands, Greece, Cyprus, and Spain have already expressed discontent with the sanctions and with the stalemated war in Ukraine. And one exceedingly anti-Russian government, the United Kingdom, has left the European Union via Brexit.

In this respect, Europe may be diminishing its political deference to the United States, currently the most anti-Russian, pro–Cold War of the major powers, along with the UK, and finally edging toward its own foreign policy. If so, what this means for the heralded "transatlantic alliance" may depend on whether or not Trump reaches out for pro-détente allies in Europe.

Just how much relations with Russia are in flux is indicated even by outgoing President Obama. He recently stopped referring to the United States as "the indispensable nation" in world affairs and termed it instead "an indispensable nation," suggesting America might have equal partners. And whereas he once dismissed Russia as a weak "regional power," he has revised that formulation considerably. Now, according to Obama, "Russia is an important country. It is a military superpower… It has influence around the world. And in order for us to solve many big problems around the world, it is in our interest to work with Russia and obtain their cooperation." This is the traditional language of détente.

False Narratives, Not "Fake News,"
Are the Danger

November 30

DESPITE THE (LARGELY BOGUS) FUROR OVER "fake news," entrenched false narratives of the new Cold War are the real threat to US national security and to the détente policies that President-Elect Trump suggests he might pursue. I have commented on them intermittently in recent years, but it is important at this crucial political moment to reiterate five of them:

1. That Russian President Putin is solely responsible for the new Cold War and its growing dangers on several fronts, from the confrontation over Ukraine to Syria. If this is true, there is no need for Washington to rethink or change any of its policies, but it is not true.

2. That President Obama's declared intention, in 2014, to "isolate Putin's Russia" in international affairs has been successful, and therefore Putin is desperate to be released from the political wilderness. This too is untrue. Since 2014, Putin has been perhaps the busiest national leader of any major power on the world stage, from China and India to the Middle East and even Europe. Arguably, the world is changing profoundly, and Putin is more attuned to those changes than is the bipartisan US foreign-policy establishment.

3. That Washington's Cold War policies toward Russia have strengthened the vaunted US-European "transatlantic alliance," as exemplified by NATO's buildup on Russia's western borders. In reality, a growing number of European countries are trending away from Washington's hard-line policies toward Moscow, among them France, Austria, The Netherlands, Italy, Hungary, and others, perhaps even Germany. And this does not include Brexit, which removed hard-line London from European policy-making. This does not mean these countries are becoming "pro-Russian," as crude media coverage would have it, but less anti-Russian for the sake of their own national interests.

4. That "Russia's aggression," its "invasion," is the primary cause of the Ukrainian crisis, which is still the political epicenter of the new Cold War. In reality, the underlying cause is a civil war that grew out of Ukraine's diverse history, politics, social realities, and culture. This means that negotiations, not more war, are the only solution.

5. The orthodox US narrative of the Syrian civil war has, on the other hand, suddenly changed. While Obama was negotiating with Putin for joint US-Russian military action in Syria, "terrorists" were said to be entrenched in Aleppo and other anti-Assad strongholds. Since that diplomacy failed, the *New York Times*, the *Washington Post*, CNN, and other mainstream media have rewritten the narrative to pit Syrian, Russian, and Iranian forces against benign anti-Assad "rebels" and "insurgents." In Iraq, in Mozul, however, the US-led war is said to be against "terrorists" and "jihadists." Thus, in Aleppo, Russia is reported to be committing "war crimes" while in Mozul these are called "collateral damages."

All of us live according to the stories we tell ourselves. When policy-makers act according to false narratives, the result is grave dangers, as we are now experiencing in the new Cold War. To escape these dangers, Washington must first get the history right, particularly of its own role in creating it.

Cold War Hysteria vs. National Security

December 15

SINCE THE PRESIDENTIAL ELECTION, ALLEGATIONS HAVE grown that Kremlin cyber-invasions of the Democratic National Committee and dissemination of its materials severely damaged Hillary Clinton's campaign and contributed to Donald Trump's victory. Thus far, no actual evidence has been made public to support these unprecedented and exceedingly dangerous charges.

Nor are the motives being attributed to Russian President Putin credible. Why would a Kremlin leader whose mission has been to rebuild Russia with economic and other partnerships with the West seek to undermine the political systems of those countries, not only in America but also in Europe, as is being alleged?

Judging by the public debate among Russian policy intellectuals close to the Kremlin, it is not clear that it so favored the largely unknown, inexperienced, and unpredictable Trump. But even if Putin was presented with the possibility of stealing and publicizing DNC emails, he certainly would have understood that such crude Russian interference in a US election would become known and thus work in favor of Clinton, not Trump.

Nonetheless, these Trump-Putin allegations are inspiring an alarming Cold War hysteria in the American political-media establishment, still without facts to support them. One result is more neo-McCarthyite slurring of people who dissent from this narrative. A December 12 *New York Times* editorial alleged that Trump had "surrounded himself with Kremlin lackeys." And Senator John McCain ominously warned that anyone who disagreed with his longstanding political jihad against Putin "is lying."

A kind of witch hunt may be unfolding of the kind the *Washington Post* tried to instigate with its now discredited "report" of scores of American websites said to be "fronts for Russian propaganda." It could spread to higher levels. For example, Trump's nominee for secretary of state, Rex Tillerson, is charged with being "a friend of Putin" as a result of having struck a major deal for ExxonMobil for Russian oil reserves. Surely Tillerson was obliged to do this as the company's CEO.

Several motives seem to be behind this bipartisan campaign against the President-elect, who is being associated with all manner of Russian misdeeds. One is to reverse the Electoral College vote. Another is to exonerate the Clinton campaign from its electoral defeat by blaming Putin instead and thereby trying to maintain the Clinton wing's grip on the Democratic Party. Yet another is to delegitimize Trump even before he is inaugurated. And no less important, to prevent the détente with Russia that Trump seems to want.

We therefore face the growing possibility of two profound and related crises. One is an ever more perilous Cold War with Russia. The other is a new American president so politically paralyzed he cannot cope with such dangers as previous presidents have done.

Part III

Unprecedented Dangers

2017

Did Putin Really Order a "Cyber–Pearl Harbor"?

January 4

CONFRONTATIONS BETWEEN WASHINGTON AND MOSCOW—NOW EXTEND-ING from the Baltic region, Ukraine, and Syria to the American polit-ical system itself—are becoming more dangerous than was the US-Soviet nuclear confrontation over Cuba in 1962. Unlike in 1962, when the Kennedy administration made public evidence of Soviet missile silos under construc-tion on the neighboring island, the Obama administration has presented no concrete evidence that the Kremlin, directed by President Putin, hacked the Democratic National Committee and arranged for damaging materials to be disseminated in order to put Donald Trump in the White House.

Nonetheless, even as a number of independent cyber experts doubt the plausibility of White House intelligence reports, powerful political interests are inflating the story to imply that a US warlike act of retaliation is required. A *Washington Post* editorial on Dec. 31, for example, declared that America had suffered "a real cyber-Pearl Harbor" at Putin's hands. The motives of these political interests vary, as we have seen, from exonerating Hillary Clinton of her defeat to crippling Trump before he even enters the White House. In resolving the Cuban Missile Crisis wisely, President Kennedy did not have to cope with these kinds of debilitating public divisions and toxic allegations.

Today's hysteria, suffused with growing neo-McCarthyism and a witch hunt–like search for "Putin's friends" in the United States, first and foremost, of course, Trump himself, are making any rational, fact-based discourse nearly impossible. Public discussion is urgently needed regarding NATO's buildup on Russia's western borders, the civil/proxy wars in Ukraine and Syria, and more generally a less confrontational US policy toward Russia. With the *New York Times*, the *Washington Post*, and their echo chambers on cable-TV networks labeling anyone who rethinks US policy a "Trump apologist" and "Putin apologist," civil discourse so vital to democratic resolutions, and to US national security, has become nearly impossible.

Trump and Putin have tried to diminish the hysteria. Putin's attempt, declining to adopt the traditional Cold War tit-for-tat approach of immediately expelling 35 American "intelligence operatives" from Russia, raises a question about the Obama administration. Did whoever advised the president to expel 35 Russians and their families within 72 hours understand the order would violate the hallowed tradition of Russian New Year's Eve, the most sentimental of holidays, which families spend together at home, not in clubs or otherwise dispersed? If so, it was a malicious decision that enabled Putin to be magnanimous toward the American families affected in Russia. On the other hand, if Obama's advisers did not know this simple fact, it may explain his disastrous Russia policies since taking office.

Meanwhile, Putin has his own political problems. His generals, tasked with taking the Syrian city of Aleppo, had already protested his repeated "humanitarian ceasefires" as thwarting their mission. Now hard-liners are asking why Putin gave such a "soft" response to Obama's sanctions and expulsions as retaliation for Russia's purported role in the US presidential election. This too Obama should have been made to understand by his advisers. Was he? Or was Obama determined to prevent Trump from changing the soon-to-be former president's approach to Russia?

The Real Enemies of US Security

January 11

N OT SURPRISINGLY, NOW THERE IS MORE: allegations that the Kremlin possesses compromising materials, from sexual to financial, that would enable it to "blackmail" President-elect Trump. The leaked "documents" were first gleefully trumpeted by CNN on January 10 and quickly followed by a tsunami of echoing media stories. The allegedly incriminating documents themselves were then published by *BuzzFeed*—all raising serious questions about the sub-tabloid reporting of admittedly "unsubstantiated," even "unverifiable," allegations, though few people raised any. More importantly, who planned this obviously coordinated strike against Trump, and why?

At least two conflicting interpretations are possible. Either Trump is about to become a potentially treasonous American president. Or powerful domestic forces are trying for other reasons to destroy his presidency before it begins. Even if the allegations are eventually regarded as untrue, they may permanently slur and thus cripple Trump as a foreign-policy president, especially in trying to cope with the exceedingly dangerous new Cold War with Russia. That itself would constitute a grave threat to American national security—one created not by Trump or Putin but by whoever is responsible for these new "revelations."

Their timing is suspicious. They come on the heels of the just-released "Intelligence Community's" utterly vacuous "Assessment" that Kremlin leader Putin directed a campaign, including hacking of the Democratic National Committee, intended to discredit Mrs. Clinton and put Trump in the White House. Anti-Trump media widely trumpeted this story. But even the determinedly anti-Trump, anti-Putin *New York Times* "analysis", by Scott Shane on January 7, initially had reservations. It found that the much awaited "intelligence community" report was "missing…hard evidence to back up the agencies' claims"—that there was an "absence of any proof".

The anti-Trump "dossier" said to have been compiled by a former British intelligence agent, Christopher Steele, and leaked to CNN and *BuzzFeed*, is no more convincing. Despite Steele's claims of "Kremlin sources," it seems culled from long circulating Russian, American, UK, and other NATO scuttlebutt, of the "Intel" variety.

Even before the latest "revelations," there has been an unprecedented media campaign to defame Trump as a would-be traitor in his relations with Russia. On the evening of January 4, a CNN paid contributor characterized the next president as a Russian "fifth columnist." No one on the panel dissented or demurred. Subsequently, *Washington Post* columnists warned that Trump might commit "treason" as president or even replicate with Putin the notorious 1939 Nazi-Soviet Pact. Another columnist set out the articles of Trump's impeachment even before his inauguration. Here too nothing so poisonous, or potentially detrimental to national security, or to the institution of the presidency itself, has occurred in modern American history, if ever.

Predictably, anti-Trump media are warning him, and the public, against being "skeptical" about the quality and motives of US intelligence agencies.

Given the long history of the CIA's misleading American presidents into disastrous wars, from the Bay of Pigs and Vietnam to Iraq and Libya, why would anyone think this is sound advice? National security requires a president who is able to evaluate critically intelligence reports or have people around him who can do so.

All this comes on the eve of Rex Tillerson's hearings for confirmation as secretary of state. Few doubt that Tillerson was a successful CEO of the global ExxonMobil Corporation, though some are charging that in doing so he too became "a friend of Putin."

This unfortunate occasion is a moment to make a somewhat related point. The United States does not need a "friend" in the Kremlin, as President Bill Clinton liked to boast he had in the often compliant and intoxicated Boris Yeltsin, but a national-security partner whose nation's interests are sufficiently mutual for sustained cooperation—for détente instead of Cold War. In this regard, Tillerson, whose professional success was based on reconciling national economic interests, would appear to be well qualified, though he too is being defamed for suggesting any kind of cooperation with Moscow, no matter the benefits to US national security.

What might Putin himself think about this political uproar in the United States? His own leadership motives are usually and wrongly surmised solely from the fact that he is "a former KGB agent," which appears to be his middle name in US media coverage. However formative that biographical circumstance may have been, it does enable Putin to analyze intelligence reports and understand politics inside national intelligence agencies.

His reaction to the US Intelligence Community Assessment may therefore have been shock over the embarrassing paucity of the report. He might even have reconsidered his long-sought cooperation between Russian and US intelligence in the fight against international terrorism. Putin might now conclude, they need us more than we do them. Considering the recent antics of US "Intel," he might not be wrong.

Ukraine Revisited

February 8

WITH FIGHTING HAVING ESCALATED BETWEEN THE US-backed Kiev government and Russian-backed rebels in Donbass, we must focus yet again on Ukraine's pivotal role in the new Cold War since 2013–2014. Here again, as we have seen elsewhere, widely disseminated false narratives obscure what really happened.

The orthodox US account that Russian President Putin alone is responsible for the new Cold War hangs largely on his alleged unprovoked "aggression" against Ukraine in 2014 and ever since. (The narrative is sustained in part by the near-total absence of American mainstream reporting of what is actually happening in Kiev-controlled or rebel-controlled territories.) In fact, Putin's actions both in Donbass, where an indigenous rebellion broke out against the overthrow of the legally elected president in Kiev three years ago, and in Crimea, which had been part of Russia for more than 200 years (about as long as the United States has existed), was a direct reaction to the longstanding campaign by Washington and Brussels to bring Ukraine into NATO's "sphere of influence."

That itself was a form of political aggression against the centuries of intimate relations between large segments of Ukrainian society and Russia, including family ties. At the very least, it was reckless and immoral for Washington and the European Union to impose upon Kiev a choice between Russia and the West, thereby fostering, if not precipitating, civil war. And to flatly reject Putin's counter-proposal for a three-way Ukrainian-Russian-EU economic relationship. In this regard, Washington and the EU bear considerable responsibility for the 10,000 who have died in the ensuing Ukrainian civil and proxy war. They have yet to assume any responsibility at all.

A false narrative also quickly emerged to explain the recent escalation of fighting along the ceasefire zone in Ukraine. There are no facts to support the US political-media establishment's contention that Putin initiated the escalation—all reported facts point to Kiev—or any logic whatsoever. Why would Putin, who has openly welcomed Trump's détente initiative, seek to provoke or challenge the new American president at this critical moment? Whether or not Kiev was actively encouraged by anti-détente forces in

Washington is unclear, but a real possibility. (Inflammatory remarks made by Senators John McCain and Lindsay Graham in Ukraine, in January, now circulating on a video, may be telling evidence.) If so, the blood of the 40 or more who died in the January–February fighting is on their hands as well.

What are the chances of Trump-Putin cooperation to end the Ukrainian crisis? If the country is not to fragment into two, three, or more parts, a united Ukraine will have to be militarily non-aligned (that is, not a member of NATO) and free to have prosperous economic relations with both Russia and the West.

The Minsk Accords, drafted by Germany and France and endorsed by Moscow and Kiev, would have moved Ukraine in this direction, but have been repeatedly thwarted, primarily by Kiev. Whether or not full backing for Minsk by both Trump and Putin, particularly the provision giving rebel territories some degree of home rule, would end the Ukrainian civil war is far from certain. It might even result in the overthrow of the current Kiev government by well-armed ultranationalist forces. But for now there is no peaceful alternative.

Even if Trump and Putin adopt a wise joint policy toward Ukraine, neither leader has much political capital to spare at home. Trump is opposed by virtually across-the-political-spectrum opposition to any kind of agreements with Russia, not the least regarding Ukraine. And Putin can never be seen at home as "selling out" Russia's "brethren" anywhere in southeast Ukraine. Whether the two leaders have the wisdom and determination to end Ukraine's tragic and utterly pointless war, which has left the country nearly in ruins, remains to be seen.

Kremlin-Baiting President Trump

February 15

THE TSUNAMI OF ALLEGATIONS THAT PRESIDENT Trump has been seditiously "compromised" by the Kremlin continues to mount. *New York*

Times guru-columnist Thomas Friedman repeated the charge yet again on February 15. He too did so without any verified facts. The lack of any non-partisan high-level protest against this Kremlin-baiting of Trump is deeply alarming. It has become, it seems, politically correct.

Promoted by Hillary Clinton's campaign in mid-2016 and even more after her defeat, and exemplified now by the strident innuendos of MSNBC's Rachel Maddow and almost equally unbalanced CNN panels and newspaper editorial pages, the practice is growing into a kind of latter-day McCarthyite red-baiting and hysteria. Such politically malignant practices are to be deplored anywhere they appear, without exception, whether on the part of conservatives, liberals, or progressives. Whatever the motives, the slurring of Trump, which is already producing calls for his impeachment, poses grave threats to US and international security and to American democracy itself.

One or more of the allegations against Trump may turn out to be true, as might be almost anything in politics, but no actual evidence has been presented for any of the allegations. Without facts, all of us—professors, politicians, doctors, journalists, pundits—are doomed to malpractice or worse. A special investigation might search for such facts, but it is hard to imagine a truly objective and focused probe in the current political atmosphere.

For now, there are no facts or logic to support the following six related allegations that Trump has been treasonously "compromised" by Putin's Kremlin:

1. Trump has "lavished praise" on Putin, as the *Times* charged on February 12, echoing many other media outlets. All Trump has said is that Putin is "a strong leader" and "smart" and that it would be good "to cooperate with Russia." These are empirically true statements. They pale in comparison with, for example, FDR's warm words about Stalin, Nixon's about Leonid Brezhnev, and particularly President Bill Clinton's about Russian President Boris Yeltsin, whom he compared favorably with George Washington, Abraham Lincoln, and FDR. Only against the backdrop of unrelenting US media demonizing of Putin could Trump's "praise" be considered "lavish." Unlike virtually every other mainstream American politician and most media outlets, Trump has simply refused to vilify Putin—as in declining to characterize him as "a killer," for which there is also no evidence.

2. Trump and his associates have had, it is charged, business dealings in Russia and with Russian "oligarchs." Perhaps, but so have scores of major American corporations, from Delta Airlines, McDonald's, Wendy's, KFC, and Starbucks to Ford, Procter & Gamble, and several energy giants. Unavoidably, some of their Russian partners are "oligarchs." Moreover, unlike many international hotel chains, Trump tried but failed to build his

own affiliate, or anything else permanent, in Russia. The "Russian assets" about which his son once spoke evidently referred to condos and coops in the United States sold to cash-bearing Russians in search of a luxury brand and who did not need mortgages. New York City and South Florida are among those prime and entirely legitimate markets. It is said that Trump's tax returns, if revealed, would expose incriminating Russian money. Perhaps— but also an allegation, not a fact.

3. Trump's "associate," and briefly campaign manager, Paul Manafort, is alleged to have been "pro-Russian" when he advised Ukrainian President Victor Yanukovych, who was subsequently deposed unconstitutionally during the Maidan "revolution" in February 2014. As I already pointed out, this, to be polite, is uninformed. A professional political "adviser," Manafort was well paid, like many other American electoral experts hired abroad. But his advice to Yanukovych was to move politically and economically toward the ill-fated European Union Partnership Agreement, away from Russia, as Yanukovych did in order to get votes beyond his constituency in southeastern Ukraine. (Nor was the unsavory Yanukovych, whom Putin loathed for this and other reasons, considered pro-Russian in Moscow prior to his crisis in late 2013, when Putin got stuck with him.)

4. In January, as we know, a "dossier" of "black" or "compromising" material purporting to document how the Kremlin could blackmail Trump was leaked to CNN and published by *Buzzfeed*. Compiled by a former British intelligence official, Christopher Steele, whose shadowy partners in various countries abetted his commercial projects, the "report" was initially contracted by one of Trump's Republican primary opponents and then taken up and paid for by the Clinton campaign. Its 30-odd pages are a compilation of the entirely innocent, unverified, preposterous, and trash for sale in many political capitals, including London, Moscow, Kiev, Baltic capitals, and Washington. More recently, CNN exclaimed that its own intelligence leakers had "confirmed" some elements of the dossier, but thus far nothing that actually compromises Trump. Generally, more fact checking is done at tabloid magazines, lest they be sued for libel. (Nonetheless, Senator John McCain, a rabid opponent of any détente with Russia, acquired and gave a copy of the dossier to the FBI. No doubt the agency already had copies, bits of which had been floating around for months, but understood McCain wanted it leaked. And so it was, by someone.)

5. But the crux of pro-Kremlin allegations against Trump was, and remains, the charge that Putin hacked the DNC and disseminated the stolen emails through WikiLeaks in order to put Trump in the White House. A summary of these "facts" was presented in the declassified report released by the US "Intelligence Community" and widely published in January 2017. Though it has since become axiomatic proof for Trump's political and media enemies, as I pointed out earlier, virtually nothing in the "Assessment's" some 13 pages of text (or Steele's dossier) is persuasive—or entirely logical. For example, would Trump, a longtime hotelier, really commit "acts of sexual perversion" in a VIP suite he did not control, especially in Moscow, where audio and video bugging had long been rumored? Indeed, those who accept the Intelligence Community Assessment (ICA) as canon seem not to have noticed the nullifying disclaimer its authors buried at the end: "Judgments are not intended to imply that we have proof that shows something to be a fact."

In reality, about half the ICA pages are merely assumptions—or "assessments"—based on surmised motivations, not factual evidence of a Kremlin operation on behalf of Trump. The other half is a pointless and badly outdated evaluation deploring broadcasts by the Kremlin-funded television network RT. Not addressed is the point made by a number of American hacking experts that Russian state hackers would have left no fingerprints, as US intelligence claimed they had. Indeed, the group Veteran Intelligence Professionals for Sanity believes that the damaging DNC documents were not hacked but leaked by an insider. If so, it had nothing to do with Russia. (The NSA, which has the capacity to monitor the movement of emails, was only "moderately confident" in the report it co-signed, while the CIA and FBI were "highly confident," even though the FBI inexplicably never examined the DNC computers.)

There is another incongruity. At his final presidential press conference, Obama referred to the DNC scandal as a leak, not a hack, and said he did not know how the emails got to WikiLeaks—this despite allegations by his own intelligence agencies. (No one seems to have asked Obama if he misspoke!) On the other side of this alleged conspiracy, nor is it clear that Putin so favored the clearly erratic Trump that he would have taken such a risk, which if discovered, as I also pointed out earlier, would have compromised Trump and greatly favored Clinton. (Judging from discussions in Kremlin-related Russian newspapers, there was a serious debate as to which American presidential candidate might be best—or least bad—for Russia.)

6. Finally, there is the resignation (or firing) of General Michael Flynn as Trump's national security adviser for having communicated with Russian representatives about the sanctions imposed by Obama just before leaving

the White House and before Trump was inaugurated. Flynn may have misled Vice President Mike Pence about those "back-channel" discussions, but they were neither unprecedented nor incriminating, so far as is known.

Other American presidential candidates and presidents-elect had communicated with foreign states before taking office—as Richard Nixon seems to have done to prevent a Vietnam peace agreement that would have favored Hubert Humphrey, and as Ronald Reagan seems to have done with Iran to prevent release of its American hostages before the election. In fact, this was and remained a common practice. Obama's own top Russia adviser, Michael McFaul, told the *Washington Post* on February 9 that he visited Moscow in 2008, before the election, for talks with Russian officials. The *Post* reporter characterized this as "appropriate conduct." Certainly, it was not unprecedented.

Nor was Flynn's. More generally, if Flynn's purpose was to persuade the Kremlin not to overreact to Obama's December sanctions, which were accompanied by a provocative threat to launch a cyber attack on Moscow, this was wise and in America's best interests. Unless our political-media establishment would prefer the harshest possible reaction by Putin, as some of its Cold War zealots apparently do.

All this considered, it is less Putin who is threatening American democracy than is the Kremlin-baiting of President Trump without facts. Less Putin who is endangering US and international security than are the American enemies of détente who resort to such practices. Less Putin who is degrading US media with "fake news" than is the media's fact-free Kremlin-baiting of Trump. And less the "former KGB thug" who is poisoning American politics than are US intelligence leakers at war against their new president.

President Eisenhower eventually stopped Joseph McCarthy. Who will stop the new McCarthyism before it spreads even more into the "soul of democracy"? Facts might do so. But in lieu of facts there are only professional ethics and patriotism.

Putin's Own Opponents of Détente

February 22

T HE RUSSIAN POLICY ELITE CLOSELY FOLLOWS US publications, especially "leading" papers like the *New York Times*. It would have reacted
strongly—as should American readers—to a series of articles in the *Times*
from February 16 through February 19 on the theme of a "Trump-Putin axis"
in the White House, as columnist Paul Krugman so elegantly phrased it on
February 17. Indeed, the entire February 19 *Times Sunday Review* was substantially devoted to this extraordinary, though now commonplace, allegation.

But Russian analysts would have focused even more—as should we—
on an ominous statement quoted approvingly by *Times* columnist Nicholas
Kristof, on February 16, that "the bigger issue here is why Trump and people
around him take such a radically different view of Russia than has been the
case for decades." The clear message: any critical thinking about US policy
toward Russia since the 1990s is now under suspicion—and perhaps criminal. No wonder some members of the Russian elite have concluded that
the slurring of the new US president and all American proponents of better
relations means there will be no new détente.

This can only please Putin's own opponents of "cooperation" with the
United States. There is, of course, a spectrum of policy views in the Russian
political elite. Some strongly favor a new détente with Washington, but we
should not discount those—rarely, if ever, noted in US media—that equally strongly do not. Generally known as "state nationalist patriots," these
Russians insist that détente has been historically catastrophic for Russia and
thus is unpatriotic.

Their opposition echoes in part the centuries-long divide between
Russian Westernizers and traditionalist Slavophiles, but it is also pointedly
contemporary. Today's Russian foes of détente argue that the Gorbachev-
Reagan-Bush rapprochement of the late 1980s and early 1990s led to the
end of the Soviet Union and Russia's collapse as a great power. And that
the Yeltsin-Clinton "partnership" during the 1990s resulted in a decade of
Russia's humiliation at home and abroad.

They add, not incorrectly, that the US repeatedly lied or broke promises to Gorbachev and Yeltsin and even to Putin himself during Moscow's

détente-like "reset" with Washington, and will do so again under President Trump. If nothing else, Putin must not be seen at home as following in the tradition of Gorbachev and Yeltsin. (Yes, to make the point again, this means that Putin is not an "autocrat" whose will despotically becomes policy.)

Embracing Trump as a détente partner would pose other problems for Putin. As head of a vast multi-ethnic state, with some 20 million Muslim citizens, Putin cannot be associated with anti-Muslim aspects of Trump's immigration policies. Nor can he consider as a "bargaining chip" Moscow's increasingly close relations with China or even Iran. (The "China card," played by Henry Kissinger on behalf of President Richard Nixon, is no longer applicable.) Even nuclear-weapons reductions, the most attainable détente achievement, along with cooperation in Syria, is no longer so straight-forward. For Putin, it is inextricably tied to the missile-defense systems Washington is installing around Russia. Trump would need to revise this Obama policy as well.

There is another historical echo in the new struggle over détente. As during the 40-year Cold War, those known as "hardliners" or "hawks" both in Washington and Moscow have again formed an unholy, if inadvertent, axis.

The "Fog of Suspicion"

March 8

ONCE RESPECTABLE AMERICAN MEDIA ARE RECKLESSLY feeding neo-McCarthyist impulses inherent in the Russiagate frenzy. This could indeed become a political witch hunt ensnaring Americans with legitimate "contacts" with Russia—scholars, corporate executives and independent business people invested in Russia, diplomats, performers, journalists themselves, and many others.

On March 6, for example, the *New York Times*' Charles Blow, echoing his fellow columnists, applauded the "gathering fog of suspicion" in the hope it will bring down President Trump. MSNBC contributed a two-hour kangaroo tribunal on "The Trump-Putin Power Play" (no question mark) featuring "experts" without any doubts (or much actual knowledge) on their minds. A CNN "documentary" on Putin—"The Most Powerful Man in the World"—provided the kind of elliptical narrative needed to explain his "war" on America, and to inspire more hysteria. Both MSNBC and CNN regularly feature prosecutorial "former intelligence officials" whose misinformed statements about Russia's leadership can only give the CIA and US "Intel" generally a bad reputation. Specialists with dissenting analyses and points of view are effectively excluded. In this enveloping "fog," the accompanying clamor for "investigations" may only make things worse.

Not surprisingly, the "fog of suspicion" is chilling, even freezing, public discourse about worsening US-Russian relations, which should be a compelling media subject. As the political-media establishment "redirects" Trump away from his campaign promise of détente with Russian President Putin, some university scholars, think-tank specialists, and journalists are reluctant to speak candidly, at least publicly. As are US CEOs in pursuit of profits in Russia, who would normally welcome Trump's détente as their predecessors embraced the Nixon-Kissinger détente with Soviet Russia in the 1970s. Also not surprisingly, only one or two members of Congress have publicly expressed any principled alarm over the mounting hysteria. Most seem willing to accept the anti–national security mission of Senator Lindsay Graham to make 2017 "the year of kicking Russia in the ass."

This absence of statesmanship prevails in Washington even as three new Cold War fronts become more fraught with the possibility of hot war. In the Baltic and Black Sea regions, on Russia's borders, where NATO's unprecedented buildup continues and is provoking equally dangerous forms of Russian "brinkmanship." In Syria, where the growing number of American troops are increasingly in military proximity to the Russian-Syrian alliance, another realm of lethal mishaps waiting to happen. And in Ukraine, where recent developments show again that the US-backed Kiev government is hostage to armed ultranationalists and where that civil and proxy war could easily become a much larger conflagration with Russia.

There is also the wildly hyperbolic charge that Putin, like his worst Soviet predecessors, is now at war against the entire "liberal world order," including the European Union. This too is trumpeted by influential American media, but for this too there are no facts or logic. Why would Putin want to destroy the EU, an essential trading partner? Why would he undermine European politicians who favor ending sanctions against Russia, as is being alleged?

More generally, is Putin really the cause of Europe's multiple crises today in ways that the superpower Soviet Union never was? And what is this international "order" that has featured so many wars, many of them US ones, since the Soviet Union ended in 1991?

The blaming of Russia for America's domestic shocks—for Hillary Clinton's defeat and for President Trump, in particular—is political evasion now being projected onto the entire "liberal world order." This is indeed a "fog," but not the one of "suspicion" the *Times*, the *Washington Post*, cable "news," and other mainstream media are busy promoting.

Neo-McCarthyism Is Now Politically Correct

March 22

I HAVE BEEN SHARPLY CRITICIZED, PARTICULARLY BY self-professed liberal and progressive Democrats, for warning that Russiagate allegations against President Trump, whatever their still unverified validity, are growing into a kind of widespread Russophobic neo-McCarthyism. Recall that the original premise of McCarthyism was the existence of a vast Soviet Communist conspiracy inside America. Now consider, in addition to previous examples I have already given, more recent echoes of that era.

At recent House hearings, Democratic Representative Adam Schiff warned of a "Russian attack on our democracy." He meant the Kremlin's alleged hacking of the DNC and allegations that the Trump campaign had "colluded"—that is, conspired—with the Kremlin.

As the session unfolded, representative after representative, most of them Democrats, demanded the "unmasking" of Americans who had or have "contacts" with Russia. Under suspicion, it seemed, was anyone who traveled frequently to Russia, married a Russian, written or spoken critically about

US policy toward Russia (as the *New York Times'* Nicholas Kristof warned in an example I cited earlier), or, as another Democrat put it, otherwise done "Putin's bidding." He was referring to the new Secretary of State Rex Tillerson in his previous role as CEO of ExxonMobil.

Most alarming perhaps was the spectacle of FBI Director James Comey emerging in the role of his distant predecessor J. Edgar Hoover as a great authority on Russian malignancies—in this case, on the politics of "Putin's Russia" and Putin himself, including his personal motives, plans, and more. And yet, when asked what he thought about Gazprom—Russia's giant natural gas company, producer of more than a third of Europe's energy, and very often cited as a major pillar of Putin's power—Comey said he had not heard of it. And there was the spectacle of Schiff, who elaborating on the purported "collusion" as "one of the most shocking betrayals of our democracy in history," seemed to morph into McCarthy himself.

Congress, of course, was not acting in a political vacuum. For months, mainstream media, mostly associated with the Democratic Party—from the *Times* and the *Washington Post* to the *New Yorker*, *Politico*, MSNBC, CNN, and NPR—have promoted the theme of a Trump-Putin conspiracy and now a "Trump-Putin regime" in the White House.

Little wonder that related aspects of neo-McCarthyism have become politically correct. On March 20, MSNBC's Chris Matthews declared that loyal "Americans don't go to Russia." In a tweet on March 14, the *Atlantic's* David Frum proposed that someone "should stake …out" a Russian Embassy concert, in Washington, in memory of the Red Army Choir that perished in a plane crash and "photograph who attends."

Adumbrations of the 1950s are bipartisan. For a disagreement in the Senate, John McCain accused his fellow Republican Senator Rand Paul of "working for Vladimir Putin." And Trump's new UN ambassador, Nikki Haley, proclaimed, "We should never trust Russia." (If implemented, her diplomatic axiom would invalidate decades of US nuclear arms control agreements with Moscow.)

Lest anyone think the present danger is any less than was that of Soviet Russian Communism, we have *Post* columnist Dana Milbank warning, on March 21, of "the red menace of Vladimir Putin's Russia." Considering recent American media coverage, he might well think Communists still control the Kremlin.

The political logic inherent in all of this is obvious—and ominous. The question is how many influential Americans, if any, will at long last stand publicly against it.

Yevtushenko's Civic Courage

April 5

YEVGENY YEVTUSHENKO, RUSSIA'S GREAT POET-DISSENTER, DIED on April 1. I may not be fully objective about him, having known him for many years. Not well in the late 1970s and early 1980s, when I lived off and on in Moscow among Soviet-era dissidents, though a bit from our encounters there and in New York. But very well from 1985, when Mikhail Gorbachev began the perestroika reforms and I regained my Soviet entry visa, denied since 1982. So well that Zhenya, as his friends called him, was the godfather of my younger daughter, born in 1991.

Mindful of the adage that a great writer in Russia is more than a writer, Yevtushenko was for decades the nation's—and perhaps the world's—most famous and popular poet. He used his talent and position to champion the cause of historical and political justice and then a Soviet democratic reformation, as attempted by Gorbachev in the late 1980s. Long before Gorbachev's "glasnost" summoned radical reformers into public action, Yevtushenko acted boldly at great political and personal risk.

Western observers not known for protesting anything in their own countries often criticized Yevtushenko for having been officially tamed and corrupted by privilege, and still do so. They do not know the scores of writers, dissidents, and cultural works his private interventions helped, even saved. Or the impact of his (not so) private letter to Soviet leader Leonid Brezhnev protesting the Soviet invasion of Czechoslovakia in 1968. Many of his poems, and his riveting public readings, inspired at least two generations of Soviet reformers, including Gorbachev, as he later acknowledged.

At least two of Yevtushenko's most famous poems had a direct impact on public affairs. "The Heirs of Stalin" warned the nation in 1962 that powerful forces behind the scenes were seeking to overthrow Soviet leader Nikita Khrushchev, in part for his anti-Stalinist revelations, as they finally did in 1964. And "Babi Yar" broke the official Soviet taboo against discussion of the Jewish Holocaust.

Zhenya's death causes me to wonder again why established American figures—in the media, Congress, universities, cultural life, and elsewhere—have not protested abuses now engulfing US politics in a wave of McCarthy-like hysteria. They have far less to lose than did Yevtushenko. A torrent of fact-free allegations and slurring of people has flowed for months from leading newspapers and television networks, but exceedingly few, if any, Americans in a prominent position to protest have done so.

When *New York Times* columnist Charles Blow declares that "the Russians did interfere in our election. This is not a debatable issue"—why does no one protest that it is in fact debatable? Or when Blow slurs Secretary of State Rex Tillerson as a compromised friend of Russian President Putin? Or when other baseless allegations are made almost nightly by MSNBC and CNN hosts and panelists? Or when hyperbolic claims of a vast "Russian threat" to democracy everywhere were declared at the Senate "investigation" earlier this month? Some prominent Americans have grave doubts about this political and media conduct, but they are silent. Do they lack the civic courage that Yevtushenko exhibited for decades while treading a political razor's edge?

Such behavior, along with large policy issues, were exhibited in another way by the US response to the recent terrorist act on a St. Petersburg subway. Downplaying it generally, too many American commentators suggested that Putin was himself behind the explosion that killed or maimed scores of Russian citizens—in order, it was said, to deflect attention from public protests against official financial corruption. Again, there is no evidence or plausible logic for these shameful innuendoes.

They also directly threaten US national security. Ever since the 9/11 actual attack on America, inescapably recalled by subsequent attacks on European cities, the imperative of a US-Russia alliance against international terrorism has been abundantly clear. So are the readiness and capabilities of Russia—which has suffered in this regard more than any other Western nation—to help. Time and again such an alliance has been thwarted, primarily by powerful forces in the US establishment.

President Trump indicated he wanted this alliance. The tragedy in St. Petersburg should have been occasion enough to warrant one. But it may again be thwarted, now by the Kremlin-baiting of Trump and the nearly indifferent reaction by the US political-media establishment to the most recent act of terrorism in Russia.

When Yevgeny Yevtushenko turned his pen against the powerful, repressive forces of Soviet neo-Stalinism and anti-Semitism, he risked his life and his family's. What do privileged Americans who understand the ongoing folly but remain silent have to lose?

"Words Are Also Deeds"

April 12

THE US POLITICAL-MEDIA ESTABLISHMENT HAS EMBRACED three fraught narratives for which there is still no public evidence, only "Intel" allegations. One is, of course, "Russiagate," as it is being called: that Kremlin leader Putin ordered a hacking of the DNC and disseminated its emails to help put Donald Trump in the White House. The second is that Syrian President Assad, Putin's ally, ordered last week's chemical-weapons attack on Syrian civilians, including young children. A new third faith-based narrative, promoted by MSNBC in particular, now links the other two: Trump's recent missile attack on a Syrian military air base was actually a Putin-Trump plot to free the new American president from the constraints of "Russiagate" investigations and enable him to do Putin's bidding.

In addition to the absence of any actual evidence for these allegations, there is no logic. The explanation that Putin "hated Hillary Clinton" for protests that took place in Moscow in 2011 is based on a misrepresentation of that event. (The protested parliamentary election actually resulted in Putin's party losing its constitutional majority in the Duma.) And why would Assad resort to the use of chemical weapons, thereby risking all the military, political, and diplomatic gains he has achieved in the past year and half, and while he had Russian air power at his disposal as an alternative? The emerging sub-narrative that Putin lied in 2013, when he and President Obama agreed Assad would destroy all of his chemical weapons, is based on another factual misrepresentation. It was the United Nations and its special agency that verified the full destruction of those weapons, not Putin.

The Russian adage "words are also deeds" is true, it seems. Trump's missile attack on Moscow's ally Syria probably had a domestic political purpose—to disprove the narrative that he is somehow "Putin's puppet." If so, the American mainstream media that has promoted this narrative for months is deeply complicit. Meanwhile, the Kremlin, which watches these narratives unfold politically in Washington, has become deeply alarmed, resorting to its own fraught words. The No. 2 leader, Prime Minister Dmitri Medvedev, declared that US-Russian relations have been "ruined," a statement I do not recall any previous Soviet or post-Soviet leader ever having made. Medvedev added that the two nuclear superpowers are at "the brink" of war.

Understanding that Medvedev is regarded as the leading pro-Western figure in Putin's inner circle, imagine what the other side—state patriots, or nationalists, as they are called—is telling Putin. Still more, the Kremlin is warning that Trump's missile attack on Syria crossed Russia's "red lines," with all the warfare implications this term has in Washington as well. And flatly declaring the mysterious use of chemical weapons in Syria to have been a "provocation," Putin himself warned that forces in Washington were planning more such "provocations" and military strikes. In short, while the Kremlin does not want and will not start a war with the United States, it is preparing for the possibility.

Meanwhile, Trump's new secretary of state, Rex Tillerson, had just arrived in Moscow for talks with Russian leaders. Whether or not Putin himself would met with Tillerson was still uncertain. Putin may be an authoritarian leader, the "decider," but influential forces were strongly against him meeting with an American secretary of state in the immediate aftermath of such a US "provocation." Whatever the case, Tillerson's visit is vitally important.

Tillerson is well known to Putin and other Kremlin leaders. On behalf of ExxonMobil, he negotiated with them one of Russia's largest energy deals, granting access to the nation's vast oil resources beneath frozen seas. Putin personally approved the agreement, which oil giants around the world had sought. He would not have done so had he not concluded that Tillerson was a serious, highly competent man. (For this achievement on behalf of a major American corporation, US media continue to slur Tillerson as "Putin's friend.")

The Kremlin will therefore expect candid answers from Tillerson to questions related to the looming issue of war or peace. Are the fact-free narratives now prevailing in Washington determining factors in Trump's policy toward Russia? Are they the reason Trump committed the "provocation" in Syria? Does this mean Trump no longer shares Russia's essential strategic premise regarding the civil and proxy war in Syria—that the overthrow of Assad would almost certainly mean ISIS or another terrorist army in Damascus, an outcome the Kremlin regards as a dire threat to Russia's national security?

And, most fundamentally, who is making Russia policy in Washington: President Trump or someone else? Putin, it should be recalled, asked the same question publicly about President Obama, when the agreement he and Obama negotiated for military cooperation in Syria was sabotaged by the US Department of Defense.

The answers that the experienced Tillerson—he had his own corporate global state department and intelligence service at ExxonMobil—gives may do much to determine whether or not the new Cold War moves even closer to the brink of hot war in Syria. To avert that dire possibility, American mainstream media should return to their once professed practice of rigorously fact-checking their narratives with an understanding that words are indeed also deeds.

Wartime "Tears" in Moscow, Cold War Inquisition in Washington

May 10

G ROWING UP IN SMALL-TOWN KENTUCKY IN the aftermath of World War II, I looked forward to the annual V-E (Victory in Europe) Day remembrance, on May 8, particularly the parades featuring floats and veterans in their uniforms. Apparently it is no longer observed as a major American holiday across the United States. In sharp contrast, Victory Day, May 9, remains the most sacred Russian holiday, a "holiday with tears."

And so it was this year. The day was marked by commemorations across the vastness of Russia, not only by the traditional military parade on Moscow's Red Square. A remarkable new feature, "The Immortal Regiment," has recently been added—millions of people, among them President Putin, walking together through a myriad of streets bearing portraits of family members who fought in what is known as The Great Patriotic War, very many of whom did not return. The annual events are promoted by the government, as US media unfailing point out, but the "holiday with tears" is profoundly authentic for an overwhelming majority of the Russian people, and for understandable historical reasons.

Most Americans today believe "we defeated Nazi Germany," as President

Obama wrote on the 70th anniversary of the end of World War II. It is a misconception fostered by Hollywood films that portray the US landing at Normandy in June 1944 as the beginning of the destruction of Hitler's Germany.

In truth, America won the war in the Pacific, against Japan, but the Soviet Union fought and destroyed the Nazi war machine on the "Eastern Front" almost alone from 1941 to 1944, from Moscow, Kursk, and Stalingrad, and eventually to Berlin in 1945. Some 75 to 80 percent of all German casualties were suffered on the Eastern Front. By the time US and British forces landed at Normandy, Hitler had insufficient divisions to withstand the invasion, too many of them destroyed or still fighting oncoming Soviet forces from the east.

Soviet losses were almost unimaginable. More than 27 million citizens died, 60 to 70 percent of them ethnic Russians. Some 1700 cities and towns were all but destroyed. Most families lost a close or extended member. Perhaps most tellingly, only three of every hundred boys who graduated from high school in 1941–42 returned from the war. This meant that millions of Soviet children never knew their fathers and that millions of Soviet women never married. (They were known as "Ivan's widows," more than a few doomed to lonely lives in the often-harsh post-war Soviet Union.)

This is an enduring part of Russia's "holiday with tears." This is in large measure why so many Russians, not just the Kremlin, have watched with alarm as NATO has crept from Germany to their country's borders since the late 1990s. Why they resent and fear Washington's claims on the former Soviet republics of Ukraine and Georgia. And why they say of NATO's ongoing buildup within conventional firing range of Russia, "Never has so much Western military power been amassed on our borders since the Nazi invasion in June 1941." This is the "living history" that underlies Russia's reaction to the new Cold War.

Again in sharp contrast, on May 8 and 9 in Washington, today's Russia was being portrayed at renewed Senate hearings as an existential threat, as having committed an "act of war against America" by "hijacking" the 2016 presidential election on behalf of President Trump. By end of day on May 9, Trump's firing of FBI Director James Comey was said to be an attempt to cover up that collusion.

After nearly a year, no actual facts have yet been presented to support the allegation. On the other hand, evidence has appeared that for more than a year elements of the US Intelligence Community—almost certainly the CIA and FBI—have been engaged in shadowy operations designed to link Trump to Putin's Kremlin. I've called this "Intelgate" and urged it be investigated first and foremost. Intel leaks and "reports," in evident "collusion" with the failed Clinton campaign, have driven the Russiagate narrative from the outset, amplified almost daily by a mainstream media that shows no interest at all in Intelgate.

Which brings us to Trump's (and before him Obama's) thwarted effort to forge an anti-terrorist alliance with Moscow. Russia has suffered more from jihadist terrorism than has any other Western country. For many Russians, it is becoming an existential threat reminiscent of German fascism in the 1930s. Therefore, they naturally want another wartime alliance with the United States. But Russia's tearful memories and real present-day perils do not interest Russiagate zealots, who are focused on Trump's firing of Comey. (Considering his acts detrimental to her campaign, a President Hillary Clinton would almost certainly also have replaced Comey.)

None of this seems to matter to representatives of the Democratic Party or to Washington's bipartisan cold warriors. They prefer pursuing still fact-free allegations. On May 8-9, they should instead have gone to Moscow to commemorate the historic allied victory in World War II. But they were following recent precedent: President Obama pointedly boycotted the 70th anniversary commemoration in Moscow in 2015.

Terrorism and Russiagate

May 31

IT CANNOT BE EMPHASIZED TOO OFTEN: international terrorism—a modern-day phenomenon that controls territory, has aspects of statehood, commands sizable fighting forces and agents in many countries, and is in pursuit of radioactive materials to make its bombings incalculably more lethal—is the No. 1 threat to the world today. Coping with this existential danger requires an international alliance of governments, first and foremost between the United States and Russia.

President Trump has suggested, publicly and privately, an anti-terrorism coalition with Russian President Putin. At each stage of the negotiations, the media's Russiagate (no need for quote marks) narrative—has intervened in ways that jeopardize, if not sabotage, the diplomatic process.

We now have more instances. Allegations that Trump betrayed intelligence secrets to Russian Foreign Minister Lavrov during an Oval Office meeting and discussed with him his firing of FBI Director Comey. And that the president's son-in-law and aide, Jared Kushner, participated in an attempt to establish a secret "back channel" of communication with Moscow prior to Trump's inauguration. These allegations, like many others, are uninformed.

Putin has repeatedly sought a US-Russian anti-terrorism alliance for nearly 17 years, at least since the 9/11 attacks on America. Each time the prospect seemed real, at least to Moscow, it was thwarted by forces in Washington.

This time, therefore, especially given misgivings by some of his senior advisers, Putin needed from Trump personally, via Lavrov, answers to two questions. Did the two sides agree about the exchange of high-level intelligence required for such an alliance? Trump responded by sharing a piece of classified information about a terrorist threat to American and Russian passenger airliners. In doing so, Trump did nothing unprecedented, improper, or probably even revelatory. (The source involved Israel, whose intelligence agencies work closely with their Russian counterparts on matters involving terrorism.)

Second, Putin needed to know whether Trump, reeling under accusations of being a "Kremlin puppet" and facing a myriad of investigations at home, could be a reliable anti-terrorism partner. Trump responded by saying he had fired Comey, whom he thought, not unreasonably, had been inspiring some of the allegations against him. However inelegantly expressed by Trump, these were necessary discussions with Lavrov if the US-Russian alliance against terrorism was to proceed.

Nor was the Trump team's search for a back channel of communications with Moscow, whether through Russian officials or private American citizens, as Kushner then was, unprecedented or improper for a President-elect, as I previously detailed. The former diplomat Jack Matlock has said he did it for President-elect Jimmy Carter, as did then–private citizen Michael McFaul for President-elect Obama—in Moscow, no less. It is likely that Henry Kissinger, whom Putin knows and trusts, was also involved on behalf of President-elect Trump. (It's worth recalling that President John F. Kennedy used both a private American citizen and the Soviet ambassador in Washington as a back channel during the Cuban Missile Crisis.)

Trump, however, had a special problem. Regular communications with the Kremlin eventually end up, of course, both in official Russian and American channels. Convinced that US intelligence agencies had been behind the allegations against him since the summer of 2016, and particularly the steady stream of leaks to the media, Trump reasonably worried about initiating his back channel through any US institution or agency. Hence attempts by Kushner, and possibly others, to begin privately with the Russian ambassador to Washington. Not unreasonably, not improperly, though perhaps ineptly.

The real issue Americans must decide is what is more compelling: the need for a US anti-terrorism alliance with Russia or the still-undocumented allegations called Russiagate? The lethal bombings in Manchester and in a St. Petersburg metro station are more evidence, if any is still needed, that American subways and arenas are not immune.

"Details After the Sports"

June 21 / June 28

THE LATE COMEDIAN GEORGE CARLIN HAD a still telling routine. A local radio newscaster begins his report: "Nuclear war in Europe. Details after the sports." Consider some recent "details" you may have missed in leading American media.

On June 18, a US plane shot down a Syrian military aircraft. Allied with Syria and fighting there at its government's official invitation, unlike American forces which are there in violation of international law, Moscow regarded this as a provocative act of war. After a nearly 24-hour pause while the Putin leadership debated its response, the Russian military command announced that henceforth any US aircraft flying where Russia and Syria were conducting operations would be "targeted"—that is, warned to leave immediately or be shot down.

A red line had been crossed by the United States, as the Soviet Union had done in Cuba in 1962. This time, Washington wisely retreated, as Moscow did in the Cuban Missile Crisis. The Department of Defense announced it would "reposition" its war planes away from Russian-Syrian operations.

But this does not mean the danger of a Cuba-like crisis has been eliminated in Syria (or elsewhere). The Trump administration is threatening to attack Syria if President Assad "again" uses chemical weapons, thereby creating the real risk of a "false flag." Independent investigators, notably Seymour Hersh and Theodore Postol, have raised serious doubts as to whether Assad actually used chemical weapons previously, in 2013 or this April. Their findings were nowhere explored in the American mainstream media.

Nor was another recent episode. A NATO warplane above the Baltic Sea came perilously close to a Russian aircraft carrying Minister of Defense Sergei Shoigu, probably Russia's most popular political figure after President Putin. Had something worse happened, it too might well have led to war between the two nuclear superpowers.

Such "details" in current US-Russian relations are deleted or obscured by the media's fixation on Russiagate—allegations that Trump and Putin "colluded" to put Trump in the White House. Here too there are important new "details" you may have missed. Russiagate's core allegation is based officially—leaving aside the private and easily disputed Steele "dossier"—on the January 2017 US "Intelligence Community Assessment." We now know this report was not based on a consensus of all "seventeen US intelligence agencies," as implied, but on "handpicked analysts," possibly from only the CIA.

We learn this directly from former CIA Director John Brennan and former Director of National Intelligence James Clapper. Brennan, we also now know, was hardly an objective CIA director, having explained in his recent House testimony that any Americans who have contacts with Russians can embark "along a treasonous path" and "do not know they are on a treasonous path until it is too late."

Brennan's contempt for the trustworthiness of Americans was matched by Clapper's contempt for Russians. He told NBC's *Meet the Press*, on May 8, that "Russians ... are typically, almost genetically driven to co-opt, penetrate ..." and thus "genetically driven" to attack American democracy. No mainstream media have explored these revelations about President Obama's apparently paranoid CIA director and ethnically biased National Intelligence director.

Instead, they have continued to parrot what is now an established falsehood. The most indicative example is Maggie Haberman, a leading *New York Times* reporter on Russiagate and regular CNN panelist. On June 26, she wrote that President Trump "still refuses to acknowledge a basic fact agreed upon by 17 American intelligence agencies ... Russia orchestrated the attacks and did it to help get him elected." But it is Ms. Haberman and the *Times* that refuse "to acknowledge a basic fact." And they are far from alone. On June 26, *Washington Post* columnist Richard Cohen repeated the same falsehood about "17 American intelligence agencies," as do almost daily CNN and MSNBC.

On June 25, the *Post* added another dubious "detail" that went unnoticed. Buried in an interminable "investigative" article claiming to prove Putin's "crime of the century," was something meant to be a bombshell: Obama's White House knew about Putin's personal role in Russiagate from a mole—either human or technical—in his Kremlin inner circle. Logic alone discredits the story. If US Intel had acquired a listening source in Putin's closed circle, it would be one of the great espionage feats in history—a present and future asset so precious that no official would dare leak it (a treasonous capital crime) to the *Washington Post*.

One day, all of these reckless media malpractices may be critically exposed by historians and schools of journalism, though they do not do so today. One day we may learn, to use an expression I first heard from a former British intelligence agent more than 40 years ago, that documents like the ICA report and Steel's dossier are mostly "rubbish in and rubbish out." In real time, however, such "details"—with their deletions, distortions, and distractions—are a major reason why we are slouching toward war with Russia, as in Syria.

Cold-War News Not "Fit to Print"

July 19 / August 9

THE MAINSTREAM NARRATIVE OF THE NEW Cold War, now including Russiagate, continues to exclude important elements that do not conform to its orthodoxies. Typically, the narrative is driven by stories in the *New York Times* and the *Washington Post*, often based on anonymous Intel sources, and amplified for hours, even days, on CNN and MSNBC. As for the exceptionally influential *Times*, its front-page credo, "All the News That's Fit to Print," seems to have become "All the News That Fits." Here are more recent examples:

News that Trump and Putin met privately after their formal "summit" meeting in Hamburg earlier in July was treated as a sinister development. Omitted was the history of previous summit meetings. For example, Reagan and Gorbachev met alone with their translators in February 1986, when they agreed that the abolition of nuclear weapons was a desirable goal. That did not happen, but the following year they became the first and only leaders ever to abolish an entire category of those weapons. Moreover, in the long history of summits, advisers of American, Soviet, and post-Soviet leaders frequently thought it wise to arrange some "private time" for their bosses so they could develop a political comfort level for the hard détente diplomacy that lay ahead.

History is also frequently missing in other media accounts. When it turned out that a Russian lawyer wanted to speak to Donald Trump Jr. about "orphans," at a now infamous meeting at Trump Tower, this was derided as a laughable Russiagate cover-up. But the issue is serious both in Russia and for some in the United States. In 2012, Putin signed a bill banning future American adoptions of Russian orphans. (Thousands had been adopted by American families since the 1990s.) It was generally thought to have been Putin's retaliation for the US Congress' Magnitsky Act, which sanctioned Russian "human rights violators."

Several other aspects of this saga are rarely, if ever, reported. One is that the account of the Magnitsky affair given by William Browder, a onetime American financial operator in Russia who spearheaded the US legislation, uncritically repeated by US media, has been seriously challenged. Another is that Putin was already, prior to the Magnitsky Act, under considerable Russian public and elite pressure to end American adoptions because several adopted children had died in the United States. Yet another is the pain of more than 40 American families who had virtually completed the formal adoption process when the ban was enacted, leaving their children stranded in Russia.

Still more, there is the possibility that Putin might enable at least some of these Russian children to come to their would-be American families as a détente concession to Trump. But similarly unreported, Putin needs a "sanctions" concession from Trump.

In December 2016, on his way out of the White House, President Obama seized two Russian diplomatic compounds in the United States, both Russian private property, and expelled 35 Russian diplomats as intelligence agents. Putin has yet to retaliate tit for tat, as has long been traditional in such matters, by seizing American facilities in Moscow and expelling an equal number of US diplomats. Here too Putin is under Russian public and elite pressure—lest he look "soft"—to retaliate. US media reporting on Russiagate, however, probably makes it politically impossible for Trump to reverse any of Obama's sanctions, even if it helped to avoid yet another crisis in US-Russian relations and abet the détente he seems to want.

Other facts and context were missing from reports of Trump Jr.'s meeting with the Russian lawyer, which was initiated by an offer of "Kremlin dirt" on Hillary Clinton and thus portrayed as exceptionally sinister. But at that very time, June 2016, the Clinton campaign was already paying the former British intelligence officer, Christopher Steele, to collect "Kremlin dirt" on Trump—an enterprise that became known as the anti-Trump or Steele "dossier" and a foundation of Russiagate. In addition, by then, a staffer at the Clinton campaign or the DNC was collecting "black" information on Trump from officials of the US-backed Ukrainian government. Both acts of "opposition research," however commonplace in American politics, may have been deplorable, but only Clinton's was actually operationalized and productive. Nothing of the sort seems to have come of Trump Jr.'s meeting.

Consider also the US Senate's proposed economic sanctions against Russia, applauded by mainstream media. Largely uninformed, as are most of Congress' contributions to the new Cold War, they would penalize European energy corporations, and possibly American ones as well, involved in any vital (or profitable) undertakings that include Russian energy companies. Heavily dependent on Russian energy, European governments are furious over the Senate sanctions. This looming rift in the transatlantic alliance has barely been reported here, though it is a major story in Europe.

Ignorance or Russiagate spite has also obscured, perhaps entirely undermined, a potentially vital development. In Hamburg, Trump and Putin agreed that the two sides should work toward regulating cyber technology, including hacking, in international affairs. Certain that Putin had "hacked American democracy" in 2016, though still without any evidence, the US political-media establishment protested so vehemently that Trump seemed to withdraw from this agreement. But it is urgently needed, if only because cyber-hacking, with its capacity to penetrate strategic infrastructures, increases the chances of nuclear war by mishap or intent. Here too orthodox media coverage of "Russiagate" has become a direct threat to American and international security.

What's fit to print also ignores the possible significance of new French President Emmanuel Macron's decision to hold state visits both with Putin and then Trump. American commentary has offered trivial explanations without considering that Macron may be trying to adopt the tradition of the founder of the Fifth Republic, Charles de Gaulle—aloof from both Moscow and Washington, and even NATO, during the preceding Cold War. If so, this too would not fit the US media's orthodox narrative.

Finally, there is Russia's own internal politics, no longer reliably reported by US media. A recent trip to Moscow confirmed my own perception that the political situation there is also worsening due primarily to Cold War fervor in Washington, including Russiagate and proposed new sanctions. Contrary to US opinion, Putin has long been a moderate, restraining force in his own political establishment, but his space for moderation is shrinking. Thus far, his response to various US sanctions was the least he could have done. Much harsher political and economic counter-measures are being widely discussed and urged on him. For now, he resists, explaining, "I do not want to make things worse."

But as always happens in times of escalating Cold War, the pro-American faction in Russian politics is being decimated by Washington's policies. And the space for anti-Kremlin and other opposition is rapidly diminishing. This too appears to be news not fit to print.

Historical Monuments, From Charlottesville to Moscow

August 17

CONFRONTATIONS OVER MEMORIAL REMNANTS OF THE Confederacy, in Charlottesville and elsewhere, revived a theme that has long interested me: similar political legacies of American slavery and of Stalin's Great Terror, which engulfed the Soviet Union from the mid-1930s until the despot's

death in 1953. Having grown up in the Jim Crow South and later become
a historian of the Stalinist and post-Stalinist eras, I understand, of course,
profound differences between the black victims of slavery and the victimiza-
tion caused by the Stalinist Terror. But I also see some similar historical and
political consequences. Notably:

• Both events victimized many millions of people and were formative
chapters in the histories of the two political systems and societies.

• For decades, in both countries, subsequent generations were not taught
the stark truth about these monstrous historical events. I did not learn in
Kentucky schools, for example, that many founding fathers of American
democracy had been slave owners. Similarly, the beginning of partial
truth-telling about Stalin's Terror began in the Soviet Union only in the
mid-1950s and early '60s, under Nikita Khrushchev, and was then stopped
officially for another 20 years until Mikhail Gorbachev's rise to power in
1985, when the Terror was fully exposed as part of his glasnost, or truth-telling, reforms.

• Both traumas— great and prolonged crimes, to be exact—produced citizens with very different life experiences and conflicting narratives of their
own lives and their nation's history. The result was constant political, social,
and even economic conflicts during the course of many years, some of them
dramatic and violent. Eventually, descendants both of the victims and the
victimizers were in the forefront. (My book *The Victims Return* focuses on this
dimension of the Stalinist Terror and its aftermath.)

• One aspect of the controversy in both countries has been conflict over
existing monuments and other memorializing sites established decades ago
honoring leading victimizers in the American slave and Soviet Stalinist eras,
and what to do about them in light of what is now known about these historical figures. Recent events in Charlottesville are only one example, as are
ongoing Russian controversies about sites that still honor Stalin—notably
his bust behind the Lenin Mausoleum on Red Square—and his "henchmen."

• A profound, even traumatic, historical-political question underlies
these conflicts in both countries. How to separate the "crimes" committed by
the historical figures still honored from glorious national events with which
their names are also associated—in the American case, with the founding
of American democracy; in the Russian case, with the great Soviet victory
over Nazi Germany, led by Stalin? And if the "crimes" are paramount, who
else, and what else, should be deleted from places of honor in the respective national histories? No consensus regarding this ramifying question has

been achieved in either society. Both have their consensus-seekers and their "alts," with no resolution in sight.

Which brings us, very briefly, to Putin, whose place in this saga needs to be considered more fully later on. Since coming to power in 2000, he has played an essential but little-understood role in trying to cope with this decades-long controversy in Russia. It has not been, contrary to widespread opinion in American media, the role of a neo-Stalinist.

In order to rebuild a Russian state that would never again disintegrate, as it had in 1917 and again in 1991, Putin needed an effective degree of historical consensus about the conflicting Tsarist, Soviet, and post-Soviet pasts. Unlike many previous Kremlin rulers, Putin has not sought to impose a new historical orthodoxy through censorship and the educational system but to let society—through historians, journalists, broadcast and movie producers, and others—sort out history by presenting their rival perspectives. As a result, there is almost no historical censorship in Russia today.

Even more telling symbolically is the matter of memorials. In America, it bears repeating, there is still no national museum or memorial dedicated solely to the history of slavery. In 2015, there opened in Moscow, with Putin's essential political and financial backing, a large, modern-day State Museum of the History of the Gulag, the penal labor camps in which millions of Stalin's victims languished virtually as slaves and often died. Still more, on October 30, Putin will personally commemorate the first-ever national monument, in the center of Moscow, memorializing the memory of Stalin's victims.

Many Russians will not approve. A recent survey of opinion found Stalin to be "the most admired figure in history." Americans should not be surprised. As William Faulkner reminded us, such past eras are never really past.

The Lost Alternatives of
Mikhail Gorbachev

August 24

T HE YEAR 2017 MARKS THE 30TH anniversary both of Gorbachev's formal introduction of his democratization policies in the Soviet Union and of the Intermediate-Range Nuclear Forces Treaty he signed with President Reagan, the first—and still only—abolition of an entire category of nuclear weapons.

For me personally, 2017 also marks the anniversary of my first meeting with Gorbachev, in Washington in November 1987. Over the years, our relationship has grown into a personal family friendship. It has included many private discussions about politics, past and present. The most recent, three hours over dinner, was in late July at a restaurant near Gorbachev's home, about a 50-minute drive from Moscow. Also present were my wife Katrina vanden Heuvel—publisher and editor of *The Nation*—and Dmitri Muratov, editor of the independent newspaper *Novaya Gazeta*, of which Gorbachev is a minority owner.

I asked Gorbachev, on this multiple 30th anniversary, whether he felt his legacies, and his place in history, had been lost in light of events after 1987 and especially since he left power in 1991. He has addressed variations of these questions many times over the years, often in English translation.

Now 86 and in poor health, but mentally as engaged as ever, Gorbachev reiterated two points he has made before. Regarding democracy in Russia, it is a long process with forward and backward stages, but ultimately inevitable because more than one generation of Russians now adheres to the democratic values he promoted while in power. Regarding the new Cold War, he ascribes the largest responsibility to US and European leaders, particularly American ones, who failed to seize the opportunity he (and Reagan) left behind. My own thoughts on these issues will not surprise readers.

Circumstances today, certainly in the US political-media establishment, could hardly be more unlike they were when Gorbachev was Soviet leader and shortly after. Hopes for a strategic partner in the Kremlin have given way to nearly consensual assertions that the current Kremlin leader, Vladimir Putin, poses a worse threat to democracy everywhere and to US national security than did even his Soviet Communist predecessors. Hopes 30 years ago for a world without Cold War and nuclear buildups on both sides have been vaporized by unrelenting Cold War politics in Washington and by inclinations, both in Washington and Moscow, favoring another nuclear arms race. The alternatives presented by Gorbachev are no longer discussed, or even remembered, lost in a haze of historical amnesia.

Nor is there any meaningful public discussion in the United States of who—how, when, and why—those alternatives were squandered during the past 30 years. To the extent they are discussed, the nearly unanimous American explanation is that Putin's "aggressive" policies abroad and undemocratic ones at home were, and remain, solely responsible.

As I have argued, this is an exceedingly unbalanced explanation that requires deleting many causal factors that unfolded before and after Putin came to power in 2000. Among them, Washington's decision to expand NATO eastward to Russia's borders after the Cold War purportedly ended; President George W. Bush's unilateral withdrawal from the Anti-Ballistic Missile Treaty; the West's annexation of Kosovo, which the Kremlin cited as a precedent for its annexing of Crimea; and regime-change policies by several US presidents, from Iraq and Libya to, more surreptitiously, Ukraine in 2014.

None of this is discussed in the US mainstream media, partly because of the exclusion of opposing voices and partly because any Americans suggesting these alternative explanations for the new Cold War are being traduced as "pro-Kremlin" and "Putin apologists," even in progressive publications that once deplored such defamatory discourse.

Which should remind us of another great achievement by Gorbachev in the late 1980s, the introduction of glasnost—unfettered journalism and history writing in the Soviet Union—that led to the end of Soviet censorship but also to "more glasnost" impulses around the world, including in the US media. This too seems to have been lost, displaced by secrecy, a pervasive lack of candor, and other media malpractices in the United States. What we have been told, and not told, for example, about Russiagate allegations reflects a lack of glasnost at the top and lack of willingness in the mainstream media to ferret out anything that does not suggest the culpability of President Trump. Almost everything else is ignored, marginalized, or maligned, even when put forth by well-credentialed observers.

Analyzing the end of Gorbachev's democratization policies in post-Soviet Russia is more complex. Having set out my interpretation in my book *Soviet Fates and Lost Alternatives*, I will note only several factors that also unfolded before Putin came to power.

They included the undemocratic way the Soviet Union was ended surreptitiously in December 1991; the all-but-unprecedented decision by Russia's first post-Soviet president, Boris Yeltsin, to use tank cannons to abolish a popularly elected parliament—indeed, an entire constitutional order—in October 1993 and to replace it with one with fewer checks on what became a super-presidency; Yeltsin's brutal wars against the breakaway province of Chechnya; the rigging of his reelection in 1996; and the oligarchic plundering of Russia and attendant impoverishment of a majority of Russian citizens while he was in power. Again, these, and other developments under Yeltsin in the 1990s, are the essential starting point for any analysis of Putin's role in the reversal of Russia's democratization initiated by Gorbachev. For many American commentators, however, the Yeltsin 1990s remain a rose-tinted period of "democratic transition" and US-Russian solidarity.

Are Gorbachev's lost alternatives retrievable? It's hard to be optimistic. We are probably closer to actual war with Russia today than ever before in history. President Trump, who seemed to want to reverse bipartisan US policies that contributed so significantly to the new Cold War, is said to have been defeated or dissuaded in this regard by "adults" who themselves represent those previous policies.

The absence of debate and glasnost in the mainstream American media encourages silent opponents of Washington's Cold War policies to remain mute. Western Europe may, for various reasons, eventually rebel against Washington's anti-Russian policies and adopt its own approach to Moscow. But as Gorbachev demonstrated, leaders are needed for transformational alternatives. And time is running out.

Meanwhile, Mikhail Sergeevich Gorbachev, having lived long beyond his greatest achievements, watches and hopes, however faintly.

Does Putin Really Want to "Destabilize the West"?

September 6

A T THE CENTER OF RUSSIAGATE AND near abolition of US diplomacy toward Russia today is the accusation that Putin wants to "destabilize

Western democracies," from America to Europe. As with so many other new Cold War narratives, there is no persuasive historical evidence or political logic for this sweeping allegation.

Putin came to power in 2000 with the expressed mission of rebuilding, modernizing, and stabilizing Russia, which had collapsed into near-anarchy and widespread misery during the decade following the end of the Soviet Union. He sought to do so, in very large measure, through expanding good political and economic relations with democratic Europe.

Until the Ukrainian crisis erupted in 2014, much of Putin's success and domestic popularity was based on an unprecedented expansion of Russia's economic relations with Europe and, to a lesser extent, with the United States. Russia provided a third or more of the energy needs of several European Union countries while thousands of European producers, from farmers to manufacturers, found large new markets in Russia, as did scores of US corporations. As late as 2013, the Kremlin was employing an American public-relations firm and recruiting Goldman Sachs to help "brand" Russia as a profitable and safe place for Western investment. Along the way, Putin emerged, despite some conflicts, as a partner among European leaders and even American ones, with good working relations with President Bill Clinton and (initially) with President George W. Bush.

Why, then, would Putin want to destabilize Western democracies that were substantially funding Russia's rebirth at home and as a great power abroad while accepting his government as a legitimate counterpart? Putin never expressed such a goal or had such a motive. From the outset, in his many speeches and writings, which few American commentators bother to read—even though they are readily available in English at Kremlin.ru—he constantly preached the necessity of "stability" both at home and abroad.

Putin's vilifiers regularly cite questionable "evidence" for the allegation that he has long, even always, been "anti-American" and "anti-Western. They say he previously had a career in the Soviet intelligence services. But so did quite a few Western-oriented Russian reformers during the Gorbachev years. They say Putin opposed the US invasion of Iraq. But so did Germany and France. They say he fought a brief war in 2008 against the US-backed government of the former Soviet republic of Georgia. But a European investigation found that Georgia's president, not the Kremlin, began the war.[35]

Putin is also accused of pursuing a number of non-Western and thus, it is said, anti-Western policies at home. But this perspective suggests that all foreign "friends" and allies of America must be on America's historical clock, sharing its present-day understanding of what is politically and socially "correct." If so, Washington would have considerably fewer allies in the world, not only in the Middle East. Putin's reply is the non-Soviet principle of national and civilizational "sovereignty." Each nation must find its own way at home within its own historical traditions and current level of social consensus.

In short, had Putin left office prior to 2014, he would have done so as having been, certainly in the Russian context, a "pro-Western" leader—a course he generally pursued despite NATO's expansion toward Russia's borders, US regime -change policies in neighboring countries, and criticism in high-level Russian circles that he had "illusions about the West" and was "soft" in his dealings with it, especially the United States.

Everything changed with the Ukrainian crisis in 2014, as a result of which, it is asserted, Russia "aggressively" annexed Crimea and supported Donbass rebels in the ensuring Ukrainian civil war. Here began the sweeping allegation that Putin sought to undermine democracy everywhere, and eventually the American presidential election in 2016. Here too the facts hardly fit, as we have already seen but need to recall.

Throughout 2013, as the European Union and Washington wooed Ukraine's elected president, Viktor Yanukovych, with a bilateral economic partnership, Putin proposed a tripartite agreement including Russia, Ukraine's largest trading partner. The EU and Washington refused. The crisis erupted when Yanukovych asked for more time to consider the EU's financial terms, which also included ones involving adherence to NATO's policies.

Putin watched as initially peaceful protests on Kiev's Maidan Square devolved by February 2014 into Western-applauded armed street mobs that caused Yanukovych, still the constitutional president, to flee and put in power an ultranationalist, anti-Russian government. It seemed to threaten, not only vocally, ethnic Russians and other native Russian-speakers in Eastern Ukraine as well as the historical and still vital Russian naval base at Sevastopol, in Crimea, and that province's own ethnic Russian majority. Given those circumstances, which were imposed on him, Putin seemed to have had little choice. Nor would have any imaginable Kremlin leader.

A vital episode amid the February 2014 crisis has been forgotten—or deleted. The foreign ministers of three EU countries (France, Germany, and Poland) brokered a compromise agreement between the Ukrainian president and party leaders of the street protesters. Yanukovych agreed to an early presidential election and to form with opposition leaders an interim coalition government. That is, a democratic, peaceful resolution of the crisis. In

In NYC, 2003.

In Moscow, 1959.

Playing in Goat Park.
NYC circa 1978.

Under Russian student painting of Nikolai Bukharin.

At gravesite of Anna Larina, Bukharin's widow. Moscow, 2005.

At Amagansett Book Fair, 2018.

In NYC apartment doing research.

Harriman Institute debate with Michael McFaul, 2018.

At Novaya Gazeta for his 80th birthday party.

With Mikhail Gorbachev. Moscow, Lenin Hills, 2005.

Leaving Literary Gazette newspaper after Gorbachev spoke to editors and journalists. Moscow, 1992.

At Novaya Gazeta, with Mikhail Gorbachev. December 2018.

Gorbachev toasting us on our 40th wedding anniversary, at Novaya Gazeta. December 4, 2017.

At Gorbachev's favorite restaurant outside of Moscow, with Dimitry Muratov, editor, Novaya Gazeta.

At Gorbachev Foundation, with Professor Archie Brown, Gorbachev, Conference on End of Cold War, 2016.

At poet Yevgeny Yevtushenko's dacha, with "Zhenya" and Masha Yevtushenko. Peredelkino, 1987.

With Anna Larina at her dacha in Zhutovsky.

With Dan Rather and CBS cameraman, on Red Square. Summer 1987.

With Foreign Minister Sergei Lavrov, at Foreign Ministry, 2012.

At the Moscow Museum of the Gulag, with its
founder and Gulag victim, Anton Antonov
Ovsyenko.

At "The View" meeting Jerry Lee Lewis, 2015.

Overlooking Red Square, with Nika (2 months old). July 1991.

In Red Square, interviewing Gorbachev during Reagan-Gorbachev Summit. July 1987. (Foreign Minister Edward Shevarnadze and Ideology Minister Alexander Yakovlev flank them).

With a small part of his political Matryoshka doll collection. NYC, circa 2012.

a phone talk, President Obama told Putin he would support the agreement. Instead, it perished within hours when rejected by ultranationalist forces in Maidan's streets and occupied buildings. Neither Obama nor the European ministers made any effort to save the agreement. Instead, they fully embraced the new government that had come to power through a violent street coup.

The rest, as the cliché goes, is history. But if Ukraine is indicative, who actually destabilized its flawed, even corrupt, but legal constitutional democracy in 2014? Putin or the Western leaders who imposed an untenable choice on Ukraine and then abandoned their own negotiated agreement?

Will Russia Leave the West?

September 13

SOME FATEFUL QUESTIONS ARE RARELY, IF ever, discussed publicly. One is this: As the established post-1991 "liberal world order" disintegrates and a new one struggles to emerge, where will Russia, the world's largest territorial country, end up politically? The outcome will be fateful, for better or worse.

Geographically, of course, Russia cannot leave the West. Its expanses include vast Far Eastern territories and peoples and a long border with China, but also major European cities such as St. Petersburg and Moscow. For that reason alone, Russia has long been, to varying degrees at various times, both a European and non-European country. Geography, it is said, is destiny, but history is more complex.

The deep divide among Russia's political and intellectual elites between Slavophiles, who saw Russia's true destiny apart from the West, and Westernizers, who saw it with the West, originally debated passionately in the 19th century, has never ended. Arguably, it was only exacerbated by the country's subsequent political history.

It was apparent in the Soviet Communist Party in the 1920s, when rival factions debated and fought over the nature and future of the 1917 Revolution. The long Stalin era, from 1929 to 1953, imposed aspects of Western modernization on the country, such as literacy, industrialization, and urbanization, but also strong elements of what some historians called "Oriental Despotism." These conflicting aspects of the West and the East underlay the struggle, most significantly inside the Communist Party but not only, between anti-Stalinist reformers and neo-Stalinist conservatives during subsequent decades.

Even during the 40-year "Iron Curtain" Cold War, Soviet Russia, for all its elements of isolation, remained linked to the West. The official Communist ideology, however formal, was inherently Western and internationalist. The European nations entrapped in the Soviet Bloc (East Germany, Czechoslovakia, Hungary, Poland, and others) retained their Western currents, as did the Soviet Baltic republics. Those currents flowed from their own Communist parties into the Soviet Russian political establishment. Not surprisingly, many of Mikhail Gorbachev's close advisers who influenced his *perestroika* program for a Westernizing reformation of the Soviet system had themselves been strongly influenced by ideological trends and developments in Soviet Bloc European countries. (A number of them had lived in Prague, for example.)

When the Soviet Union ended in 1991, due largely to Gorbachev's democratizing reforms, it was widely assumed—in Washington, Europe, and by pro-Western factions in Moscow—that Russia was now or would soon be, after a short "transition," an integral part of the US-led West. And yet today, just more than 25 years later, Russia is reviled in Washington and parts of Europe as the "No. 1 threat to the West." Even though this widespread perception is without factual basis, we must ask, what went wrong?

The Western notion that all Soviet anti-Communist "reformers" were pro-Western was mistaken. If we take into account provincial political and intellectual elites, the majority were, and remain, modern-day Slavophiles—a circumstance I was surprised to discover while living in Russia in the 1970s and 1980s—and who now manifest themselves in various forms of "Euro-Asianism" and Russian nationalism. Their influence, abetted by the growing role of the Russian Orthodox Church, whose "ideology" lacks the Western elements of "Communism," has increased very significantly since 1991.

More important were two shocks for Russia that followed the end of the Soviet Union and of the preceding Cold War. First came the social, economic, and demographic catastrophe of the 1990s, associated with Western-promoted democracy and capitalism. Here it is necessary to note again that

Putin is regularly misquoted as having said the end of the Soviet Union caused "the greatest catastrophe of the 20th century." He said instead, "one of the greatest catastrophes," and for the majority of Russians it was a catastrophe.

The second shock was the onset of the new Cold War, for which Washington and much of Europe blame Russia for every mishap, from the Ukrainian crisis of 2014 to the election of President Trump. Many political and intellectual Russians, probably most, do not believe these allegations. They conclude instead that the West seeks only to exclude, isolate, and weaken Russia, no matter Russia's actual intentions. (Here it's also worth noting that while in Soviet times I encountered very little authentic anti-Americanism in Russia, today it is much more widespread among both older and younger generations.)

In addition, educated Russians, with far more access to information than is commonly understood in the West, see Western, particularly American, policies and actions that they interpret as intended to isolate Russia: the expansion of NATO to the country's borders; economic sanctions, along with warnings, as by Senator Jeanne Shaheen, that any "business" with Russia is undesirable; Russophobic demonizing of Putin and thus Russia itself; violations of diplomatic treaties and norms, as occurred recently at the Russian Consulate in San Francisco, suggesting that Washington may no longer want any diplomatic relations with Moscow—or, considering efforts to ban Russia's media outlets *RT* and *Sputnik*, even information relations. As a result, the conclusion of the late, but still influential, Russian philosopher Aleksandr Zinoviev is increasingly quoted as retrospective wisdom about the preceding Cold War: Western foes "were shooting at Communism, but they were aiming at Russia."

Also not surprisingly, Russia is pushing back against, even retreating from, the West. The surge of Slavophile-like ideological movements is one soft expression of this backlash. A more tangible example is Moscow's growing economic self-sufficiency from the West and reorientation toward non-Western partners, from China and Iran to the BRICS countries more generally. There are other manifestations, including, of course, military ones. Meanwhile, the fastest-growing segments of Russia's populace are its millions of Islamic citizens and immigrants from Central Asia. Eventually, demography will influence politics, if it is not already doing so.

All of these Eastern-bound developments may or may not eventually take Russia politically out of the West. If so, this will be clearer after Putin is no longer the country's leader. One indication is that none of his potential successors now visible are, in the Russian context, as "pro-Western" as Putin has been since he came to power in 2000.

What would it mean if Russia leaves—or is driven from—the West politically? Most likely a Russia—with its vast territories, immense natural resources, world-class sciences, formidable military and nuclear power, and UN Security Council veto—allied solidly with all the other emerging powers that are not part of the US-NATO Western "world order" and even opposed to it. And, of course, it would drive Russia increasingly afar from the West's liberalizing influences, back toward its more authoritarian traditions.

The Silence of the Doves

September 20 / September 27

A PERILOUS PARADOX: WHY, UNLIKE DURING THE 40-year Cold War, is there no significant American mainstream opposition to the new and more dangerous Cold War? In particular, from the 1960s through the 1980s, there were many anti–Cold War, or pro-détente, voices in the American political-media-corporate establishment—in the White House, Congress, State Department, political parties, influential print and broadcast outlets, universities and think tanks, major US corporations, even in elections.

That is, debates about Washington policy toward Moscow were the norm during the preceding Cold War, at the very top and at grassroots levels. as befits a democracy. As to the former, I can provide personal testimony. In November 1989, the first President George Bush convened at Camp David virtually his entire national-security team to attend a debate between myself—I was then at Princeton and, as now, a pro-détente advocate—and Harvard professor Richard Pipes, a renowned "hardliner," on the pressing issue of whether the détente under way with the Soviet Union under Gorbachev should be expanded or reversed.

And yet, today, despite escalating perils in US-Russian relations from the

Baltic region and Ukraine to Syria, despite the circumstance that Russia's ruling elites are no longer Communists but professed capitalists, there is virtually none of that. Even the well-organized grassroots anti-nuke movement that once animated pro-détente politics in elections has all but vanished. In the vernacular of the preceding Cold war, political struggles between American "hawks" and "doves" no longer exist. Everywhere, hawks prevail and doves are silent, even in corporations with major Russian investments.

I cannot explain this exceedingly dangerous paradox, only point out some partial factors:

The longtime demonization of Russian President Putin has been an inhibiting factor since the early 2000s. The vilification of President Trump has intensified it. Mainstream Americans skeptical about Washington's Russia policies worry about being labeled "pro-Putin" and/or "pro-Trump." That anyone need worry about such slurs is deplorable, but they do.

There is also the neo-McCarthyism that has grown considerably since Trump's election. As official investigations into alleged "collusion with Russia" become more promiscuous and well-funded campaigns to ferret out "Russian disinformation" in US media unfold, a self-censoring chill has descended on policy discussions. No one wants to be suspected of "collusion with the Kremlin" or of conveying "Russian propaganda." Nor is this merely self-censorship. Major media outlets regularly exclude critics of Washington's Russia policy from their news reports, opinion pages, and TV and radio broadcasts.

On the other hand, some have argued that the persistence and prevalence of Cold War politics is best explained by a nativist American social tradition that "needs an enemy," and more often than not Russia has been assigned this role. Having grown up in Kentucky and lived in Indiana, Florida, New York, and New Jersey, I find no evidence for this "blame the people" explanation. Nor do periodic opinion surveys.

The fault lies with America's governing elites. Two recent developments illustrate that conclusion. US political-media elites fully expected that post-Soviet Russia would become, during the "transition" of the 1990s, Washington's junior and compliant partner in world affairs. When Russia took a different course after 2000, Washington elites blamed not their own illusions and ill-conceived policies but Putin. More recently, as the US-led "liberal world order" shows signs of disintegrating, from Europe to the Middle East, with disparate symptoms from Brexit to Trump's election—US elites and "thought leaders," rather than consider profound historical factors and their own prior policies, again resort to blaming "Putin's Russia."

Where are the liberal Democrats and progressives who once opposed Cold War extremes? Many present-day ones are in the forefront of the new manias. Russiagate allegations did not begin with Trump's election but in the summer and fall of 2016 with pro- Democratic media, led by the *New York Times*, seeding the notion of a "Trump-Putin" conspiracy. Hillary Clinton herself, her campaign already funding the Steele "Dossier," branded Trump a "Putin puppet" in their August televised debate. And when President Obama imposed new sanctions on Russia in December 2016, he cited what became known as Russiagate as a reason, still without presenting any proof.

Congress is now driving Russiagate, with Democrats, many of them self-professed liberals, still in the forefront, among them Representatives Adam Schiff, Jackie Speier, Eric Swalwell, and Maxine Waters, along with Senators Mark Warner and Richard Blumenthal. Abandoning journalistic standards of verifiable evidence, reliable sources, and balanced coverage, the *Times*, joined by the *Washington Post*, are publishing even more sweeping allegations as virtual facts. (For their practices, see the many critical articles by the award-winning journalist Robert Parry at consortiumnews.com.) That print news is amplified almost nightly on pro-liberal MSNBC and CNN. Smaller liberal and progressive outlets are playing the same role.

Not surprisingly, celebrities are also trumpeting Russiagate's most reckless charge that in 2016 America "came under attack by the Russian government." In a recent video produced by Hollywood liberals, Morgan Freeman intoned, "We are at war."

Don't blame trendy celebrities. According to the eminent liberal Democratic intellectual Robert Reich, Russia committed an "unprecedented attack on our democracy," the professor apparently having forgotten or discounted Pearl Harbor and 9/11. And in a major foreign-policy speech on September 21, the "maverick" Bernie Sanders told the Democratic Party, "We now know that the Russian government was engaged in a massive effort to undermine one of our greatest strengths: The integrity of our elections, and our faith in our own democracy." In reality, we do not "know" that.

We do know what many liberal Democrats and progressives once did, but no longer do. They evince no skepticism about intelligence and media Russiagate allegations, despite contrary evidence. They do not protest the growing criminalization of customary "contacts" with Russia—financial, diplomatic, even conjugal, while still promoting the truly "fake news" anti-Trump "Dossier."

Most liberals and progressive express no interest in the role of Obama's Intel chiefs in Russiagate. And even less interest in evidence that Trump's campaign was in fact surveilled by the FBI, as the president later claimed. Instead, Democrats, including liberals, have turned the intelligence agencies into an iconic source of testimony (and leaks). Indeed, Obama's director of national intelligence, James Clapper, whose ethnic slurs about Russians as inherently subverting did not perturb liberals either, is on the advisory board of Hollywood's "Committee to Investigate Russia," which scripted Morgan Freeman.

Above all, liberals once would have been shocked into protest by a recent *Times* article characterizing Special Counsel Robert Mueller's investigative methods as "aggressive tactics," "shock-and-awe tactics to intimidate witnesses and potential targets." Methods, as one source put it, "to strike terror in the hearts of people in Washington." But there is no liberal outrage, no ACLU actions, only articles applauding Mueller for his "scrupulousness" and egging him on, as by Ryan Lizza in the *New Yorker*. Not even when the *Times* suggests that Mueller, unable to find evidence of electoral "collusion," might be "on a fishing expedition" reminiscent of past abuses.

Liberal Democrats even seem indifferent to the slouching toward forms of media censorship. Some of it is soft, such as excluding contrarian voices. But there are adumbrations of harder censorship—official and unofficial campaigns to purge "Russian disinformation and propaganda" from American media, even if expressed by Americans as their own opinion. Thus we have Obama's former UN ambassador, Samantha Power, demanding that we "enhance our vigilance" and her longing for media "gatekeepers" and "umpires." This too betrays not only a disregard for the First Amendment but also contempt for American voters, who presumably, zombie-like, have no critical minds of their own. The normally loquacious ACLU, PEN, and other civil-liberties guardians remain silent.

Privately, some liberal Democrats justify their new illiberalism by insisting it is necessary for the "Resistance" against Trump. But history has long shown that ends-justify-means reasoning does not end well for liberals—or anyone else. Or maybe mainstream "doves" are silent because there no longer are any. This too is, of course, without precedent and exceedingly dangerous.

Has NATO Expansion Made
Anyone Safer?

October 18

TWENTY YEARS AGO, IN 1997, PRESIDENT Bill Clinton made the decision to expand NATO eastward. In order to placate post-Soviet Russia, then weak but heralded in Washington as America's "strategic friend and partner," the Russian-NATO Founding Act was also adopted. It promised that expansion would not entail any "permanent stationing of substantial combat forces." Today they are encamped on Russia's borders and growing. Have twenty years of NATO's expansion actually created the international security it promised?

The expansion of the US-led military alliance, which began in Germany with 13 member states and now stretches to Russia with 29, is the largest and fastest growth of a "sphere of influence" (American) in modern peacetime history. Throughout the process, with hypocrisy that does not go unnoticed in Moscow, Russia has been repeatedly denounced for seeking any sphere of security of its own, even on its own borders.

NATO expansion included two broken promises that the Kremlin has not forgotten. In 1990, the Bush administration and other Western powers assured Soviet leader Gorbachev that, in return for Russia agreeing to a united Germany in NATO, the alliance would "not expand one inch to the east." (Though denied by a number of participants and pro-NATO commentators, the assurance has been confirmed by other participants and by archive researchers.)

The other broken promise is unfolding today as NATO builds up its permanent land, sea, and air power near Russian territory, along with missile-defense installations. NATO "enlargement," as its promoters benignly termed it, continues. Montenegro became a member in 2017 and the "door remains open," Western officials say repeatedly, to the former Soviet republics of Georgia and Ukraine.

NATO is more than the world's largest military alliance. With lavishly funded offices, representatives, think tanks, and other advocates not only in Brussels but in many Western capitals, it is also a powerful political-ideological-lobbying institution—perhaps the world's most power-ful corporation, taking into account its multitude of bureaucratic employees in Brussels and elsewhere.

NATO is also very big business. New members must purchase Western-made weapons, primarily US ones. The alliance has, that is, diverse corpo-rate interests that it vigorously promotes. In the United States alone, scarce-ly a week passes without promotional "news" and commentary produced by NATO-affiliated institutes and authors or based on NATO sources. (The Atlantic Council is an especially prolific source of these media products.)

Asking whether "enlarged" NATO has actually resulted in more insecu-rity than security requires considering the consequences of several wars it led or in which some of its member states participated since 1997:

• The Serbian war in 1999 resulted in NATO's occupation and annex-ation of Kosovo, a precedent cited by subsequent annexationists, including Russia when it took back Crimea from Ukraine in 2014.

• The 2003 Iraq War was a catastrophe for all involved and a powerful factor behind expanding organized terrorism, including the Islamic State, and not only in the Middle East. The same was true of the war against Libya in 2011, no lessons of Iraq having been learned.

• NATO promises that Georgia might one day become a member state was an underlying cause of the Georgian-Russian war of 2008, in effect a US-Russian proxy war. The result was the near ruination of Georgia, where NATO remains active today.

• Similarly persistent NATO overtures to Ukraine underlay the crisis in that country in 2014. It resulted in Russia's annexation of Crimea, the still ongoing Ukrainian civil war in Donbass, and another US-Russian proxy war. Meanwhile, US-backed Kiev remains in deep economic and political crisis, and Ukraine fraught with the possibility of a direct US-Russian mili-tary conflict.

• There is also, of course, Afghanistan, initially a NATO war effort, but now the longest (and possibly most un-winnable) war in American history.

Any rational calculation of the outcomes of these NATO wars adds up to far more military and political insecurity than security—at most a pseudo-se-curity of simmering crises.

NATO expansion has also bred political-ideological insecurities. The alliance's incessant, ubiquitous media saturation and lobbying in Western capitals, particularly in the United States, has been a major driving force behind the new Cold War and its rampant Russophobia. One result has been the near-end of American diplomacy toward Russia and the almost total militarization of US-Russian relations. This alone is a profound source of insecurity—including the possibility of war with Russia.

During these same 20 years, the enormous resources devoted to NATO expansion have scarcely contributed anything to resolving real international crises, among them economic problems in Europe that have helped inspire its own secessionist movements; international terrorism in the Middle East and the refugee crisis; the danger of nuclear proliferation, which NATO has abetted by spurring a new nuclear arms race with Russia; and others.

Nor has NATO's vast expansion resolved its own internal crises. They include growing military cooperation between NATO member Turkey and Russia; and undemocratic developments in other member states such as Hungary and Poland. And this leaves aside the far-reaching implications of the emerging anti-NATO alliance centering around Russia, China, and Iran—itself a result of NATO's 20-year expansion.

Now consider arguments made by NATO- expansion promoters over the years:

• They say the small Baltic and other Eastern European countries previously victimized by Soviet Russia still felt threatened by Russia and therefore had to be brought into the alliance. This makes no empirical sense. In the 1990s, Russia was in shambles and weak, a threat only to itself. And if any perceived or future threat existed, there were alternatives: acting on Gorbachev's proposed "Common European Home"—a security agreement including all of Europe and Russia; bilateral security guarantees to those once-victimized nations, along with diplomacy on their own part to resolve lingering conflicts with Russia, particularly the disadvantaged status of their ethnic Russian citizens. This argument makes no historical sense either. The tiny Baltic states nearest to Russia were among the last to be granted NATO membership.

• It is also said that every qualified nation has a "right" to NATO membership. This too is illogical. NATO is not a non-selective college fraternity or the AARP. It is a security organization whose sole criterion for "enlargement" should be whether or not new eastern members enhance the security of its current members. From the outset, it was clear, as many Western critics pointed out, it would not.

• Now, it is belatedly argued, Russia has become a threat under Vladimir Putin. But much of what is decried as "Putin's aggression" abroad has been the Kremlin's predictable responses to US and NATO expansionist policies. There is a related negative consequence. Moscow's perception that it is increasingly encircled by an "aggressive" US-led NATO has had lamentable, and also predictable, influence on Russia's internal politics. As NATO expanded, space for democracy in Russia diminished.

For the sake of international security, NATO expansion must end. But is there a way to undo the 20-year folly? Member states taken in since the late 1990s cannot, of course, be expelled. NATO expansion could, however, be demilitarized, its forces withdrawn back to Germany, from which they crept to Russia's borders.

This may have been feasible in the late 1990s or early 2000s, as promised in 1997. Now it may seem to be a utopian idea, but one without which the world is in ever graver danger—a world with less and less real security.

More Double Standards

October 25

MOSCOW AND WASHINGTON HAVE CONFLICTING NARRATIVES—EXPRESSED regularly in their mass media and periodic diplomacy—regarding the history, causes, and nature of the new Cold War. Not surprisingly, both narratives are often self-serving and unbalanced. But the near-consensual US version features an array of double standards that ought to be of grave concern.

I have previously commented on some of these double standards. Moscow is condemned for wanting a sphere of security, or absence of Western military bases, near its borders, while the US-led NATO military alliance has expanded from Germany to countries directly on Russia's borders. (Imagine a Russian-Chinese "sphere" in Canada or Mexico.) NATO's military build-up around Russia is frequently justified by "Putin's lies and deceits." But Kremlin complaints about American "lies and deceit" can hardly be challenged, including the 1990 promise that NATO would "not expand one inch to the east" and the Obama administration's pledge in 2011 that a UN Security Council resolution permitting use of force against Libya would not seek to remove its leader Gaddafi, who was tracked down and assassinated.

And then there is professed alarm over Moscow's very few military bases abroad while Washington has some 800.

Now we have more American double standards. When Russian air power and the Syrian army "liberated" the Syrian city of Aleppo from terrorists last year, the US political-media establishment denounced the operation as "Russian war crimes." No such characterizations appeared in coverage of the subsequent US-led "liberation" of the Iraqi city Mosul or Syria's Raqqa, where destruction and civilian casualties may have been considerably greater than in Aleppo. Indeed, on October 19, *Washington Post* columnist David Ignatius was awed by "the overwhelming, pitilessly effective military power of the United States" displayed in Raqqa.

Moscow's nonviolent "annexation" of Crimea in 2014—the Kremlin and most Russian citizens regarded it as "reunification"—continues to inspire anti-Russian sanctions by Washington. American media explain that Crimea was the first forcible modern-day realignment of borders and territory. This narrative omits the Balkan wars in the 1990s and the fate of what was once Yugoslavia, and particularly the US-led NATO annexation of the Serbian province of Kosovo, after a long bombing campaign, in 1999. It also omits secession movements since Crimea—Brexit and the recent Catalonia and Kurdish referenda.

As an outgrowth of their Russiagate coverage, US media now allege that the Kremlin, using its foreign broadcast outlets and social media everywhere, has promoted white-supremacist, neo-Nazi movements in the West, particularly in the United States. Some of this commentary gives the impression that the Kremlin actually created racial conflict in America or is primarily responsible for "exacerbating" it. Meanwhile, the US establishment has virtually nothing to say about the truly ominous growth of extreme-right-wing, even neo-Nazi, movements in US-backed Ukraine.

We will return to this phenomenon later, but briefly stated: with the tacit support, indifference, or impotence of the Kiev government, these movements, some well-armed, are rehabilitating and memorializing Ukrainian Jew-killers during the World War II German occupation—rewriting history in their favor, erecting memorials and renaming public places in their honor, occasionally directly threatening Ukrainian Jews.

Though well-reported in foreign and alternative media, these signs of a rebirth of fascism in a large European country—one supported politically, financially, and militarily by Washington—are rarely, if ever, covered by American mainstream media, notably the *New York Times* and the *Washington*

Post. Where is the balance between these unreported realities and daily allegations of some murky "Russian" divisive posts in American social media?

Finally, also almost daily, American media report that the Kremlin "meddled" in the US 2016 presidential election, warning, "They will be back!" There is as yet no actual evidence in these hyperbolic media accounts, nor any historical balance. Leave aside that Washington and its representatives have "meddled" in nearly every Russian election since the early 1990s. Leave aside even the Clinton administration's large-scale, on-site involvement in Russian President Yeltsin's reelection in 1996. Do note, however, the recent scholarly finding—reported in the *Post* on September 7, 2016—that from 1946 to 2000 (prior to Putin), the United States and Russia interfered in 117 foreign elections.

When pointed out, our new Cold Warriors denounce criticism of these US double standards as "moral equivalence" and pro-Kremlin "whataboutism." But facts being facts, their self-apologetics are really an extreme expression of "American exceptionalism."

The Unheralded Putin—
Official Anti-Stalinist No. 1

November 8

I N NOVEMBER 1961, AT THE FIRST SOVIET Communist Party Congress that publicly condemned Stalin's crimes, the leader, Nikita Khrushchev, unexpectedly called for a national memorial to the tens of millions of victims of the despot's nearly 25-year reign. During the following decades, a fierce political struggle raged between anti-Stalinists and pro-Stalinists, sometimes publicly but often hidden inside the ruling Communist Party, over whether the victims should be memorialized or deleted from history through repression and censorship.

This year, on October 30, anti-Stalinists finally won the struggle when President Putin personally inaugurated a large memorial sculpture, in the center of Moscow, named "Wall of Sorrow" depicting the victims' fate. Though nominally dedicated to all victims of Soviet repression, the monument was clearly—in word, deed, and design—focused on the Stalin years from 1929 to 1953.

I have spent decades studying the Stalin era, during which I came to know many surviving victims of the mass terror and personally observed aspects of the struggle over their place in Soviet politics and history. (I recount these experiences in my book *The Victims Return: Survivors of the Gulag After Stalin.*) As a result, I and my wife of many years, Katrina vanden Heuvel, felt a compelling need to be present at the ceremony on October 30. Having been assured access to the semi-closed event, attended perhaps by some 300 officials, representatives of anti-Stalinist memorial organizations, aged survivors, relatives of victims, and the mostly Russian press)—we flew to Moscow.

It was a special occasion featuring three speakers: Putin, the patriarch of the Russian Orthodox Church, and a representative of a leading memorial organization, Vladimir Lukin. (I have known Lukin since 1976, when he was a semi-dissident outcast in Moscow. Many years later he was Russian ambassador to Washington.) The formal ceremony began just after 5 pm and lasted, after choir hymns, about 45 minutes. At first, I felt the long-anticipated event was marred by the dark, cold, rainy weather, until I heard someone quietly remark, "The heavens are weeping for the victims."

In the context of other anti-Stalinist speeches by Soviet and post-Soviet leaders over the years, Putin's remarks seemed heartfelt, moving, even profound. Without mentioning their names, he alluded to the crucial roles played in the anti-Stalinist struggle by Khrushchev and Mikhail Gorbachev, whose glasnost policies made public the full dimensions of Stalin's mass terror.

One of Putin's remarks seemed especially important. After allowing that many events in Russian history were the subject of legitimate debate, he said Stalin's long terror was not. Other controversial episodes may have their historical pluses and minuses, but the Stalinist terror and its consequences were too criminal and ramifying for any pluses. This, he seemed to emphasize, was the essential lesson for Russia's present and future.

Russia's media being diverse these days, they reacted in three conflicting ways to the memorial monument and Putin's role, at least in Moscow. One was with full approval. Another, expressed in a protest by a number of Soviet-era dissidents, most now living abroad, objected to a memorial to historical victims as "cynical" while there are still victims of repression in Russia. The third view, asserted by ultranationalists, opposed any official condemnation of Stalin's "repression" as detrimental because it weakened the nation's will to "repress" US and NATO encroachment on Russia's borders and the West's "fifth column" inside Putin's own political establishment.

Nonetheless, official state sponsorship of the memorial monument was a historic development—not only a much belated tribute to Stalin's victims and millions of surviving relatives but acknowledgment of the (Soviet) Russian state's prolonged act of criminality. Putin's personal role in the ceremony made this all the more emphatic.

And yet, American media coverage of the October 30 event was characteristic of its general reporting on Russia today—either selectively silent or slanted to diminish the significance of the event, whether out of historical ignorance or a need to vilify everything Putin does and says. The title of the *New York Times* report, on October 30, was representative: "Critics Scoff as Kremlin Erects Monument to the Repressed." Not atypically, the article also contained an untrue assertion, reporting that the Kremlin "has never opened the archives from the [Stalin] period." As all historians of the Soviet period, and any informed Moscow journalist, know, those archives have opened ever wider since the 1990s. This is true of the Soviet Communist Party archive, which holds most of Stalin's personal documents, where I work during periodic visits to Moscow.

But the media malpractice is larger. The persistent demonizing of Putin portrays him as a kind of crypto-Stalin who has promoted the rehabilitation of the despot's reputation in Russia. This is also untrue. Putin's rare, barely semi-positive public references to Stalin over the years relate mostly to the Soviet victory over Nazi Germany, from which, however great Stalin's crimes, he cannot truthfully be separated. For better or worse, Stalin was the wartime Soviet leader.

Nor was October 30 the first time Putin had appeared at a public memorialization of Stalin's victims. He had done so previously, and is still the only Soviet or post-Soviet leader ever to do so. Above all, as I know from my sources, Putin personally made possible politically and financially, against high-level opposition, the creation not only of the new memorial monument but, a few years earlier, a large State Museum of the History of the Gulag, also in Moscow.

It is true that Stalin's reputation in Russia today is on the rise. But, as I explained earlier, this is due to circumstances that Putin does not control, certainly not fully. Pro-Stalin forces in the Russian political-media-historical establishment have used their considerable resources to recast the murderous tyrant in the image of a stern but benign leader who protected "the people" against foreign enemies, traitors, venal politicians, and corrupt bureaucrats.

In addition, when Russia is confronted with Cold War threats from abroad, as it perceives itself to be today, Stalin reemerges as the leader who drove the Nazi war machine from Russia back to Berlin and destroyed it along the way. Not surprisingly, in the recent survey of popular attitudes toward historical figures I cited before, Stalin topped the most-admired list. That is, his reputation has fallen and risen due to larger social and international circumstances. Thus, during the very hard economic times of the Yeltsin 1990s, Stalin's reputation, after plunging under Gorbachev, began to rise again.

It is often reported that Putin's relative silence about controversial subjects in modern Russian history is a kind of sinister cover-up or censorship. Again, this misinterpretation fails to understand two important factors. Like any state, Russia needs a usable, substantially consensual history for stability and progress. Achieving elite or popular consensus about the profound traumas of the Tsarist, Soviet, and post-Soviet pasts remains exceedingly difficult, if not impossible.

Putin's approach, with rare exceptions, has been twofold. First, he has said little judgmental about controversial periods and events while encouraging historians, political intellectuals, and others to argue publicly over their disagreements, though "civilly." Second, and related, he has avoided the Soviet practice of imposing historical orthodoxy though heavy-handed censorship and other forms of suppression. Hence Putin's refusal to stage state events during this 100th anniversary year of the 1917 Revolution—not, as is widely reported, because he "fears a new revolution." He left the public celebrations to the large Russian Communist Party, for which 1917 remains sacred.

American media also regularly assert that Russia has never grappled publicly with, "confronted," its dark Stalinist past. In fact, from 1956 to his overthrow in 1964, Khrushchev permitted waves of revelations and judgments about the crimes of the Stalin era. They were mostly stopped under his immediate successors, but under Gorbachev there was, as was commonly said at the time, a kind of "Nuremberg Trial of the Stalin Era" in virtually all forms of Soviet media. It has continued ever since, though to a lesser degree, with less intensity, and facing greater pro-Stalin opposition. Again, Americans might consider that in Moscow there are two state-sponsored national memorials to Stalin's millions of victims—the Gulag Museum and the new monument. In Washington, there are none specifically dedicated to the millions of American slaves.

Nonetheless, the new memorial to Stalin's victims, however historic, will not end the bitter controversy and political struggle over his reputation, which began with his death 64 years ago. The dispute will continue, not primarily because of one or another Kremlin leader, but because millions of relatives of Stalin's victims and their victimizers still confront each other and will do so for perhaps at least another generation. Because the Stalin era was marked both by the mountain of crimes and the mountain of national achievements I discussed earlier, which even the best-informed and most well-intended historians still struggle to reconcile or balance. And because the nearly 30-year Stalinist experience still influences Russia in ways no less than does a Kremlin leader, even Vladimir Putin, however good his own intentions.

Russiagate Zealots vs. National Security

November 15

AMERICA IS NOW IN UNPRECEDENTED DANGER due to two related crises. A new and more perilous Cold War fraught with the possibility of hot war between the two nuclear superpowers on several fronts, especially in Syria. And the worst crisis of the American presidency in modern times, which threatens to paralyze the president's ability to deal diplomatically with Moscow. (As a reminder, Watergate never accused President Nixon of "collusion with the Kremlin" or his election having been abetted by a Russian "attack on American democracy.")

What Trump did in Vietnam last week was therefore vitally important and courageous, though uniformly misrepresented by the American mainstream media. Despite unrelenting Democratic threats to impeach him for "collusion with the Kremlin," and perhaps even opposition by high-level members of his own administration, Trump met several times, informally and briefly, with Russian President Putin. Presumably dissuaded or prevented by top advisers from having a formal lengthy meeting, Trump was nonetheless prepared. He and Putin issued a joint statement urging cooperation in Syria, where the prospects of a US-Russian war had been mounting. And both leaders later said they had serious talks about cooperating on the crises in North Korea and Ukraine.

What Trump told the US press corps after his meetings with Putin was even more remarkable—and defiantly bold. He reiterated his longstanding position that "having a relationship with Russia would be a great thing—not a good thing—it would be a great thing." He is right: it would be an essential thing for the sake of US national security on many vital issues and in many areas of the world, and should be a priority for both political parties.

Trump then turned to Russiagate, saying that Putin had again denied any personal involvement and that the Russian leader seemed sincere. Trump quickly added that three of President Obama's top intelligence directors—the CIA's John Brennan, Office of National Intelligence's James Clapper, and the FBI's James Comey—were "political hacks," clearly implying that their comments about Russiagate have been and remain less than sincere. He also suggested, correctly, that Russia had been too "heavily sanctioned" by Washington to be the national-security partner America needs.

The immediate reaction of liberal and progressive Russiagaters was lamentably predictable, as was that of their Cold War allies Brennan, Clapper, and Senator John McCain, who never saw the prospect of war with Russia he didn't want to fight. Racing to their eager media outlets, they denounced Trump's necessary diplomacy with Putin as "unconscionable."

Columnist Charles Blow, who from his regular perch at the *New York Times* and on CNN influences many Democrats, followed suit, accusing the president of "a betrayal of American trust and interests that is almost treasonous." He quickly deleted "almost," declaring Trump's presidency to be "a Russian project" and Trump himself "Putin's dupe." In full retro mode, Blow characterized the US president as Putin's "new comrade," apparently unaware that both leaders are known to be anti-Communists.[36]

It's hard not to conclude that promoters of Russiagate have no concern for America's actual national-security interests and indeed, in this regard, are actively undermining those interests. To the extent that Russiagate's crippling of Trump as a foreign-policy president is becoming a major part of the Democratic Party's electoral platform, can the party really be trusted to lead the nation?

Trump's diplomatic initiatives with Putin in Vietnam also demonstrate that a fateful struggle over Russia policy is under way at high levels of the US political-media establishment. Whatever else we may think of the president—I did not vote for him and I oppose many of his other policies—Trump has demonstrated consistency and determination on one existential issue: Putin's Russia is not America's enemy but a national-security partner our nation vitally needs. The president made this clear again following the scurrilous attacks on his negotiations with Putin: "When will all the haters and fools out there realize that having a good relationship with Russia is a good thing, not a bad thing."

Another indication that Trump is prepared to fight for his Russia policy was also noteworthy. He sent his own CIA director to speak with William Binney, a leading member of Veteran Intelligence Professionals for Sanity, which recently published a study concluding that the theft of emails from the Democratic National Committee during the 2016 presidential campaign was not a remote hack by Russia—the foundational allegation of Russiagate—but an inside job. Russiagate zealots quickly dismissed Binney as a "crackpot conspiracy theorist," but he is hardly that.

A retired longtime NSA official, Binney and his colleagues produced a serious alternative explanation of what happened at the DNC. Highly technical aspects of the VIPS report have been seriously contested, including by members of the organization itself, but it cannot be lightly dismissed. It is no more "crackpot conspiracy theory" than was the January 2017 Intelligence Community Assessment that alleged, without the slightest evidence, as we saw, that Putin personally ordered what became known as the "attack on American democracy."

Trump also pointed out, as have others, that the ICA report was not the produce of "17 intelligence agencies" but of a few hand-picked "analysts." He seems to have been suggesting, as I have, that an Intelgate, instead of Russiagate, should first be investigated. This too enraged Democrats, who now defer to US intel chiefs as iconic truth-tellers. They apparently have no memory of the 1976 Senate Church Committee report on gross abuses by US intelligence agencies over the years, including foreign assassinations and violations of Americans' privacy at home, or even their malpractices during the run-up to the not-so-remote Iraq War.

We are clearly at a fateful crossroads in US-Russian relations and in the history of the American presidency. The crux should be American national security in the fullest domestic and international respects, not whether we are Trump supporters or members of the "Resistance." Reckless denunciations make both crises worse. The only way out is nonpartisan respect for verified facts, logic, and rational civil discourse, which Russiagate seems to have all but vaporized, even in once-exalted places.

Russia Is Not the "No. 1 Threat"

November 27

I N THE 1990S, THE CLINTON ADMINISTRATION embraced post-Soviet Russia as America's "strategic partner and friend." Twenty years later, twenty-six since the end of the Soviet Union, the US policy establishment, from liberals to conservatives, insists that "Putin's Russia" is the No. 1 threat to American national security. The primary explanation for how this bipartisan axiom came about, as I have long argued, is to be found in Washington, not Moscow. Whatever the full explanation, it is myopic and itself a threat to US national security.

Threats can be real, uninformed misperceptions, or manufactured by vested interests. In today's real world, Russia is not even among the top five, which are these:

1. Russiagate. Since the late 1940s, when both the United States and the Soviet Union acquired atomic and then nuclear weapons, the first existential duty of an American president has been to avoid the possibility of war with Russia, a conflagration that could result in the end of modern civilization. Every American president has been politically empowered to discharge that duty, even during the most perilous crises, until now.

The still unverified but ever-more-persistent allegations that President Trump has somehow been compromised by the Kremlin and may even be its agent are the number-one threat to America because they hinder, if not cripple, his ability to carry out that existential duty. Recently, for example, his negotiations with Russian President Putin to replace US-Russian conflicts in Syria with cooperation were treated as "treasonous"—not by a successor publication of the John Birch Society but in the pages of the *New York Times* and by other leading media.

Still more, Russiagate alleges that "we were attacked by Russia" during the 2016 presidential election, an act likened to a "political Pearl Harbor." What could be more reckless than to insist we are already at war with the other nuclear superpower? Lest there is any doubt about the gravity of the national-security threat represented by Russiagate, imagine President John F. Kennedy so burdened with such allegations during the 1962 Cuban Missile Crisis. It is unlikely he could have negotiated its peaceful resolution as he did.

2. The demonization of Putin. This too, as I have documented, is unprecedented. No Soviet or post-Soviet leader was ever so wildly, baselessly vilified as Putin has increasingly been for more than a decade. Demonizing Putin has become so maniacal that leading "opinion-makers" seem to think he is a Communist. Joy Reid of MSNBC actually said so, but more telling is the breathless warning on March 30 by *Washington Post* columnist Dana Milbank about "the red menace of Vladimir Putin's Russia."

Mainstream media consumers may be excused for thinking that somehow the Soviet Communist "menace" has been reborn in Moscow, and as an even more fearsome threat. Trump's own CIA Director at the time, Mike Pompeo, evidently believes this uninformed nonsense, or wishes us to do so. Warning that "we still face a threat from the Russians," he explains: "They're Russians, they're Soviets.... pick a name."[37]

Demonizing Putin and "Putin's Russia" as a ramifying threat. It is hard to imagine the plausibility of Russiagate without such a master villain in the Kremlin. And it all but excludes, in effect delegitimizes, the national-security partner most needed by Washington—whoever sits in the Kremlin—in the nuclear age.

3. ISIS and other international terrorist organizations in pursuit of radioactive material to lace with their explosives. This threat would be number one if the US political-media establishment had not conjured up the preceding ones.

Little more needs be said about the looming danger. Imagine even small quantities of radioactive material aboard the planes of 9/11, mixed with the bombs of Paris, Boston, and many other cities, spewed in the air by the fiery explosions and borne by the wind—and wonder if those areas would be inhabitable today. Now consider the value and willingness of Moscow, so often a target of terrorism, as a security partner in this regard given its experiences, sprawling presence between East and West, and exceptional intelligence capabilities. Unlike Russiagate allegations, the threat of terrorism has been amply verified.

4. The proliferation of states with nuclear weapons. In 1949, there were two. Today there are nine. In a new era of transnational ethnic and religious hatreds and wars, such fanaticisms could easily overwhelm the taboo against using forbidden weapons. Iran and North Korea are not the only states capable of acquiring nuclear weapons and the means to deliver them. (Every time the United States militarily attacks a non-nuclear state, others feel the imperative to acquire them as a deterrent.) US-Russian cooperation is essential for preventing more proliferation of all weapons of mass destruction, but threats No. 1 and 2 are preventing Trump from achieving this, even if he wants to do so.

5. Climate change—the science is sound—along with global income inequality, which breeds misery, resentments, fanaticism, and thus terrorism around the world. (According to a report by Scott Shane and others in the *New York Times* on November 7, "The richest 1 percent of the world's population now owns more than half of global wealth, and the top 10 percent owns about 90 percent.") These growing threats rank below the others only because of what a US-Russian bilateral partnership could achieve now. These two require a much larger international alliance and considerably more time.

Why are neither Russia nor China on this list? Russia—because it represents no threat to the United States at all (apart from a nuclear accident or miscalculation) except those Washington and NATO have themselves created. China—because its historical moment as a very great power has come. It may be an economic and regional rival to the United States, but an actual threat (at least thus far) only if Washington also makes it one. The expanding alliance between Russia and China, itself significantly a result of unwise Washington policy-making, is a separate subject.

Why Russians Think America Is Attacking Them

December 20

For 18 months, much of the US establishment has told us, preposterously and without real evidence, that "Russia attacked America" during the 2016 president election. On the other hand, many Russians—in the policy elite, the educated middle class, and ordinary citizens—believe "America has been at war with Russia" for 25 years, and for understandable reasons.

US commentators attribute these views to "Kremlin propaganda." It is true that Russians, like Americans, are strongly influenced by the mass media, especially television. It is also true that Russian television news reporting and commentary are no less politicized than their US counterparts.

But elite and educated Russians are generally better informed and more independent-minded about our political life than most of us are about theirs. They have much more regular access to American news and opinions—from cable and satellite TV, US-funded Russian-language broadcasts and Internet sites, and from Russian sites, such as inosmi.ru, that translate scores of US media articles daily. (Recent prohibiting steps taken by the Department of Justice against *RT* and *Sputnik* can only further diminish American information about Russia.)

Above all, Russians are strongly influenced by what they call "living history." They remember the history of US policy toward post-Soviet Russia since the early 1990s, especially episodes they perceived as having been warlike or acts of "betrayal and deceit"—promises and assurances made to Moscow by Washington and subsequently violated, such as the following:

Presidents Reagan and George H.W. Bush negotiated with the last Soviet Russian leader, Mikhail Gorbachev, what they said was the end of the Cold War on the shared, expressed premise that it was ending "with no losers, only winners." (For this crucial mutual understanding, see two books by Jack F. Matlock Jr., both presidents' ambassador to Moscow: *Reagan and Gorbachev: How the Cold War Ended* and *Superpower Illusions: How Myths and False Ideologies Led America Astray–And How to Return to Reality*.) But readers will recall that in 1992, during his reelection campaign against Bill Clinton, Bush suddenly declared, "We won the Cold War." This anticipated the triumphalism of the Clinton administration and the implication that post-Soviet Russia should be treated as a defeated adversary, as Germany and Japan were after World War II. For many knowledgeable Russians, including Gorbachev himself, this was the first American betrayal.

For the next eight years, in the 1990s, the Clinton administration based its Russia policy on that triumphalist premise, with wanton disregard for how it was perceived in Russia or what it might portend. The catastrophic "shock therapy" economics imposed on Russia by President Boris Yeltsin was primarily his responsibility, but that draconian policy was emphatically insisted on and (meagerly) funded by Washington. The result was the near ruination of Russia—the worst economic depression in peacetime, the disintegration of the highly professionalized Soviet middle classes, mass poverty, plunging life expectancy, the fostering of an oligarchic financial elite, the plundering of Russia's wealth, and more.

All the while, as we have seen, the Clinton administration lauded Yeltsin as its "democrat" and clung to him, as did most leading US political figures, media, and many other influential Americans. Re-making post-Soviet Russia became an American project, as countless American "advisers" encamped to

Moscow and other cities. So many that Russians sometimes said their country had been "occupied." (I treated this subject at the time in my book *Failed Crusade: America and the Tragedy of Post-Soviet Russia.*)

In 1999, Clinton made clear that the crusade was also a military one. He began the still-ongoing eastward expansion of NATO, now directly on Russia's borders. That so many Russians see NATO's unrelenting creep from Berlin to within artillery range of St. Petersburg as "war on Russia" hardly needs explanation. Moreover, herein lies the second "betrayal and deceit" that has not been forgotten.

As readers already know, in 1990, in return for Gorbachev's agreement that a reunited Germany would be a NATO member, all of the major powers involved, particularly the first Bush administration, promised that NATO "would not expand one inch to the east." Many US participants later denied that such a promise had been made, or claimed that Gorbachev misunderstood. But documents just published by the National Security Archive in Washington, on December 17, prove that the assurance was given on many occasions by many Western leaders, including the Americans. The only answer they can now give is that "Gorbachev should have gotten it in writing," implying that American promises to Russia are nothing more than deceit in pursuit of domination.

In 1999, Clinton made clear that NATO expansion was not the non-combat policy Russia had been told it would be. For three months, US-led NATO war planes bombed tiny Serbia, Russia's traditional Slav ally, in effect annexing its province of Kosovo. Visiting Moscow at the time, I heard widely expressed shock, dismay, anger, and perceptions of yet another betrayal, especially by young Russians, whose views of America were rapidly changing from ones of a benign well-wisher to a warlike enemy. Meanwhile, also under Clinton, Washington began its still-ongoing campaign to diminish Moscow's energy sales to Europe, thereby also belying US wishes for Russia's economic recovery.

George W. Bush's administration continued Clinton's winner-take-all approach to post-Soviet Russia. More than any NATO member, Putin's government assisted the United States in its war against the Taliban in Afghanistan after the events of 9/11, saving American lives. In return, Putin expected a genuine US-Russian partnership in place of the pseudo-one Yeltsin had received.

Instead, by 2002, Bush had resumed intrusive "democracy promotion"—interference, or, in today's Russiagate parlance, "meddling"—in Russian politics and NATO expansion eastward. No less fatefully, Bush unilaterally withdrew from the Anti-Ballistic Missile Treaty, the cornerstone of Russian nuclear security. That led to the ongoing process of ringing Russia with anti-missile installations, now formally a NATO project.

In 2008, President Bush tried to fast-track Georgia and Ukraine—both former Soviet republics and Moscow's "red lines" into NATO. Though vetoed by Germany and France, a NATO summit that same year promised both eventual membership. Hardly unrelated, in August Georgian President Mikheil Saakashvili, a Washington protégé, launched a sudden military assault on the Russian protectorate of South Ossetia, inside Georgia, killing a number of Russian citizens. Seeing Saakashvili as an American proxy, the Kremlin intervened.

President Obama came to office promising a "new era of American diplomacy," but his approach to Russia was no different and arguably even more militarized and intrusive than that of his predecessors. During the White House's short-lived "reset" of relations with the Kremlin, then occupied by President Dmitri Medvedev, Obama's vice president, Joseph Biden, told a Moscow public audience, and then Putin himself, that Putin should not return to the presidency. (In effect, Obama and Biden were "colluding" with their imagined partner Medvedev against Putin.)

Other "meddling" was also under way. The Obama administration, notably Secretary of State Hillary Clinton, stepped up intrusive "democracy promotion" by publicly criticizing Russia's parliamentary and presidential elections. Though welcomed by Putin's street opponents, many Russians saw her remarks as characteristic American arrogance.

By 2011, the Obama administration, presumably having lost interest in its own "reset," now betrayed its own partner, President Medvedev, by breaking its promise not to use a UN Security Council resolution in order to depose Libyan leader Gaddafi. Readers will recall that he was tracked by US-NATO war planes and murdered—sodomized with a bayonet—in the streets, a gruesome end Mrs. Clinton later laughingly rejoiced over. All the while, Obama, like his predecessors, pushed NATO expansion ever closer to Russia, eventually to its borders.

Given this history, the fateful events in Kiev in 2014 seem almost inevitable. For anti-Russian NATO expansionists in Washington, Ukraine remained "the biggest prize" in their march from Berlin to Russia, as Carl Gershman, head of the official US regime-change institution, the National Endowment for Democracy, candidly proclaimed in the *Washington Post* on September 26, 2013.

The ensuing crisis led to yet another broken US commitment. In February

2014, readers will also recall, Obama assured Putin that he supported a negotiated truce between Ukrainian President Yanukovych and the Maidan street protesters. Within hours, the protesters headed toward Yanukovych's official residence, and he fled, yielding to the US-backed anti-Russian regime now in power.

Then or later, Obama did not, for whatever reasons, ultimately prefer real diplomacy with Russia. He repeatedly refused, or stepped back from, Moscow's offers of cooperation against ISIS in Syria, until finally Putin, after months of pleading, acted on his own in September 2015. Typically, Obama left office by imposing more sanctions, essentially economic warfare, on Russia—this time for the unproven allegations of Russiagate. Indeed, his sanctions included an unprecedented and reckless threat of covert cyber attacks on Russia.

It is through this 25-year history of "American aggression" that many Russians perceive the meaning of Russiagate. For them, a US presidential candidate, and then president, Donald Trump, suddenly appeared proposing to end the long US war against Russia for the sake of "cooperation with Russia."

Russiagate charges—Russians had seen multitudes of American "contacts" with their officials, oligarchs, politicians, wheeler-dealers, ordinary women and men, even orphans ever since the Soviet Union ended—are seen as fictions designed to prevent Trump from ending the long "war against Russia." When influential American media denounce as "treasonous" Trump's diplomacy with Putin regarding Syria and terrorism, for example, Russians see confirmation of their perceptions.

Americans themselves should decide whether these perceptions of US policy are correct or not. Perceptions are at the core of politics, and even if Russians misperceive American intentions, has Washington given them cause to do so? Put another way, is Putin really the "aggressor" depicted by the US political-media establishment or a leader responding to a decades-long "American war against Russia?"

There is one anomaly: Putin, almost alone among high Russian officials, rarely—if ever—speaks of an "American war against Russia." In the context of bellicose statements issued almost daily by the US Congress and mainstream media, might we call this statesmanship?

Part IV

War With Russia?
2018

Four Years of Maidan Myths

January 3

THE UKRAINIAN CRISIS, WHICH UNFOLDED IN late 2013 and early 2014, again requires our attention. It has become a seminal political event of the early 21st century, leading to Russia's annexation of Crimea and to the ongoing US-Russian proxy war in Donbass. It militarized and rooted the epicenter of the new Cold War on Russia's borders, indeed inside a civilization shared for centuries by Russia and large parts of Ukraine. It implanted a toxic political element in American, Russian, Ukrainian, and European politics, possibly in ways we do not yet fully understand. And it has left Ukraine in near-economic ruin, with thousands dead, millions displaced, and others still struggling to regain their previous quality of life.

The events of 2014 also led to NATO's ongoing buildup on Russia's western border, in the Baltic region, yet another new Cold War front fraught with the possibility of hot war. Making things only worse, in late 2017, the Trump administration announced it would supply the Kiev government with more, and more sophisticated, weapons, a step that even the Obama administration, which played a large detrimental role in the 2014 crisis, declined to take.

There are, as we already saw, two conflicting narratives of the Ukrainian crisis. One, promoted by Washington and the US-backed government in Kiev, blames only "aggression" by the Kremlin and specifically by Russian President Putin. The other, promoted by Moscow and rebel forces in eastern Ukraine, which it supports, blames "aggression" by Washington and the European Union. There are enough bad intent, misconceptions, and misperceptions to go around, but on balance Moscow's narrative, almost entirely deleted from US mass media, is closer to the historical realities of 2013–2014.

One myth has been particularly tenacious in Western accounts: what occurred on Kiev's Maidan Square in February 2014 was a "democratic revolution." Whether or not it eventually turns out to have been a "revolution" can be left to future historians, but it hardly seems like one now. Most of the oligarchic powers that afflicted Ukraine before 2014 remain in place four years later, along with their corrupt practices. As for "democratic," removing a legally elected president by threatening his life, as happened to Viktor Yanukovych in February 2014, did not qualify. Nor did the preemptory way the new government was formed, the constitution changed, and pro-Yanukovych parties banned. Yanukovych's overthrow involved people in the streets, but it was a coup.

How much of it was spontaneous and how much directed, or inspired, by high-level actors in the West remains unclear, but a related myth again needs to be dispelled. The rush to seize Yanukovych's residence was triggered by snipers who killed some 80 or more protesters and policemen on Maidan. It was long said that the snipers were sent by Yanukovych, but it has now been virtually proven that the shooters were instead from Right Sector, a neo-Nazi group that was among the protesters on the square.[38]

The anti-democratic origins of today's Kiev regime continue to afflict it. Its president, Petro Poroshenko, is intensely unpopular at home, as are his leading would-be successors. The government remains pervasively corrupt. Its Western-financed economy continues to flounder. And for the most part, Kiev still refuses to implement its obligations under the 2015 Minsk II peace accords, above all granting the rebel Donbass territories enough home rule to keep them in a unified Ukrainian state.

Meanwhile, Poroshenko's government remains semi-hostage to armed ultranationalist battalions, whose ideology and symbols include proudly neo-fascist ones—forces that hate Russia and Western "civilizational" values, to which Maidan was said to aspire, almost equally. The Donbass rebel "republics" have their own ugly traits, but they fight only in defense of their own territory against Kiev's armies and are not sponsored by the US government.

Making things worse, the Trump administration now promises to supply Kiev with more weapons. The official pretext is plainly contrived: to deter Putin from "further aggression against Ukraine," for which he has shown no desire or intention whatsoever. Nor does it make any geopolitical or strategic sense. Neighboring Russia can easily upgrade its weapons to the rebel provinces.

There is also the danger that Kiev's wobbly regime will interpret the American arms as a signal from Washington to launch a new offensive against Donbass in order to regain support at home, but which is likely to end again in military disaster for Kiev. If so, it could bring neo-fascists, who may acquire some of the American weapons, closer to power and the new US-Russian Cold War closer to direct war between the nuclear superpowers. (US trainers will need to be sent with the weapons, adding to the some 300 already there. If any are killed by Russian-backed rebel forces, even unintentionally, what will be Washington's reaction?)

Why would Trump, who wants to "cooperate with Russia," take such a reckless step, long urged by Washington's hawks but resisted even by President Obama? Assuming it was Trump's decision, no doubt to disprove Russiagate allegations that he is a lackey of the Kremlin—accusations he hears and reads daily not only from damning commentary on MSNBC and CNN, but from the once-distinguished academic Paul Krugman, who told his *New York Times* readers on November 17, 2017: "There's really no question about Trump/Putin collusion, and Trump in fact continues to act like Putin's puppet."

Even though there is every "question" and as yet no "in fact" at all, Trump is understandably desperate to end the unprecedented allegations that he is a "treasonous" president—to demonstrate there was "no collusion, no collusion, no collusion." We have here yet another example of how Russiagate has become the No. 1 threat to American national security, certainly in regard to nuclear Russia.

If the media insists on condemning Trump based on dubious narratives and foreign connections, they might focus instead on former vice president Joseph Biden. President Obama put him in charge of the administration's "Ukrainian project," in effect making him pro-consul overseeing the increasingly colonized Kiev. Biden, who is clearly already seeking the 2020 Democratic presidential nomination, bears a heavy personal responsibility for the four-year-old Ukrainian crisis, though he shows no sign of any rethinking or remorse.

In an article in *Foreign Affairs*, Biden and his coauthor, Michael Carpenter, string together a medley of highly questionable, if not outright false, narratives regarding "How to Stand Up to the Kremlin," many involving the years he was vice president. Along the way, Biden repeatedly berates Putin for meddling in Western elections. This is the same Joe Biden who told

Putin not to return to the Russian presidency during Obama's purported "reset" with then President Dmitri Medvedev, and who, in February 2014, told Ukraine's democratically elected President Yanukovych to abdicate and flee the country.

Russia "Betrayed" Not "News That's Fit to Print"

January 10

US MAINSTREAM MEDIA MALPRACTICE IN COVERING Russia has a long history. There have been three major episodes.

The first was when American newspapers, particularly the *New York Times*, misled readers into thinking the Communists could not possibly win the Russian Civil War of 1918–1920, as detailed in a once famous study by Walter Lippmann and Charles Merz and published as a supplement to the *New Republic*, August 4, 1920. (Once canonical, the study was for years assigned reading at journalism schools, but no longer, it seems.)

The second episode was in the 1990s, when virtually the entire mainstream America print and broadcast media covered the US-backed "reforms" of Russian President Boris Yeltsin, which plundered the state and brought misery to its people, as a benevolent "transition to democracy and capitalism" and to "the kind of Russia we want."[39]

The third and current episode of journalistic malpractice grew out of the second and spread quickly through the media in the early 2000s with the demonization of Vladimir Putin, Yeltsin's successor. It is now amply evident in mainstream coverage of the new Cold War, Russiagate allegations that "Russia attacked American democracy" in 2016, and by much else. Today's rendition may be the worst; certainly it is the most dangerous.

Media malpractice has various elements—among them, selective use of facts, some unverified; questionable narratives or reporting based on those "facts"; editorial commentary passed off as "analysis": carefully selected "expert sources," often anonymous; and amplifications by chosen opinion-page contributors. Throughout is the systematic practice of excluding developments (and opinion) that do not conform to the *Times*' venerable front-page motto, "All the News That's Fit to Print." When it comes to Russia, the *Times* often decides politically what is fit and what is not.

And thus the most recent but exceedingly important example of malpractice. In 1990, as readers know, Soviet Russian leader Mikhail Gorbachev agreed not only to the reunification of Germany, whose division was the epicenter of that Cold War, but also, at the urging of the Western powers, particularly the United States, that the new Germany would be a member of NATO. (Already embattled at home, Gorbachev was further weakened by this decision, which probably contributed to the attempted coup against him in August 1991.) Gorbachev made the decision based on assurances by his Western "partners" that in return NATO would never be expanded "one inch eastward" toward Russia. Today, having nearly doubled its member countries, the world's largest military alliance sits on Russia's western borders.

At the time, it was known that President George H.W. Bush had especially persuaded Gorbachev through Secretary of State James Baker's "not one inch" promise and other equally emphatic guarantees. Ever since Bush's successor, President Bill Clinton, began the still ongoing process of NATO expansion, its promoters and apologists have repeatedly insisted there was no such promise to Gorbachev, that it had all been "myth" or "misunderstanding."

Now, however, the National Security Archive at George Washington University has established the historical truth by publishing, on December 12, 2017, not only a detailed account of what Gorbachev was promised in 1990–1991 but the relevant documents themselves. The truth, and the promises broken, are much more expansive than previously known: all of the Western powers involved—the US, the UK, France, Germany itself—made the same promise to Gorbachev on multiple occasions and in various emphatic ways. If we ask when the West, particularly Washington, lost Moscow as a potential strategic partner after the end of the Soviet Union, this is where an explanation begins.

And yet, nearly a month after publication of the National Security Archive documents, neither the *Times* nor the *Washington Post*, which profess to be the nation's most important and indispensable political newspapers, has

printed one word about this revelation. (The two papers are widely important to other media, not only due to their national syndication but because
broadcast media such as CNN, MSNBC, NPR, and PBS take most of their
own Russia-related "reporting" cues from the *Times* and the *Post*.)

How to explain the failure of the *Times* and *Post* to report or otherwise
comment on the National Security Archive's publication? It can hardly be
their lack of space or disinterest in Russia, which they featured regularly in
one kind of unflattering story or another—and almost daily in the form of
"Russiagate." Given their immense news-gathering capabilities, could both
papers have missed the story? Impossible, especially considering that three
lesser publications—the *National Interest*, on December 12; *Bloomberg*, on
December 13; and the *American Conservative*, on December 22—reported on
its significance at length.

Or perhaps the *Times* and *Post* consider the history of NATO expansion
to be no longer newsworthy, even though it has been the driving, escalatory
factor behind the new US-Russian Cold War; already contributed to two
US-Russian proxy hot wars (in Georgia in 2008 and in Ukraine since 2014)
as well as to NATO's provocative buildup on Russia's borders in the Baltic
region; provoked Russia into reactions now cited as "grave threats"; nearly
vaporized politically both the once robust pro-American lobby in Moscow
politics and previously widespread pro-American sentiments among Russian
citizens; and implanted in the Russian policy elite a conviction that the broken promise to Gorbachev represented characteristic American "betrayal
and deceit."

Both Russian presidents since 2000—Putin and President Obama's "reset"
partner Dmitri Medvedev—have said as much, more than once. Putin put
it bluntly: "They duped us, in the full sense of this word." Russians can cite
other instances of "deceit," as I have already specified. But it is the broken
promise to Gorbachev regarding NATO expansion that lingers as America's
original sin, partly because it was the first of many such perceived duplici-
ties, but mainly because it has resulted in a Russia semi-encircled by US-led
Western military power.

Given all this, we must ask again: Why did neither the *Times* nor the *Post*
report the archive revelations? Most likely because the evidence fundamentally
undermines their essential overarching narrative that "Putin's Russia" is solely
responsible for the new Cold War and all of its attendant conflicts and dangers,
and therefore no rethinking of US policy toward post-Soviet Russia since 1991
is advisable or permissible, certainly not by President Donald Trump.

Therein lie the national-security dangers of media malpractice. And this example, while of special importance, is far from the only one in recent years. In this regard, the *Times* and *Post* seem contemptuous not only of their own professed journalistic standards but of their professed adage that democracy requires fully informed citizens. It also sheds ironic light on the *Post*'s new front-page mantra, "Democracy Dies in Darkness."

US Establishment Finally Declares "Second Cold War'"

January 24

FOR MORE THAN A DECADE, I have been warning about an unfolding new Cold War with Russia. Despite compelling evidence, leading US policymakers, media commentators, and scholars have adamantly denied its existence, even such a possibility. They have cited post-Soviet Russia's purported weakness; the absence of "ideological conflict"; the non-global nature of any conflicts; the benign nature of Washington policy; etc.

These new Cold War deniers were either uninformed, myopic, or unwilling to acknowledge their own complicity in the squandered opportunity for a real post-Soviet peace, even an American-Russian strategic partnership. But the deniers' most prestigious and influential foreign policy organization, the Council on Foreign Relations (CFR), has now issued a report fully acknowledging, indeed eagerly declaring, that "The United States is currently in a second Cold War with Russia."

The importance of the CFR is not easily exaggerated. As its activities, history, self-proclamations, and *Wikipedia* entry make clear, it is not an ordinary "think tank." Founded nearly a century ago, headquartered lavishly in New York City with a branch in Washington, almost 5,000 selected members, and considerable annual revenue, its aura, influential journal *Foreign Affairs*, and elite membership have long made the CFR America's most important non-governmental foreign-policy organization—certainly for politicians, business executives, media leaders, academics, and others involved with US foreign policy. Almost all of them, including presidential candidates, aspire to CFR membership or its imprimatur in one way or another. (Hence Joseph Biden's recent article in *Foreign Affairs*.)

For decades, the CFR's primary role has been—through its journal, website, special events, and multiple weekly membership sessions—to define the legitimate parameters of discussion about US foreign policy and related issues. Regarding Russia, even the Soviet Union, the CFR, as a professed bipartisan, independent, centrist organization, generally adhered to this role, and not badly. (I became a member in the 1970s and resigned in protest this year.)

The CFR featured varying, even conflicting, expertise and opinions about the 40-year Cold War and thereby fostered intellectual and policy debate. This more ecumenical, pluralist orientation largely ended, however, more than a decade ago. Opinions incompatible with Washington's growing "group think" about Russia were increasingly excluded, with very few exceptions. The CFR—much like Congress and the mainstream media—became a bastion of the new Cold War, though without acknowledging it.

Now it has done so. The CFR's new report, "Containing Russia," by two "bipartisan" veterans of the genre, both longtime CFR fellows, Robert D. Blackwill and Philip H. Gordon, could have been published during the hyperventilated early stage of the preceding Cold War, before it was tempered by the 1962 Cuban Missile Crisis, as reflected in the retrograde word "Containing."[40]

The best that can be said about the report is its banality—some 50 pages and 72 endnotes offering little more than a superficial, though devout, digest of recent mainstream media malpractices. We find here, for example, the usual unbalanced narratives of contemporary events, questionable "facts," elliptical history (when any at all), opinion and ideology passing as analysis, and not a little Russophobia.

Not surprisingly, the still unproven allegations of Russiagate are the pretext and pivot of the CFR report. (Its authors even inflate the scandal's already inflammatory rhetoric: "Moscow's ultimate objective was regime change in the United States.") Thus the first sentence of the introduction by CFR president Richard Haass: "Russia's interference in the 2016 US presidential election constituted an attack on American democracy," echoing the tacky Hollywood celebrity video produced a few months ago. The authors also repeat hyperbolic assertions equating "the attack" with Pearl Harbor and 9/11.

From this, the report goes on to refer, directly and allusively, to the alleged Kremlin-Trump "collusion," and then to project the "threat" represented by Russian President Putin, who is presented as having no legitimate Russian national interests, only "paranoia," to "worldwide" status. Again, every piece of alternative or conflicting reporting, analysis, and sourcing is omitted, as is any mention of retracted and "corrected" mainstream media articles and broadcasts. Nowhere is there any serious concern about the graver dangers inherent in this "second Cold War." In this perilous context, the CFR "recommendations" are of the back-to-the-future kind—back to the initial, unbridled, pre-1962 Cuban Missile Crisis threats, confrontations, and escalations.

Considering how this shabby—some may say shameful—report should reflect on the CFR's reputation, what was the motivation behind its publication? Recalling that it comes on the heels of similar new Cold War exhortations—Biden's article mentioned earlier, Senator Ben Cardin's similar "report" not long ago, leading newspaper editorials demanding a stronger reaction to "Russia's war on the West," and the Trump administration's own myopic doctrinal declaration last week that Russia and China are now a greater threat than is international terrorism—the CFR report's purpose seems to be threefold. To mobilize the bipartisan US policy establishment behind a radical escalation of the new Cold War. (Tellingly, it also criticizes former President Obama for not having done enough to counter Moscow's "growing geopolitical challenge".) To preclude any critical mainstream discussion of past or current US policy in order to blame only Russia. And thereby to prevent the possibility of any kind of détente, as proposed by President Trump.

The CFR report may slam the door, already nearly shut, on such discussions and policies. If so, where is any hope, any way out of this unprecedentedly perilous state of US-Russian relations? Recent opinion surveys suggest that a majority of Americans have no appetite for such reckless policies. Conceivably, they could vote to change Washington's approach to Russia. But for this they would need such candidates and time. Currently, there are neither. As during the 40-year Cold War, the CFR Report seeks to mobilize European allies behind escalating the "second Cold War." In several European countries and parties, there also appears to be little appetite for this. Americans may have to look to Europe for alternative leadership, while hoping that meanwhile Moscow does not overreact.

For now, however, the only hope is that Russiagate allegations do not prevent Trump from becoming the pro-détente president "cooperating with

Russia" he wanted to be. Even if he tries, would the Council on Foreign Relations' like-minded praetorians in Washington—who now present that traditional aspiration as evidence of criminality—permit it?

Russiagate or Intelgate?

February 7

I FIRST RAISED THE QUESTION OF "INTELGATE," perhaps coining the word, nearly a year ago. The recently released Russiagate memo, overseen by Republican Congressman Devin Nunes and declassified by President Trump, raises the question anew.

Having for years researched Soviet-era archive materials (once highly classified) in Moscow, I understand the difficulties involved in summarizing secret documents, in particular ones generated by secretive intelligence agencies. They must be put in the larger political context of the time, which can be fully understood only by using open and other sources as well. And they may be subsequently contradicted by classified materials not yet available.

Nonetheless, the "Republican memo," as it has become known while we await its Democratic counterpart, indicates that some kind of operation against presidential candidate and then President Trump, an "investigation," was under way among top officials of US intelligence agencies for a long time.

The memo focuses on questionable methods used by Obama's FBI and Justice Department to obtain a secret warrant permitting them to surveil Carter Page, a peripheral and short-tenured Trump foreign-policy adviser, and on the role played in this by the anti-Trump "dossier" complied by Christopher Steele, a former British intelligence officer whose career specialization was Russia. But the memo's implications are larger.

Steele's dossier, which alleged that Trump had been compromised by the Kremlin in various ways for several years even preceding his presidential candidacy, was the foundational document of the Russiagate narrative, at least from the time its installments began to be leaked to the American media in the summer of 2016. It has played a central role ever since, possibly even in the US Intelligence Community Assessment (ICA) of January 2017 (when *BuzzFeed* published the dossier), the same month that FBI Director James Comey "briefed" President-elect Trump on "salacious" parts of the dossier—apparently in an effort to intimidate him. Directly or indirectly, the dossier led to the special investigation headed by Robert Mueller.

Even though both the dossier and subsequent ICA report have been substantially challenged for their lack of verifiable evidence, they remain the basic sources for proponents of the Russiagate narrative of "Trump-Putin collision." The memo and dossier are now being subjected to closer (if partisan) scrutiny, much of it focused on the Clinton campaign having financed Steele's work through his employer Fusion GPS.

But two crucial and ramifying question are not being explored. Exactly when, and by whom, was this Intel operation against Trump begun? And exactly where did Steele get the "information" that he was filing in periodic installments and that grew into the dossier?

In order to defend itself against the Republican memo's charge that it used Steele's unverified dossier to open its investigation into Trump's associates, the FBI claims it was prompted instead by a May 2016 report of remarks made earlier by another lowly Trump adviser, George Papadopoulos, to an Australian diplomat in a London bar. Even leaving aside the ludicrous nature of this episode, the public record shows it is not true.

In testimony to the House Intelligence Committee in May 2017, John Brennan, formerly Obama's head of the CIA, strongly suggested that he and his agency were the first, as the *Washington Post* put it at the time, "in triggering an FBI probe." Both the *Post* and the *New York Times* interpreted his remarks in this way.[41,42] Equally certain, Brennan, as widely reported, played a central role in promoting the Russiagate narrative thereafter, briefing members of Congress privately and giving President Obama himself a top-secret envelope in early August 2016 that almost certainly contained Steele's dossier.

Early on, Brennan presumably would have shared his "suspicions" and initiatives with James Clapper, then Obama's Director of National Intelligence. FBI Director James Comey, distracted by his mangling of the Clinton private-server affair during the presidential campaign, may have joined them actively somewhat later. But when he did so publicly, in his March 2017 testimony to the House Intelligence Committee, it was as J. Edgar Hoover reincarnate—as the nation's number-one expert on Russia and its profound threat to America. (As I pointed out previously, his testimony regarding Russia was remarkably uninformed.)

The question therefore becomes: when did Brennan begin his "investigation" of Trump? His House testimony leaves this somewhat unclear, but according to a subsequent *Guardian* article, by late 2015 or early 2016 Brennan was receiving, possibly soliciting, reports from foreign intelligence agencies about "suspicious 'interactions' between figures connected to Trump and known or suspected Russian agents."[43]

If these reports and Brennan's own testimony are to be believed, he, not the FBI, was the instigator—the godfather—of Russiagate. Certainly, his subsequent frequent and vociferous public retelling of Russiagate allegations against Trump suggest that he played a (probably the) instigating role. And, it seems, a role in the Steele dossier as well.

Equally important, where did Steele get his information? According to Steele and his many stenographers—they include his American employers, Democratic Party Russiagaters, the mainstream media, and many other, even progressive, publications—the information came from his "deep connections in Russia," specifically from retired and current Russian intelligence officials in or near the Kremlin. From the moment the dossier began to be leaked to the American media, this seemed highly implausible (as reporters who took his bait should have known) for several reasons.

Steele had not returned to Russia after leaving his post there in the early 1990s. Since then, the main Russian intelligence agency, the FSB, has undergone many personnel and other changes, especially since 2000, and particularly in or near Putin's Kremlin. Did Steele really have such "connections" so many years later?

Even if he did, would these purported Russian insiders really have collaborated with a "former" British intelligence agent under what is so often said to be the ever-vigilant eye of the ruthless "former KGB agent" Vladimir Putin, thereby risking their positions, income, perhaps freedom, as well as the well-being of their families?

It was said originally that his Russian sources were highly paid by Steele. Arguably, this might have warranted the risk. But on January 2, 2018, Steele's employer and head of Fusion GPS, Glenn Simpson, wrote in the *Times* that "Steele's sources in Russia…were not paid." If the Putin Kremlin's purpose was to put Trump in the White House, why would these "Kremlin-connected" sources have contributed to Steele's anti-Trump project without financial or political gain—only with considerable risk? (There is the also the matter of factual mistakes in the dossier that Kremlin "insiders" were unlikely to have made, but this is the subject for a separate analysis.)

We now know that Steele actually had at least three other "sources" for the dossier, ones not previously mentioned by him or his employer. There was information from foreign intelligence agencies provided by Brennan to Steele or to the FBI, which we also now know was collaborating with Steele. There was the contents of a "second Trump-Russia dossier" prepared by people personally close to Hillary Clinton and who shared their "findings" with Steele.[44] And in fact, Steele himself repeatedly cites as a source a Russian emigre associate of Trump—that is, apparently an American, not Russian, citizen.

Most intriguing, there was "research" provided by Nellie Ohr, wife of a top Department of Justice official, Bruce Ohr, who, according to the Republican memo, "was employed by Fusion GPS to assist in the cultivation of opposition research on Trump. Ohr later provided the FBI with all of his wife's opposition research." Most likely, it too found its way into Steele's dossier. (Mrs. Ohr was a trained Russian studies scholar with a PhD from Stanford and a onetime assistant professor at Vassar, and thus, it must have seemed, an ideal collaborator for Steele.)

There is also the core allegation made both by Steele and the ICA report that Putin personally "ordered" and "directed" the Russiagate operation on behalf of Trump, but neither gives a persuasive or consistent motive, especially considering that if exposed—even Steele claims some top-level Kremlin officials feared the purported plot might "backfire"—it would benefit electorally only Hillary Clinton. Nor do their many media stenographers give us a coherent motive.

Some say the operation was "payback" for Clinton having encouraged protests against Putin in Moscow in 2011-2012. No, say others, it was a longer-standing Kremlin preference for Trump going back eight or more years, though this is contradicted in the Steele dossier where some Kremlin officials are said not to favor Trump. Still others say it was payback not against Clinton but for what Putin saw as the US-led doping scandal that battered the Russian Olympic team. Now it's just Putin's general desire to sow "chaos and disorder" in the West. None of these motives make sense given, as I have pointed out, Putin's initial and still ongoing hope to rebuild Russia partly through modernizing economic partnerships with a stable and prospering West, including the United States.

We are left, then, with a ramifying question: how much of the "intelligence information" in Steele's dossier actually came from Russian insiders, if any? (This uncertainty alone should stop Fox News' Sean Hannity and others from declaring that the Kremlin used Steele—and Hillary Clinton—to pump its "propaganda and disinformation" into America. These pro-Trump counter-allegations also fuel the new Cold War.)

We are left with even more ramifying questions. Was Russiagate produced by leaders of Obama's intelligence community, not just the FBI? If so, it is the most perilous political scandal in modern American history, and the most detrimental to American democracy. It would indeed, as zealous promoters of Russiagate assert, make Watergate pale in significance. (To understand more, we need to know more, including whether Trump associates other than Carter Page and Paul Manafort were surveilled by any of the intelligence agencies involved. And whether they were surveilled in order to monitor Trump himself, on the assumption they would be in close proximity to him, as the president suggested in a tweet.)

If Russiagate involved collusion among US intelligence agencies, as now seems likely, why was it undertaken? There are various possibilities. Out of loathing for Trump? Out of institutional opposition to his promise of better relations—"cooperation"—with Russia? Or out of personal ambition? Did Brennan, for example, aspire to remain head of the CIA, or to a higher position, in a Hillary Clinton administration?

What was President Obama's role in any of this? Or to resort to the Watergate question: what did he know and when did he know it? And what did he do? The same questions would need to be asked about his White House aides and other appointees involved. Whatever the full answers, there is no doubt that Obama acted on the Russiagate allegations. He cited them for the sanctions he imposed on Russia in December 2016, which led directly to the case of General Michael Flynn; to the worsening of the new US-Russian Cold War; and thus to the perilous relationship inherited by President Trump.

With all of this in mind, and assuming Trump knew most of it, did he really have any choice in firing FBI Director Comey, for which he is now being investigated by Mueller? We might also ask again, given Comey's role during Hillary Clinton's presidential campaign (for which she and her team loudly condemned him), whether as president she too would have had to fire him.

Listening almost daily to the legion of former US intelligence officers condemn Trump in the media, we may wonder if they are increasingly fearful it will become known that Russiagate was mostly Intelgate. For that we may need a new bipartisan Senate Church Committee of the mid-1970s. Once famously, it investigated and exposed misdeeds by US intelligence agencies and led to reforms that are no longer the preventive measures against abuses of power they were intended to be. (Ideally, everyone involved would be granted amnesty for prior misdeeds, ending all talk of "jail time," on the condition they now testify truthfully.)

Such a full, inclusive investigation of Intelgate would require the support of leading Democratic members of Congress. This no longer seems possible.

What Russiagate Reveals About America's Elites

February 21

RUSSIAGATE'S NEARLY TWO YEARS OF ALLEGATIONS and investigations were instigated by top US political, media, and intelligence elites. They have revealed profoundly disturbing characteristics of people who play a very large role in governing our country. Six of these barely concealed truths are especially alarming.

1. Russiagate's promoters evidently have little regard for the future of the American presidency. At the center of their allegations is the claim that the current president, Donald Trump, achieved the office in 2016 due to a conspiracy ("collusion") with the Kremlin; or to some dark secret the Kremlin uses to control him; or due to "Russian interference" in the election; or all three. This means, they say outright or imply daily, that the president is some kind of Kremlin agent or "puppet" and thus "treasonous."

Such allegations are unprecedented in American history. They have already deformed Trump's presidency, but no consideration is given to how they may affect the institution in the future. Unless actual proof is provided in the specific case of Trump—thus far there is none—they are likely to leave a stain of suspicion on, or inspire similar allegations against, future presidents. If the Kremlin is believed to have made Trump president or corrupted him, why not future presidents as well?

That is, Russiagate zealots seek to delegitimize Trump's presidency but risk leaving a long-term cloud over the institution itself. And not only the presidency. They now clamor that the Kremlin is targeting the 2018 congressional elections, thereby projecting the same dark cloud over the next Congress, even if embittered losers do not explicitly blame Putin's Kremlin.

2. Russiagate promoters clearly also have no regard for America's national security. By declaring that Russia's "meddling" in the 2016 US presidential election was "an attack on American democracy" and "an act of war" comparable to Pearl Harbor and 9/11, they are practicing the dictionary meaning of "war-mongering." Can this mean anything less than that the United States must respond with "an act of war" against Russia? It is noteworthy that Russiagaters rarely, if ever, mention the potentially apocalyptic consequences of war between the two nuclear superpowers, an abiding concern once shared by all enlightened elites.

Closely related, Russiagate accusations against Trump, whom they characterize as a "mentally unstable president," risk provoking him to stumbling into just such a war in order to demonstrate he is not the "Kremlin's puppet." By casting doubt on Trump's loyalty to America, they also limit his capacity, possessed by all American presidents since the onset of the atomic age, to avert or resolve nuclear crises through diplomatic instead of military means, as President Kennedy did in the Cuban Missile Crisis.

In short, American elites themselves have made Russiagate the number-one threat to US national security, not Russia.

3. Having found no factual evidence of such a plot, Russiagate promoters have shifted their focus from the Kremlin's alleged hacking of DNC emails to a social-media "attack on our democracy." In so doing, they reveal their contempt for American voters, for the American people.

A foundational principle of theories of representative democracy is that voters make rational and legitimate decisions. But Russiagate advocates strongly imply—even state outright—that American voters are easily duped by "Russian disinformation," zombie-like responding to signals as how to act and vote. The allegation is reminiscent of, for people old enough to remember, the classic Cold War film *Invasion of the Body Snatchers*. But let the following representatives of America's elite media speak for themselves:

• According to *Washington Post* columnist Kathleen Parker, Russia's social-media intrusions "manipulated American thought.... The minds of social media users are likely becoming more, not less, malleable." This, she goes on, is especially true of "older, nonwhite, less-educated people." *New York Times* columnist Charles Blow adds that this was true of "black folks."[45,46]

- *Times* reporter Scott Shane is straightforward, writing about "Americans duped by the Russian trolls." Evan Osnos of the *New Yorker* spells it out without nuance: "At the heart of the Russian fraud is an essential, embarrassing insight into American life: large numbers of Americans are ill-equipped to assess the credibility of the things they read."[47,48]
- Another *Post* columnist, Dana Milbank, even rehabilitates a Leninist concept. "Putin," he tells readers, "has played Americans across the political spectrum for suckers." In particular, he turned Trump's millions of voters "into the useful idiots of the 21st century." To be clear, according to Milbank's demeaning of US citizens generally, "Putin made fools of Americans."[49]

These denigrators of the American people are, of course, lead writers for some of our most elite publications. Their apparent contempt for "ordinary" citizens is not unlike a centuries-old trait of the radical Russian intelligentsia. That tradition has long viewed the Russian *narod* (people) with similar contempt, while maintaining that the rarified intelligentsia therefore must lead them, and not always in democratic ways.

4. Russiagate was initiated by political actors, but elite media gave it traction, inflated it, and promoted it to what it is today. These most "respectable" media include the *New York Times*, the *Washington Post*, the *New York Review of Books*, the *New Yorker*, and, of course, CNN and MSNBC, among others. They proclaim themselves to be factual, unbiased, balanced, and an essential component of American democracy—a "fourth branch of government."

Maybe a "branch," but far from fact-based and unbiased in its reporting and commentary on Russiagate. The media's combined loathing for Trump and "Putin's Russia" has produced, as we have seen repeatedly, one of the worst episodes of malpractice in the history of American journalism. This requires a special detailed study, though no leading media critics or elite journalism schools seem interested.

Nor are elite media outlets above slurring the reputations of anyone who dissents from contemptuous aspects of Russiagate, even members of their own elite. Recently, for example, the *Times* traduced a Facebook vice president whose study suggested that "that swaying the election was not the main goal" of Russian use of Facebook. Similarly, a brand name of liberal-progressive MSNBC, John Heilemann, suggested on air, referring to questions about Russiagate posed by Congressman Devin Nunes, "that we actually have a Russian agent running the House Intel Committee on the Republican side." The Democratic senator being interviewed, Chris Murphy, was less than categorical in brushing aside the "question."[50,51]

Not to be overlooked, elite media have done little, if anything, to protest the creeping Big Brother-like censorship programs now being assiduously promoted by other elites in government and private institutions in order to ferret out and ban "Russian disinformation," something any American might be "guilty" of entirely on his or her own. Instead, leading media have abetted and legitimized these undemocratic undertakings by citing them as sources.

5. Then there is the Democratic Party's role in promoting Russiagate. Preparing for congressional elections in 2018, this constituent component of the American two-party system seems less a vehicle of positive domestic and foreign-policy alternatives than a party promoting conspiracy theories, Cold War, and neo-McCarthyism. A number of local candidates say these electoral approaches are less their own initiatives than cues, or directives, coming from high party levels—that is, from Democratic elites.

6. Finally, but no less revealing, American elites have long professed to be people of civic courage and honor. Russiagate has produced, however, very few "profiles in courage"—people who use their privileged positions of political or media influence to protest the abuses itemized above. Hence another revelation, if it is really that: America's elites are composed overwhelmingly not of "rugged individualists" but of conformists—whether due to ambition, fear, or ignorance hardly matters.

Russiagate Amnesia or Denialism

February 28

MANY RUSSIANS, I HAVE ALREADY EXPLAINED, have an awareness of "living history"—memories of past events that continue to influence current ones. Russiagate suggests that Americans have significantly less historical awareness—or that its promoters willfully ignore past American events and practices.

A fundamental Russiagate tenet is that the Kremlin sought, primarily through social media, "to create or exacerbate divisions in American society and politics" in 2016. Even if true, there is no evidence that this purported campaign had any meaningful impact on how Americans voted in the presidential election. But even it somehow did, the social and political "divisions" were hardly comparable to those in our not so distant past.,

Those past divisions included Jim Crow segregation and the black civil-rights struggle; the social-political barricade in American life—even in families—generated by the Vietnam War; and the religious-political division over abortion rights during several electoral cycles. There were also "divisions" associated with Watergate, which drove a president from office, and with the House impeachment of President Clinton. To assert that the considerably lesser "divisions" in the country in 2016 were any less American in origin or needed to be exacerbated by Russia is a kind of amnesia or denialism uninformed by history.

Closely related is the claim that "Russian propaganda and disinformation" played in 2016 an unprecedented, oversized role in America, and continue to do so. But I recall, at least since my schoolboy days in Kentucky, that this was an everyday allegation back then as well, including during the civil-rights struggle. A primary source of those dire warnings was none other than then FBI director, J. Edgar Hoover, whose writings were often assigned in schools as cautionary readings.

Hoover's essential theme was, of course, that Americans posing as loyal citizens were actually agents of Soviet (Russian) Communist "propaganda and disinformation." That allegation was also widely used by many others, mainly for political purposes, and perhaps widely believed. When blacklisting reached Hollywood in the 1950s, films were "investigated" for latent "Communist propaganda," and purportedly found. This was a search for, so to speak, "Russian trolls" in the movies, not so unlike those said to be found today in social media.

On similar ahistorical grounds, Russiagaters go on to allege that Russia "meddled" in the 2016 US presidential election and thus committed "an act of war against America." Whatever "meddle" means—the word is both capacious and imprecise—governments have meddled in the elections of other states for centuries in one form or another. Israel has, of course, meddled in US elections for decades. More to the point, according to a study reported by the *New York Times*, on February 17, 2018, the US government ran 81 "overt and covert election influence operations" in foreign countries from 1946 to 2000. (Soviet and post-Soviet Russia ran 36 such operations during the same period.)

As readers already know, official and unofficial American institutions have been deeply involved in—meddled in—Russian political life ever since the end of the Soviet Union in 1991. The instance that should dispel any amnesia is, of course, the financial, on-site, hands-on American effort to help reelect a badly failing President Yeltsin in 1996. (There is some doubt as to whether he really was reelected). Nor was this, as we saw, covert, having been apparent at the time and US mass media later boasting about it. Two wrongs may not make a right, but less amnesia would put the lesser Russiagate allegations of "meddling," none of the truly significant ones yet having been proven, in perspective.

One way or another, to some degree or another, at least two US intelligence agencies, the CIA and FBI, have played unsavory roles in Russiagate. And yet, many mainstream American media outlets and leading Democrats are exalting them as paragons of verified, nonpartisan information, including their recurring leaks to media. This is puzzling and probably best explained by willful amnesia or denial since not a few of these same media and politicians had previously been highly skeptical, even sharply critical, of both agencies.

Leave aside well-documented CIA assassinations and FBI persecution of civil-rights leaders, including Martin Luther King, Jr. Recall instead only the quality of CIA information that led President Kennedy to the Bay of Pigs disaster, President Lyndon B. Johnson and Congress ever deeper into the Vietnam War, and the nation to the catastrophic war in Iraq, whose consequences still linger. And yet information provided by the CIA regarding Russiagate is to be accepted uncritically? Is its past role, and that of the FBI, forgotten or forgiven?

Unable to provide proof linking the Kremlin or President Trump to the alleged original sin—the hacking and dissemination of DNC emails—media investigators and special counsel Robert Mueller himself have settled for seeking and prosecuting past financial misdeeds on the part of Trump "associates," notably Paul Manafort. (Manafort's laundered millions having originated mostly in Ukraine, not Russia, why is this not actually Ukrainegate? Or Russiagate without Russia?)

Here too precedents are forgotten or deleted. The "shock therapy" urged on Moscow by Washington in the 1990s led to the creation of a small group of Russian billionaire oligarchs and the "globalization" of their wealth, lavishly between the United States and Russia. Predictable scandals ensued. Two resulted in high-profile US convictions for money laundering and other financial improprieties, not unlike the charges against Manafort.

One involved the Bank of New York, the other a Harvard University institute. Both featured Americans and "Kremlin-linked" officials of the

Yeltsin government, which the Clinton administration, to say the least, strongly supported. One scandal dwarfed the charges against Manafort financially, billions of dollars having been involved, and both did so politically. In the end, however, the Manafort and other Russiagate financial cases, like their predecessors, are likely to turn out to be mostly the everyday corruption of the 1 percent and its servitors. This too seems to have been forgotten or, considering the fully bipartisan nature of the American corruption, deleted.

A final example of amnesia is particularly remarkable and known to readers. Even though the new or "second" Cold War with Russia has been unfolding for nearly 20 years, the head of America's most prestigious think tank and foreign-affairs organization, the Council on Foreign Relations, discovered it only recently and "unexpectedly." Is such myopia on the part of one of the most acclaimed US foreign-policy experts amnesia—he did not remember what the preceding Cold War looked and sounded like—or denial of the role he and his fellow experts played in bringing about the "second" one?

Whatever the explanation, all of these "unprecedented" aspects of Russiagate are part of a new, more dangerous Cold War. We should worry that Marx's famous adage—history repeats itself, first as tragedy, then as farce—may in this case turn out to be, first as tragedy, then as something worse.

How Washington Provoked—and Perhaps Lost—a New Nuclear-Arms Race

March 7

PRESIDENT PUTIN'S SPEECH TO BOTH HOUSES of the Russian parliament on March 1, somewhat akin to the US president's annual State of the Union address, was composed of two distinct parts. The first approximately two-thirds was pitched to the upcoming Russian presidential election, on March 18, and to domestic concerns of Russian voters not unlike those of American voters: stability, jobs, inflation, health care, education, taxes, infrastructures, etc.

The latter part of the speech was, however, devoted solely to recent achievements in Russia's strategic, or nuclear, weapons. These remarks, though also of electoral value, were addressed directly to Washington. Putin's overarching point was that Russia has thwarted Washington's two-decade-long effort to gain nuclear superiority over—and thus a survivable first-strike capability against—Russia. His conclusion was that one era in Russian-American strategic relations has ended and a new one begun. This part of Putin's speech makes it among the most important he has delivered during his 18 years in power.

The historical background, to which Putin refers repeatedly for his own purposes, is important. Ever since the United States and Soviet Union, the two nuclear superpowers, acquired the ability to deliver transcontinental warheads against the other, three alternative approaches to this existential reality have informed debates and policy-making: nuclear-weapons abolition, which is a necessary goal but not an achievable one in the foreseeable future; a quest for nuclear superiority, making a devastating first-strike immune from an equally catastrophic retaliation and thus "survivable" and thinkable; and mutual security based on "Mutual Assured Destruction" (MAD), which required that both sides have roughly equal nuclear capabilities and neither strive for first-strike superiority.

During the preceding Cold War, by the late 1960s and early 1970s, both Washington and Moscow officially embraced the mutual security approach. MAD, however fearful its apocalyptic reasoning, was accepted as the safest—only rational—orientation, along with the need to maintain rough strategic parity. Hence the succession of US-Soviet nuclear arms treaties, including reductions in arsenals. Nuclear technology continued to develop, making weapons ever more destructive, but MAD and the parity principle contained the technology and kept the nuclear peace despite some near misses.

This approach reached its most hopeful apogee in the late 1980s when President Reagan and the last Soviet leader, Mikhail Gorbachev, expanded their understanding of "mutual security." They agreed that any strategic "build up" by one side would be perceived as a threat by the other, which would then undertake its own reactive buildup. They agreed to end this perilous dialectic that had driven the nuclear-arms race for decades. And in

1987, they abolished for the first (and still only) time an entire category of nuclear weapons, those borne by intermediate-range missiles.

That exceedingly hopeful opportunity, the legacy of Reagan and Gorbachev, was lost almost immediately after the Soviet Union ended in 1991—squandered in Washington, not in Moscow. Beginning in the 1990s, successive US administrations—under Bill Clinton, George W. Bush, and Barack Obama—sought de facto nuclear superiority over post-Soviet Russia. Animated by rampant post–Cold War (misconceived) triumphalism and by a perception that Russia was now too weak, demoralized, or supplicant to compete, they did so in three ways: by expanding NATO to Russia's borders; by funding ever more destructive, "precise," and "usable" nuclear weapons; and, in 2002, by unilaterally withdrawing from the 1972 Anti-Ballistic Missile Treaty.

The ABM treaty, by prohibiting wide deployment of anti–missile defense installments (each side got one exception at home), had long guaranteed mutual security based on the underlying principles of MAD and parity. Bush's abolition of the treaty in effect nullified those principles and signified Washington's quest for nuclear superiority over Russia.

Today, there are scores of deployed US missile-defense installments, now officially a NATO project, around the world, particularly on land and at sea targeted at Russia. From the beginning, Washington maintained, as it does today, that "Our missile defense has never been about Russia," only about Iran and other "rogue states." No sensible observer has ever believed this fairy tale, certainly not Moscow.

All of Russia's new nuclear weapons itemized by Putin on March 1, long in development, have been designed to evade and render useless Washington's global missile-defense program developed over decades at great financial, political, and real security costs. The US political-media establishment has mostly dismissed Putin's claims as a "bluff," "aggressive," and "saber-rattling." But these traits have never characterized his major policy statements, nor do they this one.

If even only a quarter of Putin's claims for Russia's new strategic weapons is true, it means that while Washington heedlessly raced for nuclear superiority and a first-strike capability, Moscow quietly, determinedly raced to create counter-systems, and—again assuming Putin's claims are substantially true—Russia won. From Moscow's perspective, which in this existential instance should also be ours, Russia has regained the strategic parity it lost after the end of the Soviet Union and with it the "mutual security" of MAD.

Read carefully, Putin's speech also raises vital political questions. At one point, he remarkably says "we ourselves are to blame" for the dire strategic condition in which Russia found itself in the early 2000s. Presumably he is referring to his own "illusions" about the West, particularly about Washington, to which he has previously alluded. Presumably he is also referring to his fruitless appeals to "our Western partners" for policies of mutual security instead of NATO expansion and unilateral missile-defense deployments, "illusionary" appeals for which he has sometimes been criticized by actual anti-Western forces in Russia's political-security establishment. As Putin ruefully admits, his "Western partners" did not "listen." This is compelling evidence that Putin himself changed in response to US-NATO policies during his years in power, but also that he is capable of change again, given Western initiatives.

In the speech, Putin does not comment directly on past nuclear-arms races, but he makes clear that another, more dangerous, one looms, depending on how Washington reacts to Moscow's new weapons. Washington can accept the parity—the deterrent—Russia has restored and return to full-scale nuclear arms negotiations. Or it can try again to surpass Moscow's parity.

If Washington chooses the latter course, Putin says, Moscow is fully able and ready to compete, again and again, though he makes clear he would prefer instead to commit his remaining years of leadership, legacy, and national resources to Russia's modernization and prosperity, which he spells out (yet again) in the first two-thirds of his speech. Putin insists, that is, Russia's new weapons are not for any kind of aggression but solely for its legitimate military defense and, politically, to bring Washington back to détente-like policies and particularly to nuclear arms negotiations. The Kremlin, he adds, is "ready."

Even having made a compelling and obviously proud presentation of what Russia has unexpectedly achieved, does Putin really believe Washington will "listen now"? He may still have some "illusions," but we should have none. Recent years have provided ample evidence that US policy-makers and, equally important, influential media commentators do not bother to read what Putin says, at least not more than snatches from click-bait wire-service reports. Still worse, Putin and "Putin's Russia" have been so demonized it is hard to imagine many leading American political figures or editorial commentators responding positively to what is plainly his hope for a new beginning in US-Russian relations.

If nothing else, strategic parity always also meant political parity—recognizing that Soviet Russia, like the United States, had legitimate national interests abroad. Years of American vilifying Putin and post-Soviet Russia are essentially an assertion that neither has any such legitimacy. Now, making matters worse, there is the Russiagate allegation of a Kremlin "attack" on the United States. Even if President Trump understands, or is made to understand, the new—possibly historic—overture represented by Putin's speech, would the "Kremlin puppet" charges against him permit him to seize this opportunity? Do the promoters of Russiagate even care?

History has taught that technology sometimes outruns political capacity to control it. Several of Russia's new nuclear weapons were unforeseen. (If US intelligence was not fully aware of their development prior to Putin's speech, what were those agencies doing instead?) It is no longer possible to dismiss Russia, again declared to be America's number-one threat, as anything less than a nuclear superpower at least fully equal to the United States.

If Washington does not "listen now," if instead it again strives for superiority, we may reasonably ask: We survived the preceding Cold War, but can we survive this one? Put differently, is what Putin displayed but also offered on March 1, 2018, our last chance? In any event, he was right: "This is a turning point for the entire world."

Russia Endorses Putin, the US and UK Condemn Him (Again)

March 22

US POLITICAL AND MEDIA ELITES ARE characterizing Putin's overwhelming victory in Russia's presidential election on March 18 as a "fraud" and "sham" that "does not matter." Both assertions are untrue. They are made mostly by professed authorities whose opinions about Russia are based not on actual knowledge but on political and ideological biases.

Russian presidential and parliamentary elections are, of course, far from fully free and fair. The Kremlin has overwhelming "administrative resourc-es," including unlimited funds, control of the national television networks and many newspapers, and influence over who is, and is not, on the ballot.

But the March 18 election was not greatly constricted or fraudulent. Putin's rivals, including outspoken anti-Putin ones, were permitted to debate on national television (though without Putin himself), and to conduct their campaigns throughout the country relatively freely with whatever resources they had, including in the significantly freer print media and on the nearly uncontrolled Internet. Voters knew the candidates and what they represent-ed. According to many on-site observers, there was relatively little fraud. A frequent complaint that Putin's campaign helped "get out the vote" by busing its voters to polling places is no doubt true, but also not uncommon in the United States.

In short, there is no reason to doubt the magnitude or authentic nature of Putin's victory. The Kremlin hoped for a 70 percent turnout of eligible voters with a 70 percent vote for Putin. The turnout was somewhat less, 67 percent (but larger than the just under 58 percent in the 2016 US presidential elec-tion), while Putin's victory margin, 77 percent, exceeded the Kremlin's goal.

As for its authenticity and explanation, we have the reporting even of a Moscow correspondent of the *New York Times*, which competes with the *Washington Post* for being the most unrelentingly anti-Putin newspaper. On March 18, he wrote: "Russian voters gave…Putin their resounding approval" and a "popular mandate" for his next six-year term. "There is no question that Mr. Putin is wildly popular among Russians." The *Times* correspondent concluded: "There was no need for extensive rigging…because of Mr. Putin's genuine popularity."

So widely and deeply "resounding" was Putin's victory that he got 70 percent of the vote even in Moscow, where opposition candidates usually run relatively well, in sharp contrast to his less than 50 percent in 2012. Moreover, there is ample polling and anecdotal evidence that contrary to Western impressions, Putin is exceedingly popular among the youngest vot-ers, many of whom regard him even more favorably than do middle-age and older generations. This means that the "Putin generation," as it is called, is likely to play an important political role even after he leaves the scene.

More generally, nationalistic, anti-Western candidates gained approxi-mately 20 percent of the vote, with "liberal," pro-Western ones so favored by US political-media elites less than 5 percent. Assuming that few "liberals" voted for Putin but many anti-liberals did, this too speaks volumes about cur-rent and future Russian politics—and about highly selective, if not deluded,

US media coverage. (It is often reported correctly that Alexei Navalny, the anti-corruption crusader and radical Putin opponent, was excluded from the ballot. But it is also true that preelection polls showed him with about 2 percent popular support, hardly enough to have affected the outcome.)

US commentary also attributes Putin's popularity to his "aggressive, anti-Western foreign policies." This assumes that most Russians favor policies hostile, even aggressive, toward the West, and that Putin relies on such attitudes for his power. These assumptions are also untrue or at least significantly so. Until the US-Russian proxy war in Georgia in 2008 and even prior to the Ukrainian crisis in 2014, Putin pursued cooperation with both Europe and the United States, during which his popularity ratings remained well above 60 percent. The annexation of Crimea in 2014 boosted his popular support to more than 80 percent.

The explanation is not complicated. Most Russians still credit Putin with having "saved Russia"—and their own families—from the catastrophic economic and social shock-therapy "reforms" of the Yeltsin 1990s. This "living history" remains the basis of Putin's enduring popularity, despite more recent economic hard times. And when Russians perceive their country as being under attack by foreign powers—as most Russians interpret US-NATO policies in recent years, particularly in Ukraine—they rally around a "strong leader," a reaction also not unknown in the United States.

Slurring the integrity and values of Russian voters is just that—a slur, and one on the rise in the United States, due partly to "Russiagate," though not only. Thus when Senator John McCain and others declare that Putin's victory was a "sham" and "every Russian citizen...was denied the right to vote in a free and fair election," as reported by the *Times* on March 20, they are publicly denigrating and insulting those citizens—again without the slightest factual knowledge of what they are denouncing.

The election results should give Washington's militant cold warriors serious second thoughts. Regime changers who hope US economic sanctions will turn Russia's oligarchs and even its people against Putin and depose him should by now understand that these policies are counter-productive. The Russian people rallied around Putin. And the size of his electoral victory gives him even more authority over financial oligarchs who fear the people because so many citizens still loathe them as the plunderers of the country in the 1990s. Exceedingly rich oligarchs, even those with their assets and families parked offshore and private jets on standby, understand this persistent reality and look to Putin to protect them now and in the future. The election returns confirm that he can continue to do so, if he chooses.

The election should also discredit the growing number of American commentators who equate Putin's Russia with Stalin's "totalitarianism." Proponents of this preposterous equation again reveal themselves as knowing (or caring) little about Russia's political realities today and nothing about Stalin's long terroristic rule, which destroyed millions of Soviet families.

In reality, to emphasize again, the Russian political system today is a mix of authoritarian and democratic elements, what political scientists call "soft authoritarianism." The real discussion should be the relative weight of the two components and what this may bode for Russia's future and for US-Russian relations. One thing is certain and borne out by history: Russian democratic reformers stand very little chance in conditions of Cold War and no chance at all if the new Cold War results in actual war.

Coincidentally or not, the reported assassination attempt against Sergei Skripal and his daughter in the UK has given Putin demonizers another opportunity to denigrate his reputation, no matter what Russian voters think. There are some parallels with Russiagate in the United States. Both scandals are said by high officials to have been "an act of war." Both are said to have been ordered by Putin personally. And in both cases, there are as yet no verified facts, only allegations.

As for the appalling act committed in the Skripal case, not only are there no facts, there is no common sense. Putin had no possible motive, certainly not on the eve of the Russian presidential election, with the World Cup competition in Russia upcoming, and with the toxicity of Russiagate already poisoning relations with the West. Nor did Putin ever say, as he is widely mistranslated, that "traitors" should be killed. They will, he said instead, eventually "shrivel up" (*zagnutsia*) and wither away from the self-inflicted guilt and shame of their act of betrayal. Moreover, quite a few better-known Russian intelligence defectors have lived safely in the West, sometimes publishing accounts of their feats.

Contrary to many media accounts, nor was Skripal a "Russian spy." He was a British spy, having covertly gone to work for UK intelligence in the 1990s, been arrested and convicted in 2004, and made part of an exchange of captured Russian and Western spies in 2010, which resulted in Skripal's residence in the UK. If Putin wanted him dead, why not kill him in Russia or why let him leave for the West? And if some high-placed state assassin wanted Skripal dead, why try to kill him with a lethal nerve agent that might be traceable and could harm many other people? Why not a gun, a knife, or a car "accident"?

Though the nerve agent loosely termed "Novichok" was developed in the

Soviet Union decades ago, the Organization for the Prohibition of Chemical Weapons certified in 2017 that Russia had fully destroyed all of its stockpiles and facilities for making such weapons.[52] Still more, the formula for "Novichok" was published years ago and could have been replicated by any number of competent states or individuals. And if the nerve agent was so quickly "lethal," why are the Skripals and others said to have been affected still alive and out of hospital?

There is also this crucial consideration. When Russia and the United States recruit spies in the other country, or send them there, they assure them, in so many words, "If you are caught, we will try to get you out, to bring you home." For decades, this has resulted in the kind of spy swaps of which Skripal was part in 2010. If either side seriously harms an exchanged spy, the efficacy of such exchanges and the sanctity of such intelligence agency promises are undermined, if not made invalid. As a former intelligence official, Putin above all would have understood this and thus still less have had any motive.

Which is to say, Putin's electoral victory was mostly authentic; the official version of what happened to the Skripals may not be.

Russophobia

April 4

ANALYZING WHY THE NEW COLD WAR is more dangerous than was its 40-year predecessor, I seem to have minimized the role of Russophobia. I understood its strength among some nationalities of the former Tsarist and Soviet empires now in the West, but Russophobia had not been a large causal factor, unlike anti-Communism, in the preceding Cold War. I've long been influenced by the compassionate words of George Kennan, the architect of containment, published in *Foreign Affairs* in 1951 about the Russian people:

"Give them time; let them be Russians; let them work out their internal problems in their own manner…towards dignity and enlightenment in government."

But recent Russophobic statements by former chief US intelligence officials and other influential American opinion-makers have caused me to reconsider this factor. Here are some examples:

• Former Director of National Intelligence James Clapper spoke on NBC national television about "the Russians, who typically, are almost genetically driven to co-opt, penetrate, gain favor." And former CIA Director John Brennan warned that Russians "try to suborn individuals and they try to get individuals, including US citizens, to act on their behalf either wittingly or unwittingly." Former FBI director James Comey added, "They're coming after America."[53,54,55] How would we react if these intelligence chiefs had said the same about another ethnic people? Or if Senator John McCain repeatedly characterized another nation as "a gas station masquerading as a country?"

• Russia's presidential election, a kind of referendum on Putin's 18 years as leader, gave him, as we saw, a resounding, nearly 77 percent endorsement. The election was widely dismissed by leading US media outlets as "a sham," which denigrates, of course, the integrity of Russian voters. Indeed, a leading Putin demonizer earlier characterized Russian public opinion as a "mob's opinion."[56]

• A *Rolling Stone* writer goes further, explaining that "Russia experts" think "much of what passes for civil society in modern Russia is, in fact, controlled by Putin."[57] Civil society means, of course, non-state groups and associations, that is, society itself.

• A *Washington Post* editorial headline on April 3, 2018 asks: "Is It a Crime to Worship God? According to Russia, Yes." This about a country where the Orthodox Church is flourishing and Jews are freer than they have ever been in Russian history.

• On March 7, 2018, the *Post's* international columnist, David Ignatius, downplayed the personal causality of the Kremlin leader because "President Vladimir Putin embodies this Russian paranoid ethic."

• Even a *Post* sports columnist is so afflicted that, referring to Olympic doping allegations, he characterizes Russian 2018 medal winners as representatives of "a shamed nation."[58]

• A *New York Times* columnist quotes approvingly a *Post* columnist, an expert on Russia, for asserting that "Putin's Russia" is "an anti-Western power with a different, darker vision of global politics…[a] norm-violating power."[59]

- The title of an article by CNN's Russia expert begins: "Russia's Snark."[60]
- Another prominent media commentator advises, "Treat Russia Like the Terrorist It Is." Yet another terms Russia "Gangster's Paradise."[61,62]
- A leading policy expert on Russia and former US official has decided that the West doesn't have a Putin problem: "In fact, it has a Russia problem."[63]
- Deploring Russia, the Harvard policy intellectual Graham Allison has a regret: "The brute fact is that we cannot kill this bastard without committing suicide."[64]
- According to a longtime *Fox News* Russia expert, Ralph Peters, now a guest on CNN, Putin behaves as he does "because they are Russians."[65]
- A *Post* book editor tells readers that Russians tolerate "tyrants like Stalin and Putin" because "it probably seems normal."[66]
- A prominent Russia expert and NPR commentator wonders "whether Russia can ever be normal."[67]
- And impossible to overlook, there are the ubiquitous cartoons depicting Russia as a menacing rapacious bear and alternatively as an octopus whose grasping tentacles ensnare the globe.

How to explain this rampant Russophobia? Three important but little noted books provide useful history and analyses: David S. Foglesong's *The American Mission and the "Evil Empire"*; Andrei P. Tsygankov's *Russophobia*; and, most recently, Guy Mettan's *Creating Russophobia*, which equates it with "Russo-madness."

They examine various factors: ethnic peoples, now independent states with large diasporas, and with historical grievances against both the Tsarist and Soviet empires; historical developments and immigration beginning in the 19th century; today's US military-industrial complex's budgetary need for an "enemy" after the end of the Soviet Union; other present-day anti-Russian lobbies in the United States and the absence of any pro-Russian ones.

All need to be considered, but three circumstances are certain. American attitudes toward Russia are not historically or genetically predetermined, as evidenced by the "Gorbymania" that swept the United States in the late 1980s when Soviet President Gorbachev and US President Reagan tried to end the previous Cold War. The unprecedented demonization of the current Kremlin leader, Putin, has expanded to Russia more generally. And Russophobia is much more widespread and deeper among American political and media elites than among ordinary citizens. It was, after all, elites, not the American people, who gave us the new Cold War.

Russiagate and the Risk of Nuclear War

April 18

T HE 1962 CUBAN MISSILE CRISIS REMAINS A LANDMARK event in the pre-ceding Cold War. It was the closest the United States and (then-Soviet) Russia ever came to intentional nuclear war. Its lessons have been taught ever since. No such confrontation between the two nuclear superpowers should ever be permitted again. If it happens, only diplomacy of the kind practiced by President Kennedy during the Cuban crisis, including secret negotiations, can save both countries, and the world, from catastrophe.

Accordingly, in the decades following that sobering event, Washington and Moscow enacted forms of cooperation to limit their conflicts and pre-vent a recapitulation of the Cuban episode—mutual codes of Cold War conduct; a myriad of public and secret communications; nuclear-arms agree-ments; periodic summit meetings; and other regularized processes that kept the nuclear peace.

The new Cold War has vaporized, however, most of those restraining conventions, especially since the conflict over Ukraine in 2014 and even more since Russiagate began to unfold in 2016. During the first two weeks of this April, thus arose in Syria the real possibility of a new Cuban-like crisis and of war with Russia.

The danger developed less in the context of Syrian developments than that of Russiagate. For more than a year, President Trump had been hec-tored—mainly by Democrats and much of the media—to "get tougher" with Russia and its President Vladimir Putin in order to demonstrate he was not beholden to the Kremlin.

To his credit, Trump remained publicly committed to his campaign promise to "cooperate with Russia," but while also "getting tougher." He sent weapons to Ukraine, imposed mounting economic sanctions on Moscow, and expelled large numbers of Russian diplomats, even shutting a Russian consulate in the United States, as President Obama had unwisely done. But Russiagate advocates continuously moved the goal posts of "tougher" until the end zone, war, loomed on the horizon.

As it did during the fraught days from April 7, when reports appeared that Syrian President Assad had used chemical weapons against his own people in

Douma, to the launching of US missiles against Syria on the night of April 13-14.

This might well have resulted in war with Russia because of two little-noticed red lines drawn by the Kremlin. In his speech on March 1, Putin stated that Russia's new missiles were available to protect Moscow's "allies," which clearly included Damascus. And shortly later, when perhaps scores of Russian troops were killed in Syria by US-backed anti-Assad forces, Moscow's military and civilian leadership vowed "retaliation" if this happened again. They meant Russian counter-strikes specifically against American forces in Syria and any US launchers of the weapons used. (Russian troops are embedded with many Syrian units and thus potential collateral damage.)

And yet, an evidently reluctant Trump launched more than a hundred missiles at Syria on August 13-14. Just how reluctant he was to risk a Cuban-like crisis, to risk any chance of war with Russia, is clear from what actually happened. Rejecting more expansive and devastating options, Trump chose one that gave Russia (and thus Syria) advance warning. It killed no Russians (or perhaps anyone else) and struck no essential political or military targets in Damascus, only purported chemical-weapons facilities. The Kremlin's red lines were carefully and widely skirted.

Nonetheless, the events of April were ominous and may well forebode worse to come. The very limited, carefully crafted attack on Syria was clearly not undertaken primarily for military but political reasons related to Russiagate allegations against Trump. Just how political is indicated by the fact that no conclusive evidence had yet been produced that Assad was responsible for the alleged chemical attack and that the missiles were launched as chemical weapons investigators were en route to Douma.

We might fault Trump for being insufficiently strong—politically or psychologically—to resist warfare demands that he prove his "innocence," but the primary responsibility lies with Russiagate promoters who seek obsessively to impeach the president: politicians and journalists for whom a porn actress, Stormy Daniels, seems to be a higher priority than averting nuclear war with Russia. They are mostly Democrats and pro-Democratic media, but also Republicans like Senator Lindsey Graham, who declared, "If...we back off because Putin threatens to retaliate, that is a disaster for us throughout the world." (No, senator, that is a Cuban missile crisis that was not resolved peacefully and a catastrophe for the entire world.)

More generally, as I have repeatedly warned, for the first time since the onset of the nuclear age, there is not in the White House an American president fully empowered—"legitimate" enough, Russiagaters charge—to negotiate with a Kremlin leader in such dire circumstances, as Trump has discovered every time he has tried. Or, in an existential crisis, to avert nuclear war the way President Kennedy did in 1962.

Given the escalating Cold war dynamics evidenced in recent months, not only in Syria, this generalization may be tested sooner rather than later. It doesn't help, of course, that Trump has surrounded himself with appointees who apparently do not share his opinion that it is imperative "to cooperate with Russia," but instead "adults" who seem to personify the worst aspects of Cold War zealotry and lack elementary knowledge of US-Russian relations over the years.

As President Reagan liked to say, it takes two to tango. In Moscow's policy elite, there are influential people who believe "America has been at war against Russia"—political, economic, and military—for more than a decade. Their views are often mirror images of those of Lindsey Graham and other US establishment zealots.

In this decision-making context, Putin still appears to be, in words and deeds, the moderate, calling Western leaders "our partners and colleagues," asking for understanding and negotiations, being far less "aggressive" than he could be. Our legions of Putin demonizers will say this is a false analysis, but it too should not be tested.

Criminalizing Russia

April 25

FOR MORE THAN A DECADE, THE US political-media establishment has increasingly demonized, delegitimized, and now criminalized the Russian state and its leadership. This began with the personal vilification of President Putin and has grown into a general indictment of Russia as a nation. As President Obama's former intelligence chiefs John Brennan and

James Clapper and other US authorities have told us, any Russian "linked to the Kremlin," Moscow officialdom generally, "oligarchs," or certain traits is inherently suspicious.

"Crimes" said to be committed by today's Kremlin, from America and the UK to Syria, have expanded the indictment beyond charges once leveled against Soviet Russia. The newly minted world affairs pundit Joe Scarborough, who believes the United States alone "spent the past 100 years inventing the modern age," devotes a column warning *Washington Post* readers multiple times that "our democracy is under attack by the Russians."[68,69]

There are many weightier and more far-reaching allegations. Canada's foreign minister, echoing Washington, indicts Russia for its "malign behavior in all of its manifestations...whether it is cyberwarfare, whether it's disinformation, assassination attempts, whatever it happens to be."[70]

On April 20, the Democratic National Committee, still mourning its defeat in 2016, went farther. It is seeking a formal indictment of "whatever it happens to be" by suing the Russian government for conspiring with the Trump campaign to deprive Hillary Clinton of her rightful victory in the 2016 presidential election. Central figures in this "act of unprecedented treachery" are stated to be "people believed to be affiliated with Russia."[71]

It follows, of course, that a criminal Russia—frequently termed a "mafia state," also incorrectly—can have no legitimate national interests anywhere, not on its own borders or even at home. And with such a state, it also follows, there should be no civil relations, including diplomacy, only warfare ones. Thus when a group of US senators visited Moscow in early July, another *Post* columnist, Dana Milbank, who seemed not to know or care there were precedents for the timing, indicted them for "visiting your foe on the Fourth of July" and equated it with "meeting with wounded Taliban fighters on Veterans Day."[72]

Lost, forgotten, or negated in this mania is why Russia was generally understood to matter so greatly to US national security during the 40-year Cold War that the result was myriad forms of growing and prolonged cooperation, even official episodes of détente. The reasons also apply to Russia today.

Even middle-school children presumably know the most existential reason. Like the United States, Russia possesses enormous arsenals of weapons of mass destruction, including nuclear ones. A conventional US-Russian war—as both sides are now flirting with in Syria and may soon do so in Ukraine or the Baltic region—could slip into nuclear war. As I reported earlier, at a recent meeting of Washington's highly respected Center for the National Interest, several well-informed experts thought that on a scale of 1 to 10, the chances of war with Russia today are 5 to 7.[73]

Today's Cold War includes another existential danger in the form of international terrorists in pursuit of radioactive materials to make their attacks immeasurably more devastating and the consequences more enduring. Ask real experts the chances of that happening in a major city, and of the importance of the Kremlin's full cooperation in preventing it.

Almost equally important is the reason called "geopolitical." Even after the Soviet Union, Russia remains the largest territorial country in the world. It possesses a disproportionate share of the planet's natural resources, from energy, iron ore, nickel, timber, diamonds, and gold to fresh water. It is also one of the world's leading exporters of weapons. Still more, Russia is located squarely between East and West, whose civilizations are in conflict, and part of both. Months ago, I raised the possibility that Russia might "leave the West," driven out by the new Cold War or by choice. That possibility is now said by a top Kremlin aide and ideologist to be inescapable.

Herein lies more myopia constantly perpetuated by the American media: sanctioned, criminal Russia is "isolated from the international community." This is an Anglo-American conceit. Multi-dimensional relations between "Putin's Russia" and non-Western countries such as China, Iran, India, and other BRIC nations are thriving. And it is there that most of the world's territory, people, resources, and growing markets are located. For them, Russia is not criminal but an eagerly sought partner.

Given all the warfare talk emanating from the US political-media establishment, consider also Russia's renewed military capabilities or, as strategists like to say, "capacity to project power." There is no reason to doubt Putin's March 1 inventorying of Moscow's new weapons systems. The Kremlin demonstrated its formidable military capabilities by destroying ISIS's entrenched grip on Syria following Russia's intervention in September 2015, even though most US pundits and other professed experts falsely claim this was Washington's achievement.

When there is military parity between Washington and Moscow, as during the preceding Cold War and now again, it is imperative to cooperate, not to ostracize. Otherwise, as President Reagan said when he decided to meet the Kremlin halfway in the late 1980s, there will be no winners,

There are also Moscow's under-rated capabilities for conflict resolution, not only its vote on the UN Security Council. Various recent examples could be cited, but remember Russia's essential role in the nuclear-weapons agreement with Iran; its behind-the-scenes part today in attempts to resolve the conflict with North Korea; its potential as a deciding partner in bringing peace to Syria; and the role it is likely to play when the United States finally decides to leave Afghanistan. If not criminalized, Russia can be a vital peacemaker, and there is ample reason to think that the Kremlin is ready to do so again.

Long ago, when I first developed my own "contacts" and "ties" with "Communist" Russian society and, yes, with Kremlin and many other officials, I often said and wrote, "The road to American national security runs through Moscow." The same is no less true today. This necessity may now seem futile, as US political-media elites mindlessly criminalize Russia.

On the other hand, President Trump's ambassador to Russia, Jon Huntsman, stated publicly on April 24: "My president has said repeatedly that he wants a better relationship with Russia…with Putin…. You can call it a desire for détente."[74] If so, it is imperative to support the president's initiative, even if only this one.

America's Collusion With Neo-Nazis

May 2

WE MUST RETURN YET AGAIN TO Ukraine because of what the orthodox US political-media narrative continues to omit—the still growing role of neo-Nazi forces in territories governed by US-backed Kiev. Even Americans who follow international news may not know the following:

• That the snipers who killed scores of protestors and policemen on Kiev's Maidan Square in February 2014—triggering a professed "democratic revolution" that overthrew the elected president, Viktor Yanukovych, and brought to power a virulent anti-Russian, pro-American regime—were sent not by Yanukovych, as is still widely reported, but almost certainly by the neo-fascist organization Right Sector and its co-conspirators.[75]

• That the pogrom-like burning to death of ethnic Russians and Russian-speaking Ukrainians in Odessa shortly later in 2014 reawakened memories of Nazi extermination squads in Ukraine during World War II has been all but deleted from the American mainstream narrative even though it remains a painful and revelatory episode for many Ukrainians.

• That the Azov Battalion of some 3,000 well-armed fighters, which has played a major combat role in the Ukrainian civil war and now is an official component of Kiev's armed forces, is avowedly "partially" pro-Nazi, as evidenced by its regalia, slogans, and programmatic statements, and well-documented as such by several international monitoring organizations. Congressional legislation recently banned Azov from receiving U.S. military aid, but it is likely to obtain some of the new weapons recently sent to Kiev by the Trump administration due to Ukraine's rampant network of corruption and to sympathizers in Kiev's security ministries.

• That storm troop-like assaults on gays, Roma, women feminists, elderly ethnic Russians, and other "impure" citizens are widespread throughout Kiev-ruled Ukraine, along with torchlight marches reminiscent of those that inflamed Germany in the late 1920s and 1930s. That a sacred Holocaust gravesite in Ukraine has been desecrated and looted.[76] And that police and legal authorities do virtually nothing to prevent these neo-fascist acts or to prosecute them. On the contrary, Kiev has officially encouraged this violence by systematically rehabilitating and even memorializing leading Ukrainian collaborators with Nazi German extermination pogroms during World War II. Kiev is renaming streets in their honor, building monuments to them, rewriting history to glorify them, and more.

• Or that Israel's official annual report on anti-Semitism around the world in 2017 concluded that such incidents had doubled in Ukraine and the number "surpassed the tally for all the incidents reported throughout the entire region combined." By the region, the report meant the total in all of Eastern Europe and all former territories of the Soviet Union.[77]

The significance of neo-Nazism in Ukraine and tacit US support or tolerance of it should have caused widespread outrage, but Americans cannot be faulted for not knowing these facts. They are very rarely reported and still less discussed in mainstream newspapers or on television. To learn about them, Americans would have to turn to alternative media and their independent non-mainstream writers.

Lev Golinkin is one such important American writer. He is best known for his book *A Backpack, A Bear, and Eight Crates of Vodka*, a deeply moving and highly instructive memoir of his life as a young boy brought to America by his immigrant parents from Eastern Ukraine, a place now torn by tragic civil and proxy war. But Golinkin has also been an unrelenting and meticulous reporter of neo-fascism in "our" Ukraine and defender of others who try to chronicle and oppose its growing crimes, including Ukrainian Jews.

For the record, this did not begin under President Trump but under President George W. Bush, when then President Viktor Yushchenko's "Orange Revolution" began rehabilitating Ukraine's wartime killers of Jews. It grew under President Obama, who, along with Vice President Biden, were deeply complicit in the 2014 Maidan coup and what followed. Then too the American mainstream media scarcely noticed.

Even avid followers of US news probably missed this, for example. When the co-founder of a neo-Nazi party and now repackaged speaker of the Ukrainian parliament, Andrei Parubiy, visited Washington in 2016, 2017, and 2018, he was widely feted. He spoke at leading think tanks, met with Senator John McCain, Rep. Paul Ryan, and Senator Chuck Schumer, as well as with the editorial boards of the *Washington Post* and the *Wall Street Journal*.[78] Imagine the message this official embrace sent back to Ukraine— and elsewhere.

Fascist or neo-Nazi revivalism is under way today in many countries, from Europe to the United States, but the Ukrainian case is of special importance and a particular danger. A large, growing, well-armed fascist movement has reappeared in a large European country that is the political epicenter of the new Cold War—a movement that not so much denies the Holocaust as glorifies it.

Could such forces come to power in Kiev? Its American deniers and minimizers say never, because it has too little public support (though perhaps more than Ukrainian President Poroshenko). The same was said of Lenin's party and Hitler's until Russia and Germany descended into chaos and lawlessness. Ominously, a recent Amnesty International article reports that Kiev is losing control over these radical groups and over the state's monopoly on the use of force.[79]

For four years, the U.S. political-media establishment, including prominent American Jews and their organizations, has at best ignored or tolerated Ukrainian neo-Nazism and at worst abetted it by unqualified support for Kiev. Typically, the *New York Times* may report at length on corruption in Ukraine, but not on the very frequent manifestations of neo-fascism. And when George Will laments the resurgence of anti-Semitism today, he cites the British Labor Party but not Ukraine.

When Ukrainian fascism is occasionally acknowledged, a well-placed band of pro-Kiev partisans quickly asserts—maybe, but the real fascist is America's number one enemy, Russian President Putin. Whatever Putin's failings, this allegation is either cynical or totally uninformed. Nothing in his statements over 18 years in power are akin to fascism. Nor could there be, as I explained earlier.

We are left, then, not with Putin's responsibility for the resurgence of fascism in a major European country allied with Washington, but with America's shame—and possibly an indelible stain on its reputation—for tolerating Ukraine's neo-Nazis, even if only through silence.

At least until recently. On April 23, a courageous first-term congressman from California, Ro Khanna, organized a public letter to the State Department, co-signed by 56 other members of the House, calling on the U.S. government to speak out and take steps against the resurgence of official anti-Semitism and Holocaust denialism both in Ukraine and Poland. "Ro," as he is known to many in Washington, is a rare profile in courage, as are his co-signers. Thus far, little has resulted from their wise and moral act.

In a righteous representative democracy, every member of Congress would sign the appeal and every leading newspaper lend editorial support. Not surprisingly, the mainstream media has yet even to report on Rep. Khanna's newsworthy initiative. Also not surprisingly, he has been slurred—and promptly defended by Lev Golinkin.

The previous 40-year experience taught that Cold War can corrupt American democracy—politically, economically, morally. There are many examples of how the new edition has already degraded America's media, politicians, even scholars. But the test today is how our elites react to neo-fascism in U.S.-supported Ukraine. Protesting it is not a Jewish issue. It is an American one.

"Informant" Echoes of Dark Pasts

May 23

T HE REVELATION THAT A LONGTIME CIA-FBI "informant," professor emeritus Stefan Halper, had been dispatched to "interact" with several members of Donald Trump's campaign in 2016 raises new and old issues.[80] For me, some of them revive Soviet-era memories.

A year ago, I asked if Russiagate was largely "Intelgate," pointing to compelling evidence. The revelation about Halper, essentially an Intel undercover operative, is further indication that US intelligence agencies were deeply involved in the origins and promotion of allegations of "collusion" between Trump and the Kremlin. (We do not know if other informers were deployed covertly to "investigate" the Trump campaign, what the two agencies did with Halper's information, or whether he was connected in any way to UK intelligence officer Christopher Steele and his dossier.)

The issue is not President Trump, support him or not, but two others: our own civil liberties which can be threatened by "informants" and the indifference of US organizations and media that no longer profess or defend these liberties as inalienable principles of American democracy.

Notably, the venerable ACLU has not loudly protested Intelgate or related transgressions in this regard, if at all. Why should it when the standard-setting *New York Times*, in two articles and an editorial, unconditionally defended Halper's clandestine mission. The *Times* did so by claiming that Russiagate is based on "facts" that "aren't disputed"—that "there was a sophisticated, multiyear conspiracy by Russian government officials and agents, working under direct orders from President Vladimir Putin, to interfere in the 2016 presidential election in support of Donald Trump."[81,82]

In actual fact, aspects of this narrative have been strongly questioned by a number of qualified critics, though their questioning is never printed in the *Times*. Even if there was such a "multiyear conspiracy," for example, how does the *Times* know it was carried out under Putin's "direct orders"?

It is merely an assumption based on two seriously challenged documents, as we have already seen: the January 2017 Intelligence Community Assessment and Steele's dossier. But they are enough for the *Times* to charge that Halper's targets had "suspicious contacts linked to Russia" and for its columnist Paul Krugman again, tweeting on May 19, to call them "treason." (These "Russian contacts" are so vague they could apply to many New York City taxi drivers.)

Indicative of the *Times'* coverage of Russia and Russiagate, the paper then proceeds to factual misrepresentations about three of Halper's targets. General Michael Flynn did nothing wrong or unusual in talking with the Russian ambassador to Washington in December 2016. Other presidents-elect, we have also seen, established similar "back channels" to Moscow. Carter Page was not "recruited by Russian spies." They tried to do so, but he helped the FBI expose and arrest them. And Paul Manafort had not, during the time in question, "lobbied for pro-Russian interests in Ukraine," as I and others have also pointed out more than once.

The *Times* ends by asserting what it must know to be untrue—that no information collected by Halper or Steele had been made public prior to the November 2016 election. Widely read articles alluding to that information were published as early as July 2016 by Franklin Foer and then by Michael Isikoff and David Corn.[83,84,85] The *Times* itself ran a number of insinuating "Trump-Putin" stories and editorials as well as accusatory opinion pieces by former Intel chiefs like the CIA's Michael Morell and the NSA's Michael Hayden—all prior to the election.[86,87] The allegations were so well-known that in their August debate Hillary Clinton accused Trump of being Putin's "puppet."

Of course, the *Times* was not alone among media outlets that once deplored civil-liberties abuses but justified the Halper operation. The *Washington Post* also unconditionally did so, as in a May 21 column by Eugene Robinson denouncing critics of those Russiagate practices for "smearing veteran professionals" of the agencies. Had they not dispatched Halper, Robinson exclaimed, it "would have been an appalling dereliction of duty." Proponents of civil liberties might consider Robinson's statement "appalling."

As usual, MSNBC and CNN were in accord with the *Times* and the *Post*. On May 17, for instance, CNN's Don Lemon summoned former Director of National Intelligence James Clapper himself to vouch for Halper's "informant" mission: "That's a good thing because the Russians pose a threat to the very basis of our political system." Lemon did not question Clapper about civil liberties or anything else. Nor did he book anyone who might have done so. The new cult of Intel is mainstream orthodoxy.

Not a word about constitutional civil liberties in any of this media coverage. Surely the "informant" and "contacts" themes—the Clinton-sponsored Center for American Progress recently posted 70-plus purportedly suspicious "contacts" between Trump's people and Russia—reminded some editors, writers, or producers about those practices during the McCarthy era. (If not, they should read the classic book *Naming Names*, by former *Nation* editor and publisher Victor Navasky.)

My own reminders come from, so to speak, the other side. I lived in Soviet Russia periodically from 1976 to 1982 (the year those authorities banned me from the country) among open and semi-closeted Communist Party dissidents. Those were the years of Brezhnev's "vegetarian" surveillance state. Russian friends called it "vegetarian" because the era of Stalin's mass arbitrary arrests, torture, and executions had long passed. KGB suppression now relied significantly on "softer" tactics, among them clandestine informers and accusations of "contacts with the CIA and American imperialism."

I was instructed by Moscow friends how to detect informers or, in any case, to be ever mindful "informants" might be present even at intimate gatherings of "friends." As an American living among targeted people, I tried to take every precaution to avoid being a damning "contact." In the end, though, I was cited by the KGB in cases against at least two prominent dissidents, one jailed and the other hounded. (Both later became leading human-rights figures under Gorbachev and Yeltsin: one as head of the organization Memorial, the other as founder of Moscow's Museum of the History of the Gulag.)

Surveillance was, of course, very different and far more consequential in the repressive pre-Gorbachev Soviet Union than in America today. But a number of episodes on both sides involved professors who were intelligence operatives. In the Russiagate saga, there is already Halper and the still-shadowy Professor Joseph Mifsud, who befriended the very minor, very inexperienced, and apparently clueless Trump "aide" George Papadopoulos. (Originally said to be a Russian intelligence "asset," there is some evidence that Mifsud may have worked for British intelligence. In any event, he has vanished.)

This should not surprise us. Not all US or Russian intelligence officers are assassins, recruiters, or even spies. Some are highly qualified scholars who hold positions in colleges, academies, and universities, as has long been the case both in Russia and in the United States. As a result, I myself had over the years—I will confess—knowing personal "contacts" with several Soviet and post-Soviet Russian "intelligence officers."

Two held the rank of general and were affiliated with higher-educational institutions (one as a professor), which is where I first met them. Another intelligence general I met privately headed the former KGB (now FSB) archives. The others, more junior, were working on their doctoral dissertations, a step toward promotion, in the same Stalin-era archive where I was doing research for a book.

We took many lunch and smoking breaks together. Most of our discussions focused on archival "secrets" of the Stalin Terror of the 1930s. Sometimes talk did wander to current concerns—for example, whether Kentucky bourbon, which they had not sampled but I eventually provided, was superior to Russian vodka. No other "collusion" ever resulted.

Why This Cold War is More Dangerous Than the One We Survived

June 6

A FORMAL MEETING BETWEEN PRESIDENTS TRUMP AND Putin is being seriously discussed in Washington and Moscow. Ritualized but substantive "summits," as they were termed, were frequently used during the 40-year US-Soviet Cold War to reduce conflicts and increase cooperation between the two superpowers. They were most important when tensions were highest. Some were very successful, some less so, others were deemed failures.

Given today's extraordinary political circumstances, we may wonder if anything positive would come from a Trump-Putin summit. But it is necessary, even imperative, that Washington and Moscow try because this Cold War is more dangerous than was its predecessor. By now, the reasons should be clear, but it is time to recall and update them. There are at least ten:

1. The political epicenter of the new Cold War is not in far-away Berlin, as it was from the late 1940s on, but directly on Russia's borders, from the Baltic states and Ukraine to another former Soviet republic, Georgia. Each of these new Cold War fronts is fraught with the possibility of hot war. US-Russian military relations are especially tense today in the Baltic region, where a large-scale NATO buildup is under way, and in Ukraine, where a US-Russian proxy war is intensifying.

The "Soviet Bloc" that once served as a buffer between NATO and Russia no longer exists. And many imaginable incidents on the West's new Eastern Front, intentional or unintentional, could easily trigger actual war between the United States and Russia. What brought about this situation on Russia's borders— unprecedented at least since the Nazi German invasion in 1941— was, of course, Washington's exceedingly unwise decision, in the late 1990s, to expand NATO eastward. Done in the name of "security," it has made all the states involved only more insecure.

2. Proxy wars were a feature of the old Cold War, but usually small ones in what was called the "Third World," in Africa, for example. They rarely involved many, if any, Soviet or American personnel, mostly only money and weapons. Today's US-Russian proxy wars are different, located in the center of geopolitics and accompanied by too many American and Russian trainers, minders, and possibly fighters. Two have already erupted: in Georgia in 2008, where Russian forces fought a Georgian army financed, trained, and minded by American funds and personnel; and in Syria, where in February scores of Russians were killed by US-backed anti-Assad forces. Moscow did not retaliate, but it has pledged to do so if there is "a next time," as there very well might be.

If so, this would in effect be war directly between Russia and America. The risk of a direct conflict also continues to grow in Ukraine. The country's US-backed but politically failing President Petro Poroshenko seems periodically tempted to launch another all-out military assault on rebel-controlled Donbass, which is backed by Moscow. If he does so, and the assault does not quickly fail as previous ones did, Russia will certainly intervene in eastern Ukraine with a truly tangible "invasion."

Washington will then have to make a fateful war-or-peace decision. Having already reneged on its commitments to the Minsk Accords, the best hope for ending the four-year Ukrainian crisis peacefully, Kiev seems to have an unrelenting impulse to be a tail wagging the dog of US-Russian war. Its capacity for provocations and disinformation seem second to none, as evidenced again recently by the faked "assassination and resurrection" of journalist Arkady Babchenko.

3. Years-long Western, especially American, demonization of the Kremlin leader, Putin, is also unprecedented. Too obvious to spell out again here, no Soviet Communist leader, at least since Stalin, was ever subjected to such prolonged, baseless, crudely derogatory personal vilification. Whereas Soviet leaders were regarded as acceptable negotiating partners for American presidents,

including at major summits, Putin has been made to seem to be an illegitimate national leader—at best "a KGB thug" or murderous "mafia boss."

4. Still more, demonizing Putin has generated widespread Russophobic vilification of Russia itself, or what the *New York Times* and other mainstream-media outlets have taken to calling "Vladimir Putin's Russia." Yesterday's enemy was Soviet Communism. Today it is increasingly Russia, thereby also delegitimizing Russia as a great power with legitimate national interests. "The Parity Principle," as I termed it during the preceding Cold War—the principle that both sides had legitimate interests at home and abroad, which was the basis for diplomacy and negotiations, and symbolized by leadership summits—no longer exists, at least on the American side.

Nor does the acknowledgment that both sides were to blame to some extent for the previous Cold War. Among influential American observers who even recognize the new Cold War, "Putin's Russia" alone is to blame. When there is no recognized parity and shared responsibility, there is ever-shrinking space for diplomacy, but more and more for increasingly militarized relations, as we are witnessing today.

5. Meanwhile, most of the Cold War safeguards—cooperative mechanisms and mutually observed rules of conduct that evolved over decades in order to prevent superpower hot war—have been vaporized or badly frayed since the Ukrainian crisis in 2014, as the UN General Secretary António Guterres, almost alone, has recognized: "The Cold War is back—with a vengeance but with a difference. The mechanisms and the safeguards to manage the risks of escalation that existed in the past no longer seem to be present."[88] Trump's recent missile strike on Syria carefully avoided killing any Russians, but Moscow has vowed to retaliate against the US if there is a "next time," as there may be.

Even the decades-long process of arms control may, an expert warns, be coming to an "end."[89] It would mean an unfettered new nuclear-arms race as well as the termination of an ongoing diplomatic process that buffered US-Soviet relations during very bad political times.

In short, if there actually are any new Cold War rules of conduct, they are yet to be formulated and mutually accepted. Nor does this semi-anarchy take into account the new warfare technology of cyber-attacks. What are its implications for the secure functioning of existential Russian and American nuclear command-and-control and early-warning systems that guard against an accidental launching of missiles still on high alert?

6. Russiagate allegations that the American president has been compromised by—or is even an agent of—the Kremlin are also without precedent.

These allegations, as we have seen, have already had profoundly dangerous consequences. They include the nonsensical, mantra-like declaration that "Russia attacked America" during the 2016 presidential election; crippling assaults on President Trump every time he speaks with Putin in person or by phone; and making both Trump and Putin so toxic that most American politicians, journalists, and intellectuals who understand the present-day dangers are reluctant to speak out against US contributions to the new Cold War.

7. Mainstream media outlets have, we know, played a woeful role in all of this. Unlike in the past, when pro-détente advocates had roughly equal access to influential media, today's new Cold War media continue to enforce their orthodox narrative that Russia is solely to blame. They offer not diversity of opinion and reporting but "confirmation bias." Alternative voices (with, yes, "alternative" or opposing facts) rarely appear any longer in the most influential newspapers or on national television or radio.

One alarming result is that "disinformation" generated by or pleasing to Washington and its allies has consequences before it can be corrected. The Ukrainian fake Babchenko assassination (allegedly ordered by Putin, of course) was quickly exposed, but not the official version of the Skripal assassination attempt in the UK, which led to the largest US expulsion of Russian diplomats in history before London's initial account could be thoroughly examined. This too—Cold War without debate—is unprecedented, precluding the frequent rethinking and revising of US policy that characterized the preceding 40-year Cold War.

8. Equally lamentable, and very much unlike during the 40-year Cold War, there still is virtually no significant opposition in the American mainstream to the US role in the new Cold War—not in the media, not in Congress, not in the two major political parties, not in think tanks, not in the universities, not at grassroots levels. This continues to be unprecedented, dangerous, and contrary to real democracy.

Consider again the still thunderous silence of scores of large US corporations that have been doing profitable business in post-Soviet Russia for years, from fast-food chains and automobile manufacturers to pharmaceutical and energy giants. Contrast their behavior to that of CEOs of PepsiCo, Control Data, IBM, and other major American corporations seeking entry to the Soviet market in the 1970s and 1980s, when they publicly supported and even funded pro-détente organizations and politicians. How to explain the continuing silence of their counterparts today, who are usually so profit-motivated? Are they also fearful of being labeled "pro-Putin" or possibly "pro-Trump"?

9. And then there remains the widespread escalatory myth that today's Russia, unlike the Soviet Union, is too weak—its economy too small and fragile, its leader too "isolated in international affairs"—to wage a sustained Cold War, and that eventually Putin, who is "punching above his weight," as the cliché has it, will capitulate. This too is a dangerous delusion—one that cannot be attributed to President Trump. It was, we saw earlier, President Obama who, in 2014, as approvingly reported by the *New York Times*, set out to make Putin's Russia "a pariah state."

Washington and some of its allies certainly tried to isolate Russia. How else to interpret fully the political scandals and media campaigns that erupted on the eve of the Sochi Olympics and again on the eve of the World Cup championship in Russia? Or the tantrum-like, mostly ineffective, even counter-productive cascade of economic sanctions on Moscow?

But Russia is hardly isolated in world affairs, not even in Europe, where five or more governments are tilting away from the anti-Russian line of Washington, London, and Brussels. Despite sanctions, Russia's energy industry and agricultural exports are flourishing. Moreover, geopolitically, Moscow has many military and related advantages in regions where the new Cold War has unfolded. And no state with Russia's modern nuclear and other weapons is "punching above its weight." Contrary to Washington's expectations, the great majority of Russians have rallied behind Putin because they believe their country is under attack by the US-led West. Anyone with a rudimentary knowledge of Russia's history understands it is highly unlikely to capitulate under any circumstances.

10. Finally (at least as of now), there is the growing warlike "hysteria" fueled both in Washington and Moscow. It is driven by various factors, but television talk "news" broadcasts, as common in Russia as in the United States, play a major role. Only an extensive quantitative study could discern which plays a more lamentable role in promoting this frenzy—MSNBC and CNN or their Russian counterparts. The Russian dark witticism seems apt: "Both are worst" (*Oba khuzhe*). Again, some of this American broadcast extremism existed during the preceding Cold War, but almost always balanced, even offset, by informed, wiser opinions, which are now largely excluded.

Is my analysis of the graver dangers inherent in the new Cold War itself extremist or alarmist? Some usually reticent specialists would seem to agree with my general assessment. As I reported earlier, experts gathered by a centrist Washington think tank thought that on a scale of 1 to 10, there is a 5 to 7 chance of actual war with Russia. There are other such opinions. A former head of British M16 is reported as saying that "for the first time in living memory, there's a realistic chance of a superpower conflict." And a respected retired Russian general tells the same Washington think tank that any military confrontation "will end up with the use of nuclear weapons between the United States and Russia."[90,91]

A single Trump-Putin summit cannot eliminate these new Cold War dangers. But US-Soviet summits traditionally served three corollary purposes. They created a kind of security partnership—not a conspiracy—that involved each leader's limited political capital at home, which the other should recognize and not heedlessly jeopardize. They sent a clear message to the two leaders' respective national-security bureaucracies, which often did not favor détente-like cooperation, that the "boss" was determined and they must end their foot-dragging, even sabotage. And summits, with their exalted rituals and intense coverage, usually improved the media-political environment needed to enhance cooperation amid Cold War conflicts.

If a Trump-Putin summit achieves even some of those purposes, it might pull us back from the precipice.

Summitgate vs. "Peace"

July 11

WE NEED TO REMEMBER THAT US-RUSSIAN (Soviet and post-Soviet) summits are a long tradition going back to FDR's wartime meeting with Stalin in Tehran in 1943. Every American president since FDR met with a Kremlin leader in a summit-style format at least once. Several did so multiple times. The purpose was always to resolve conflicts and enhance cooperation in relations between the two powers. Some summits succeeded, some did not, but all were thought to be an essential aspect of White House-Kremlin relations. (At least one seems to have been sabotaged. The third Eisenhower-Khrushchev meeting, scheduled for Paris in 1960, was aborted by the Soviet shoot-down of a US U-2 spy plane sent, some think, by "deep state" foes of détente.)

As a rule, American presidents have departed for summits with bipartisan support and well-wishes. President Trump's upcoming meeting with Russian President Putin, in Helsinki on July 16, is very different in two respects. US-Russian relations have rarely, if ever, been more dangerous. And never before has a president's departure—in Trump's case, first for a NATO summit and then the one with Putin—been accompanied by allegations that he is disloyal to the United States and thus, as an "expert" told *CNN*'s Anderson Cooper on June 27, someone "we cannot trust." Such defamations were once hurled at presidents only by fringe elements in American politics.

Now, however, in a kind of manufactured Summitgate scandal, we are being told this daily by mainstream publications, broadcasts, and "think tanks." According to a representative of the Center for American Progress, "Trump is going to sell out America and its allies."[92] The *New York Times* and the *Washington Post* also feature "experts"—chosen accordingly—who "worry" and "fear" that Trump and Putin "will get along."[93,94] The *Times* of London, a transatlantic bastion of Russophobic Cold War advocacy, captures this bizarre mainstream perspective in a single headline: "Fears Grow Over Prospect of Trump 'Peace Deal' with Putin."[95]

Peace, it turns out, is to be feared. A Washington establishment against "peace" with Russia is, of course, what still-unproven Russiagate allegations have wrought. A New York magazine writer summed them up by warning that the Trump-Putin summit could be "less a negotiation between two heads of state than a meeting between a Russian-intelligence asset and his handler."[96]

The charge is hardly original, having been made for months on MSNBC by the questionably credentialed "intelligence expert" Malcolm Nance and, it seems, the selectively informed Rachel Maddow. Many other "experts" are doing the same. Considering today's perilous geopolitical situation, it is hard not to conclude again that much of the American political establishment, particularly the Democratic Party, would prefer trying to impeach Trump to averting war with Russia, the other nuclear superpower. For this too, there is no precedent in American history.

Not surprisingly, Trump's dreaded visit to the NATO summit has only inflated the uncritical cult of that organization, which has been in search of a purpose and ever more funding since the end of the Soviet Union in 1991. The *Times* declares that NATO is "the core of an American-led liberal world order," an assertion that might startle some non-military institutions involved in the "liberal world order" and even some liberals. No less puzzling is the ritualistic characterization of NATO, in the same July 9 *Times* editorial, as "the most successful military alliance in history." It has never—thankfully—gone to war as an alliance, only a few "willing" member (and would-be member) states under US leadership.

Even then, what counts as NATO's "great victories"? The police action in the Balkans in the 1990s? The disasters in the aftermath of Iraq and Libya? The longest, still-ongoing US war in history, in Afghanistan? NATO's only real mission since the 1990s has been expanding to Russia's borders, and that has resulted in less, not more, security for all concerned, as is evident today.

The only "Russian threats" since the end of the Soviet Union are ones provoked by US-led NATO itself, from Georgia and Ukraine to the Baltic states. Who has actually benefited? Only NATO's vast corporate bureaucracy, its some 4,000 employees housed in its new $1.2 billion headquarters in Brussels, and US and other weapons manufacturers who profit from each new member state. But none of this can be discussed in the American mainstream because Trump uttered a few words questioning NATO's role and funding, even though the subject has been on the agenda of Washington think tanks since the 1990s.

Also not surprising, and unlike on the eve of previous summits, mainstream media have found little place for serious discussion of today's dangerous conflicts between Washington and Moscow—those regarding nuclear weapons treaties, cyber-warfare, Syria, Ukraine, Eastern Europe, military confrontation in the Black Sea region, even Afghanistan. It's easy to imagine how Trump and Putin could agree on conflict-reduction and cooperation in most of these realms. But considering the way the *Post*, *Times*, and Maddow traduced a group of US senators who recently visited Moscow, it's much harder to see how the defamed Trump could implement any "peace deals."

Nor is the unreasonably demonized Putin without constraints at home, though none like those that may cripple Trump. The Kremlin's long-delayed decision to raise the pension age for men from age 60 to 65 and for women from 55 to 60 has caused Putin's popular ratings, though still high, to drop sharply. Popular protests are under way and spreading across the country.

On another level, segments of Russia's military-security establishment still believe Putin has never fully shed his admitted early "illusions" about negotiating with an always treacherous Washington. Like their American counterparts, they do not trust Trump, whom they too view as unreliable and capricious.

Russian "hard-liners" have made their concerns known publicly, and

Putin must take them into account.[97] As has been a function of summits over the decades, he is seeking in Trump a reliable national-security partner. Given the constraints on Trump and his proclivities, Putin is taking a risk, and he knows it.

Even if nothing more specific is achieved, everyone who cares about American and international security should hope that the Trump-Putin summit at least results in a restoration of the diplomatic process, longstanding "contacts" between Washington and Moscow," now greatly diminished, if not destroyed, by the new Cold War and by Russiagate allegations. Cold War without diplomacy is a recipe for actual war.

Trump as Cold War Heretic

July 18

On July 16, President Trump held a summit meeting with Russian President Putin in Helsinki. Given fraught US-Russian confrontations from Ukraine and the Baltic and Black Sea regions to Syria, Trump had a vital national-security duty to meet with the Kremlin leader in this august way.

As with previous summits, details will come later, but the two leaders seem to have reached several important agreements. They revived a US-Russian diplomatic process tattered by recent events, apparently including negotiations to reduce and regulate nuclear weapons and thus avert a new arms race. They suggested a joint effort to prevent Iran, Russia's Middle East partner, from threatening "Israeli security," as Putin put it, on that nation's borders. They also agreed on the need for a mutual effort to relieve the "humanitarian crisis" in Syria. And there was talk of promoting US-Russian "business ties," a nebulous aspiration considering Western economic sanctions on Russia. (This may have been a signal by Trump that he would not object, as

President Obama had, if the European Union diminished or terminated its sanctions.)

Historically, in once "normal" Cold War times, these summit achievements would have been supported, even applauded, across the American political spectrum. Predictably, they were not, eliciting only a torrent of denunciation. Idioms varied, from the *Washington Post* to MSNBC and CNN, but the once-stately *New York Times*, as is now its custom, set the tone. Its front-page headline on July 17 blared: "Trump, At Putin's Side, Questions U.S. Intelligence on 2016 Election." Another headline below explained, "Disdain for U.S. Institutions, and Praise for an Adversary."

The *Times*' "reporting" itself was fulsomely prosecutorial, scarcely mentioning what Trump and Putin had agreed on. Its columnists competed to indict the American president. An early entry, on July 16, before anything was actually known about the summit results, came from Charles Blow, whose headline thundered: "Trump, Treasonous Traitor." The title of Michelle Goldberg's entry, on July 17, was less alliterative: "Trump Shows the World He's Putin's Lackey."

As I predicted in the weeks prior to the summit, the same toxic message bellowed through the realm of mainstream print and cable "news": Trump had betrayed and shamed America before the entire world. As has been the case for years regarding "the Russia threat," almost no dissenting voices were included in the "discussions," apart from a few equally unqualified Trump representatives.

The media coverage, not Trump himself at the summit, was shameful. Media were reporting "news" of the kind they wanted, amplifying leading political figures, also across the spectrum. Senator John McCain, as usual on the subject of Russia, led the vigilante posse: "No prior president has ever abased himself more abjectly before a tyrant." He added for personal emphasis: "One of the most disgraceful performances by an American president in memory." Republican Senator Bob Corker, chair of the Foreign Relations Committee echoed McCain: "A sad day for our country and everyone knows it." Democratic Senator Charles Schumer agreed, demanding that the Senate "hold the president accountable for … Helsinki."[98,99]

Most unusual, given the traditional non-political public role of Intel chiefs was former CIA director John Brennan. He quickly appeared as Trump's prosecutor and judge, declaring that the president's behavior in Helsinki "exceeds the threshold" for impeachment and, still more, "was nothing short of treasonous."[100]

Only one major political figure stood apart from and above this political-media kangaroo court, Senator Rand Paul of Kentucky. Defending the
president's meeting with Putin on behalf of US national security, Senator
Paul emerged as the only visible statesman in Congress.[101] (In the past, the
US Senate was often led by distinguished statesmen, but now by the likes of
McCain, Lindsay Graham, and other members who rarely see a war, cold or
hot, they are not eager to fight.)

Yet unproven Russiagate allegations, of course, underlay this "Trump
Derangement Syndrome," as it has been termed. Hence the charges that
in Helsinki Trump allied with Putin "against US intelligence agencies."
(Commentators wanted, it seemed, for Trump to have publicly water-board-
ed Putin into a confession of having hacked the DNC's emails.) Despite
all we now know about the role of the CIA and other intelligence operatives in the past and in Russiagate, the pursuers of Trump, particularly liberal
Democrats and their media, wish to judge him by the rectitude of "agencies"
whose sharpest critics they once were. "Derangement," indeed.

So much so that an astonishing and exceedingly wise comment by Trump,
before and again at the summit, was barely noticed or derided. Trump's
remark relates directly to the most fateful question in US-Russian relations:
Why has the relationship since the end of the Soviet Union in 1991 evolved
into a new and more dangerous Cold War?

For 15 years, the virtually unanimous American bipartisan establishment answer has been that Putin, or "Putin's Russia," is solely to blame.
Washington's decision to expand NATO to Russia's border, bomb Moscow's
traditional ally Serbia, withdraw unilaterally from the Anti-Ballistic Missile
Treaty, carry out military regime change in Iraq and Libya, instigate the
2014 Ukrainian crisis and back the coup against the country's legitimate
president, and considerably more—none of these US policies, only "Putin's
aggression," led to the new Cold War.

This explanation has long been a rigid orthodoxy tolerating no dissent,
excluding, even slurring, well-informed proponents of alternative explanations. The result has been years without real public debate, without any
rethinking, and thus no revising of the triumphalist, winner-take-all "post–
Cold War" approach first adopted by President Bill Clinton in the 1990s and
continued in spirit and most practices ever since, from President George W.
Bush to President Obama. This unassailable orthodoxy has now led to a new
Cold War fraught with possibilities of actual war with Russia.

Suddenly, whether due to common sense or wise advice, President Trump
broke with this years-long, untrue, and increasingly dangerous orthodoxy.

In a tweet on July 15, he wrote, "Our relationship with Russia has NEVER been worse thanks to many years of U.S. foolishness and stupidity." Asked in Helsinki about the new Cold War, he formulated his explanation more diplomatically: "I hold both countries responsible. I think that the United States has been foolish. I think we've all been foolish. We should have had this dialogue a long time ago."[102]

Everything in those remarks by President Trump is factually and analytically true, profoundly so. But they are also outright heresy and perhaps the real reason his meeting with Putin is being so denounced by political and media elites that have made their careers on orthodox dogmas at the expense of American and international security.

Heretics are scorned or worse, but sometimes in history they prevail. However strongly Americans may disapprove of President Trump's other words and deeds, everyone, anywhere across our political spectrum, who wishes to avoid war with Russia—again, conceivably nuclear war—must support and encourage his heresy until it is no longer heresy, until the full debate over reckless US policy since the 1990s finally ensues, and until that approach changes, as should have happened, as Trump said, "a long time ago." It is not too late, but it may be the last chance.

Sanction Mania

August 15

THE BIPARTISAN SENATE CAMPAIGN TO IMPOSE new, "crushing" sanctions on Russia needs to be seen in historical context. Broadly understood, sanctions have been part of US policy toward Russia for much of the past 100 years.

During the Russian civil war of 1918–1920, President Woodrow Wilson sent American troops to fight against the emerging Soviet government. Though the "Reds" were the established government of Soviet Russia by

1921, Washington continued to deny the USSR diplomatic recognition until President Franklin D. Roosevelt established formal relations in 1933. During much of the 40-year Cold War, the United States imposed various sanctions on its superpower rival, mainly related to technological and military exports, along with periodic expulsions of diplomats and "spies" on both sides.

Congress's major political contribution was the 1975 Jackson–Vanik Amendment. The legislation denied Moscow customary trading status with the United States, primarily because of Kremlin restrictions on Jewish emigration from the Soviet Union. Indicative of how mindlessly habitual US sanctions had become, Jackson–Vanik was nullified only in late 2012, long after the end of the Soviet Union and after any restrictions on Jews leaving (or returning to) Russia. Even more indicative, it was immediately replaced, in December 2012, by the Magnitsky Act, which purported to sanction individual Russian officials and "oligarchs" for "human-rights abuses." The Magnitsky Act remains law, supplemented by additional sanctions leveled against Russia as a result of the 2014 Ukrainian crisis and Moscow's annexation of Crimea.

Looking back over this long history, there is no evidence that any US sanctions ever significantly altered Moscow's "behavior" in ways that were intended. Or that they adversely affected Russia's ruling political or financial elites. Any pain inflicted fell on ordinary citizens, who nonetheless rallied "patriotically" around the Kremlin leadership, most recently around President Putin. Historically, sanctions were not problem-solving measures advancing American national security but more akin to temper tantrums or road rage, making things worse, than to real policy-making.

Why, then, Washington's new bout of sanction mania against Moscow, especially considering the very harsh official Russian reaction expressed by Prime Minister Dmitri Medvedev—Obama's onetime "reset" partner and generally considered the most pro-Western figure in Russia's political hierarchy? Medvedev called the Senate's proposed measures "a declaration of economic war" and promised that the Kremlin would retaliate.

One explanation is an astonishing assumption recently stated by Michael McFaul, the media-ubiquitous former US ambassador to Moscow and a longtime Russia scholar: "To advance almost all of our core national security and economic interests, the US does not need Russia."[103] Such a statement by a former or current policy-maker and intellectual may be unprecedented in modern times—and is manifestly wrong.

US "core" interests "need" Russia's cooperation in many vital ways. They include avoiding nuclear war; preventing a new and more dangerous arms race; guarding against the proliferation of weapons and materials of mass destruction; coping with international terrorists; achieving lasting peace in Syria and elsewhere in the Middle East; fostering prosperity and stability in Europe, of which Russia is a part; promoting better relations with the Islamic world, of which Russia is also a part; and avoiding a generation-long confrontation with a formidable new alliance that already includes Russia, China, Iran, and other non-NATO countries. If McFaul's assumption is widespread in Washington, as it seems to be, we are living in truly unwise and perilous times.

A second assumption is no less myopic and dangerous: the Kremlin is weak and lacks countermeasures to adopt against the new sanctions being advocated in Washington. Consider, however, the following real possibilities:

Moscow could sell off its billions of dollars of US Treasury securities and begin trading with friendly nations in non-dollar currencies, both of which it has already begun to do. It could restrict, otherwise undermine, or even shut down many large US corporations long doing profitable business in Russia, among them Citibank, Cisco Systems, Apple, Microsoft, PepsiCo, McDonald's, Johnson & Johnson, Procter & Gamble, Ford Motor Co., and even Boeing. It could end titanium exports to the United States, which are vital to American civilian and military aircraft manufacturers, including Boeing. And terminate the sale of rocket engines essential for NASA space travel and US satellite operations. The world's largest territorial country, Russia could charge US airlines higher tariffs for their regular use of its air space or ban them altogether, making them uncompetitive against other national carriers. Politically, the Kremlin could end its own sanctions on Iran and North Korea, alleviating Washington's pressure on those governments. And it could end the Russian supply transit to US troops fighting in Afghanistan used since the early 1990s.

None of this seems to have been considered by Washington's sanction zealots. Nor have four other circumstances:

Sanctions against Russia's "oligarchs" actually help Putin, whom the US political-media establishment so despises and constantly indicts. For years, he has been trying to persuade many of the richest oligarchs to repatriate their offshore wealth to Russia. Few did so. Now, fearful of having their assets abroad frozen or seized by US measures, more and more are complying.

Second, new sanctions limiting Moscow's ability to borrow and finance investment at home will retard the country's still meager growth rate. But the Kremlin coped after the 2014 sanctions and will do so again by turning away even more from the West and toward China and other non-Western partners, and by developing its own capacity to produce sanctioned imports. (Russian agricultural production, for example, has surged in recent years, becoming a major export industry.)

Third, already unhappy with existing economic sanctions against Russia, European multinational corporations—and thus Europe itself—may tilt even farther away from their capricious "transatlantic partner" in Washington, who is diminishing their vast market in the East.

And fourth, waging "economic war" is one impulsive step from breaking off all diplomatic relations with Russia. This too is actually being discussed by Washington zealots. Such a rupture would turn the clock back many decades, now in an era when there is no "globalization," or international security, without Russia.

What reason do Washington's fanatical Cold Warriors, most of them in the Senate, give for imposing new sanctions? Their professed reasons are various and nonsensical. Some say Russia must be sanctioned for Ukraine, but those events happened four years ago and have already been "punished." Others say for "Russia's aggression in Syria," but it was Putin's military intervention that destroyed the Islamic State's terrorist occupation of much of the country and ended its threat to take Damascus, an intervention that greatly benefited America and its allies, including Europe and Israel. Still others insist the Kremlin must be sanctioned for its "nerve agent" attack on Sergei Skripal and his daughter in the UK. But the British government's case against the Kremlin is less than cogent, as a reader of articles in *Johnson's Russia List* will understand.

Ultimately, the new bout of sanction mania is in response to Russia's alleged "attack on American democracy" during the 2016 presidential election. In reality, there was no "attack"—no Pearl Harbor, no 9/11, no Russian parachuters descending on Washington—only the kind of "meddling" and "interference" in the other's domestic politics that both countries have practiced, almost ritualistically, for nearly a hundred years. Whatever "meddling" Russian actors did in 2016 may well have been jaywalking compared to the Clinton administration's highly intrusive political and financial intervention on behalf of Russian President Yeltsin's reelection campaign in 1996.

We are left with the actual and perverse reason behind the new anti-Russian sanctions campaign: to thwart and punish President Trump for his policy of "cooperation with Russia." And Putin for having met and cooperated with Trump at their July Helsinki summit. This bizarre reality is more than a whisper. According to a *New York Times* "news analysis," as well as other published reports, a "bipartisan group of senators, dismayed that Mr. Trump had not publicly confronted Mr. Putin over Russia's election meddling, released draft legislation" of new sanctions against Moscow. "Passage of such a bill would impose some of the most damaging sanctions yet."[104]

Leave aside that it is not Russian "meddling" which is delegitimizing our elections but instead these fact-free allegations themselves. Remember instead that for doing what every American president since Eisenhower has done—meet with the sitting Kremlin leader in order to avoid stumbling into a war between the nuclear superpowers—in effect both Trump and Putin are being condemned by the Washington establishment, including by members of Trump's own intelligence agencies.

Who, as a result, will avert the prospect of war with Russia, a new Cuban missile–like crisis, conceivably in the Baltic region, Ukraine, or Syria? Not any leading representative of the Democratic Party. Not the current Russophobic "bipartisan" Senate. Not the most influential media outlets that amplify the warmongering folly almost daily. In this most existential regard, there is for now, like it or not, only President Donald Trump.

What the Brennan Affair Reveals

August 22

JOHN BRENNAN, FORMER PRESIDENT OBAMA'S CIA director, is back in the news. When President Trump met with Russian President Putin in Helsinki, he was scathingly criticized by much of the US political-media establishment. Brennan, however, went much farther, characterizing Trump's press conference with Putin as "nothing short of treasonous." Trump revoked Brennan's security clearance, the continuing access to classified information usually accorded to former security officials. In the political-media furor that followed, Brennan was widely heroized as an avatar of civil liberties and free speech and Trump denounced as their enemy.

Leaving aside the missed occasion to discuss the "revolving door" involving former US security officials using their permanent clearances to enhance their lucrative positions outside government, what the subsequent political-media furor obscures is truly important and ominous.

Brennan's allegation was unprecedented. No US top-level intelligence official had ever before accused an American president of treason, still more in collusion with the Kremlin. (Impeachment charges against Presidents Nixon and Clinton, I have already noted, did not involve Russia.) Brennan clarified his charge: "Treasonous, which is to betray one's trust and to aid and abet the enemy." Coming from Brennan, a man presumed to be in possession of dark secrets, as he strongly hinted, his accusation was fraught with alarming implications.[105,106]

Brennan made clear he hoped for Trump's impeachment, but in another time, and in many other countries, his allegation would suggest Trump should be removed from the presidency urgently by any means, even a coup. No one, it seems, noted this extraordinary implication with its tacit threat to American democracy. (On July 19, 2016, the *Los Angeles Times* saw fit to print an article, by James Kirchik, suggesting that the military might have to remove Trump if he were to be elected, thereby having the very dubious distinction of predating Brennan.)

Why did Brennan, a calculating man, risk making a charge that might reasonably be interpreted as sedition? The most plausible explanation is that he sought to deflect growing attention to his role as the godfather of the entire Russiagate narrative, as I suggested back in February. If so, we need to know Brennan's unvarnished views on Russia.

They were set out, alarmingly, in a *New York Times* article on August 17. Brennan's views are those of Joseph McCarthy and J. Edgar Hoover in their prime. Western "politicians, political parties, media outlets, think tanks and influencers are readily manipulated, wittingly and unwittingly, or even bought outright, by Russian operatives...not only to collect sensitive information but also to distribute propaganda and disinformation... I was well aware of Russia's ability to work surreptitiously within the United States, cultivating relationships with individuals who wield actual or potential power...These Russian agents are well trained in the art of deception. They troll political, business and cultural waters in search of gullible or unprincipled individuals who become pliant in the hands of their Russian puppet masters. Too often, those puppets are found."

All this, Brennan assures readers, is based on his "deep insight." All the rest of us, it seems, are constantly vulnerable to "Russian puppet masters" under our beds, at work, in our relationships, on our computers. Clearly, there must be no "cooperation" with the Kremlin's grand "Puppet Master," as Trump said he wanted early on. (People who wonder what and when President Obama knew about the unfolding Russiagate saga need to ask why he would keep a person like Brennan so close for so long.)

And yet, scores of former intelligence and military officials rallied around this unvarnished John Brennan, even though some said they did not entirely share his opinions. This too is revealing. They did so, it seems clear enough, out of their professional corporate identity, which Brennan represented and Trump was degrading by challenging the intelligence agencies' Russiagate allegations against him.

It's a misnomer to term these people representatives of a hidden "deep state." In recent years, they have been amply visible on television and newspaper op-ed pages. Instead, they see and present themselves as members of a fully empowered and essential branch of government. This too has gone largely undiscussed while nightingales of that branch—such as David Ignatius and Joe Scarborough in the pages of the the *Washington Post*—have been in full voice.[107,108]

The result is to further criminalize any advocacy of "cooperating with Russia," or détente, as Trump sought to do in Helsinki with Putin. A Russophobic hysteria is sweeping through the American political-media establishment, from Brennan and—pending actual evidence against her—those who engineered the arrest of the young Russian woman Maria Butina (imagine how this endangers young Americans networking in Russia) to senators preparing new "crippling sanctions" against Moscow and editors and producers at the *Times*, *Post*, CNN, MSNBC, and other media outlets. As the dangers of actual war with Russia grow, the capacity of US policy-makers, above all the president, are increasingly diminished. To be fair, Brennan may be only a symptom of this American crisis, some say the worst since the Civil War.

There was a time when many Democrats, certainly liberal Democrats, could be counted on to resist this kind of hysteria and spreading neo-McCarthyism. (Brennan's defenders accuse Trump of McCarthyism, but Brennan's charge of treason without any evidence was quintessential McCarthy.) After all, civil liberties, including freedom of speech, are directly involved—and not only Brennan's and Trump's.

But Democratic members of Congress and pro-Democratic media are in the forefront of the new anti-Russian hysteria, with few exceptions. A generally liberal historian tells CNN viewers that "Brennan is an American hero. His tenure at the CIA was impeccable. We owe him so much." In the same vein, two *Post* reporters write of the FBI's "once venerated reputation."[109,110]

Is this the historical amnesia I pointed out earlier? Is it professional incompetence? A quick Google search would reveal Brennan's less than "impeccable" record, FBI misdeeds under and after Hoover, as well as the Senate's 1976 Church Committee report of CIA and other intelligence agencies' very serious abuses of their power. Or have liberals' hatred of Trump nullified their own principles? The critical-minded Russian adage would say, "All three explanations are worst."

"Vital" US Moles in the Kremlin

August 29

FOR NEARLY TWO YEARS, MOSTLY VACUOUS, malignant Russiagate allegations have drowned out truly significant news directly affecting America's place in the world. In recent days, for example. French President Emmanuel Macron declared: "Europe can no longer rely on the United States to provide its security." He called instead for a broader kind of security "and particularly doing it in cooperation with Russia."[111] About the same time, German Chancellor Angela Merkel and Russian President Putin met to expand and solidify a crucial energy partnership by agreeing to complete the Nord Stream 2 pipeline from Russia, despite US attempts to abort it. Earlier, on August 22, the Afghan Taliban announced it would attend its first ever major peace conference—in Moscow, without US participation.

Thus does the world turn, and not to the wishes of Washington. Such news would normally elicit extensive reporting and analysis in the American mainstream media. But amid all this, on August 25, the ever-eager *New York Times* published yet another front-page Russiagate story—one that if true would be sensational. Hardly anyone seemed to notice.

According to the *Times'* regular Intel leakers, US intelligence agencies, presumably the CIA, has had multiple "informants close to...Putin and in the Kremlin who provided crucial details" about Russiagate for two years.

Now, however, "the vital Kremlin informants have largely gone silent." The *Times* laced the story with the usual misdeeds attributed to Putin and equally untrustworthy commentators, as well as the mistranslated Putin statement incorrectly having him say all "traitors" should be killed. But the article's sensation is that the US government had moles in Putin's office.

Skeptical or credulous readers will react to the *Times* story as they might. Actually, a lesser version of it first appeared, which I noted earlier, in the *Washington Post*, an equally hospitable Intel platform, on December 15, 2017. I found it implausible for much the same reasons I had previously found implausible the Steele dossier, also purportedly based on "Kremlin sources." But the *Times'* expanded version of the mole story raises new questions.

If US intelligence really had such a priceless asset in Putin's office— the *Post* story implied only one, the *Times* writes of more than one—imagine what they could reveal about Enemy No. 1 Putin's perhaps daily intentions abroad and at home. Why, then, would any American Intel official disclose this information to any media at the risk of being charged with a treasonous capital offense? And now more than once? Or, since "the Kremlin" closely monitors US media, at risk of having the no less treasonous Russian informants identified and severely punished? Presumably, this why the *Times'* leakers insist that the "silent" moles are still alive, though how they know we are not told. All of this is even more implausible, and the *Times* article asks no critical questions.

Why leak the mole story again, and now? Stripped of extraneous financial improprieties, failures to register as foreign lobbyists, tacky lifestyles, and sex having nothing to do with Russia, the gravamen of the Russiagate narrative remains what it has always been: Putin ordered Russian operatives to "meddle" in the US 2016 presidential election in order to put Donald Trump in the White House, and Putin is now plotting to "attack" the November congressional elections in order to get a Congress he wants. The more Robert Mueller and his supporting media investigate, the less actual evidence turns up. And when it seemingly does, it has to be massaged or misrepresented, lest it seem to be Russiagate without Russia.

Nor are "meddling" and "interfering" in the other's domestic policy new in Russian-American relations. Tsar Aleksandr II intervened militarily on the side of the Union in the American Civil War. President Woodrow Wilson sent troops to fight the Reds in the Russian Civil War. The Communist International, founded in Moscow in 1919, and its successor organizations financed American activists, electoral candidates, ideological schools, and pro-Soviet bookstores for decades in the United States. With the support of the Clinton administration, American electoral advisers encamped in Moscow to help rig Russian President Boris Yeltsin's reelection in 1996.

And that's the more conspicuous "meddling" apart from the decades-long "propaganda and disinformation" churned out by both sides, often via forbidden short-wave broadcasts to Soviet listeners. Unless some conclusive evidence appears, Russian social media and other meddling in the 2016 presidential election was little more than old habits in modern-day forms. (Not incidentally, the *Times* story suggests that US Intel had been hacking the Kremlin, or trying to do so, for many years. This too should not shock us.)

The real novelty of Russiagate is the allegation that a Kremlin leader, Putin, personally gave orders to affect the outcome of an American presidential election. In this regard, Russiagaters have produced even less evidence, only suppositions without facts or much logic. With the Russiagate narrative being frayed by time and fruitless investigations, the "mole in the Kremlin" may have seemed a ploy needed to keep the conspiracy theory moving forward toward Trump's removal from office by whatever means. Hence the temptation to play the mole card again now as yet more investigations generate smoke but no smoking gun.

The pretext of the *Times* story is that Putin is preparing an attack on the November 2018 elections, but the once "vital," now silent, moles are not providing the "crucial details." Even if the story is entirely bogus, consider the damage it is doing. Russiagate allegations have already delegitimized a presidential election and a presidency in the minds of many Americans. The *Times'* expanded version may do the same to congressional elections and the next Congress. If so, there is an "attack on American democracy"—not by Putin or Trump, as we saw previously, but by whoever godfathered and repeatedly inflated Russiagate.

As I have argued earlier, such evidence that exists seems to point to John Brennan and James Clapper, President Obama's head of the CIA and of National Intelligence respectively, even though attention has been focused on the FBI. If nothing else, the *Times's* new "mole" story reminds us of how central "intelligence" actors have been in this saga.

Arguably, Russiagate has brought us to the worst American political crisis since the Civil War and the most dangerous relations with Russia in history. Until Brennan, Clapper, their closest collaborators, and others deeply involved are required to testify under oath about the real origins of Russiagate, these crises will continue to grow.

Afterword

"The Owl of Minerva spreads its wings only with the falling of dusk."

—Hegel

War With Russia?, LIKE A BIOGRAPHY of a living person, is a book without an end. The title is a warning—akin to what the late Gore Vidal termed "a journalistic alert-system"[112]—not a prediction. Hence the question mark. I cannot foresee the future. The book's overarching theme is informed by past and current facts, not by any political agenda, ideological commitment, or magical prescience.

To restate that theme: The new US-Russian Cold War is more dangerous than was its 40-year predecessor, which the world survived. The chances are even greater, as I hope readers already understand, that this one could result, inadvertently or intentionally, in actual war between the two nuclear superpowers. Herein lies another ominous indication. During the preceding Cold War, the possibility of nuclear catastrophe was in the forefront of American mainstream political and media discussion, and of policy-making. During the new one, it rarely seems to be even a concern.

As I finish War *With Russia?*, the facts and mounting crises they document grow worse, especially in the US political-media establishment where, as readers also understand, I think the new Cold War originated and has been repeatedly escalated. Consider finally a few examples from the latter months of 2018, some of them not unlike political and media developments during the run-up to the US war in Iraq or, historians have told us, when the great powers "sleepwalked" into World War I:

• Russiagate's core allegations, none of them yet proven, had become a central part of the new Cold War. If nothing else, they severely constrained President Trump's capacity to conduct crisis-negotiations with Moscow while they further vilified Russian President Putin for having, it was widely asserted, personally ordered "an attack on America" during the 2016 presidential campaign. Hollywood liberals, it will be recalled, quickly omitted the question mark, declaring, "We are at war." In October 2018, the would-be titular head of the Democratic Party, Hillary Clinton, added her voice to this reckless allegation, flatly stating that the United States was "attacked by a foreign power" and equating it with "the September 11, 2001, terrorist attacks."[113]

Clinton may have been prompted by another outburst of *New York Times* and *Washington Post* malpractice. On September 20 and 23 respectively, those exceptionally influential papers devoted thousands of words, illustrated with sinister prosecutorial graphics, to special retellings of the Russiagate narrative they had assiduously promoted for nearly two years, along with the narrative's serial fallacies, selective and questionable history, and factual errors. (In the front of its issue, the *Times* reporters explained that "the goal of the project ... was to bring people back to a story they might have abandoned.")

Again, for example, the now-infamous Paul Manafort was said to have been "pro-Kremlin" during the period at issue when in fact he was pro-European Union. Again, the disgraced General Michael Flynn was accused of "troubling" contacts when he did nothing wrong or unprecedented in having conversations with a Kremlin representative on behalf of President-elect Trump. Again, the two papers criminalized the idea that "the United States and Russia should look for areas of mutual interest," once the premise of détente. And again, the *Times*, while assuring readers its "Special Report" was "what we now know with certainty," buried the nullifying acknowledgment deep in its some 10,000 words: "No public evidence has emerged showing that [Trump's] campaign conspired with Russia." (The white-collar criminal indictments and guilty pleas cited were so unrelated they again added up to Russiagate without Russia.)

Astonishingly, neither paper gave any credence to an emphatic statement by Bob Woodward—normally considered the most authoritative chronicler of Washington's political secrets—that after two years of research he had found "no evidence of collusion" between Trump and Russia. Endorsing the *Post* version, a prominent historian even assured his readers that the widely discredited anti-Trump Steele dossier—the source of so many allegations—was "increasingly plausible."[114,115]

Nor were the *Times*, *Post*, and other print media alone in these practices, which continued to slur dissenting opinions. CNN's leading purveyor of Russiagate allegations tweeted that an American third-party presidential candidate had been "repeating Russian talking points on its interference in the 2016 election and on US foreign policy."[116] Another prominent CNN figure was, so to speak, more geopolitical, warning, "Only a fool takes Vladimir Putin at his word in Syria," thereby ruling out US-Russian cooperation in that war-torn country.[117] Much the same continued almost nightly on MSNBC.

For most mainstream media outlets, Russiagate had become, it seemed, a kind of cult journalism that no counter-evidence or analysis could dent—though I try in this book—and thus itself increasingly a major contributing factor to the new Cold War. Still more, what began two years earlier as complaints about Russian "meddling" in the US presidential election became by October 2018, for the *New Yorker*[118] and other publications, including the *Times* and the *Post*, an accusation that the Kremlin had actually put Donald Trump in the White House. For this seditious charge, there was also no convincing evidence—nor any precedent in American history.

• At a higher level, by fall 2018, current and former US officials were making nearly unprecedented threats against Moscow. The ambassador to NATO threatened to "take out" any Russian missiles she thought violated a 1987 treaty, a step that would certainly risk nuclear war.[119] The Secretary of the Interior threatened a "naval blockade" of Russia.[120] In yet another Russophobic outburst, the soon-to-retire ambassador to the UN, Nikki Haley, declared that "lying, cheating and rogue behavior" are a "norm of Russian culture."[121]

These may have been outlandish statements by untutored political appointees, though they inescapably again raised the question: who was making Russia policy in Washington—President Trump with his avowed policy of "cooperation" or someone else?

But how to explain, other than as unbridled extremism, comments by a former US ambassador to Moscow, himself a longtime professor of Russian politics and favored mainstream commentator? According to him, Russia had become a "rogue state," its policies "criminal actions," and the "world's worst threat." It had to be countered by "preemptive sanctions that would go into effect automatically"—"every day," if deemed necessary.[122] Considering "crushing" sanctions then being prepared by a bipartisan group of US senators "to punish" Moscow[123], this would be nothing less than a declaration of permanent war against Russia: economic war, but war nonetheless.

• Meanwhile, other new Cold War fronts were becoming more fraught with hot war, none more so than Syria. On September 15, 2018, Syrian missiles accidentally shot down an allied Russian surveillance aircraft, killing all fifteen crew members. The cause was combat subterfuge by Israeli warplanes in the area. The reaction in Moscow was indicative—and potentially ominous.

At first, Putin, who had developed good relations with Israel's political leadership, said the incident was an accident caused by the fog of war. His own Defense Ministry, however, loudly protested that Israel was responsible. Putin quickly retreated to a more hardline position, and in the end vowed to send to Syria Russia's highly effective S-300 surface-to-air defense system, a prize long sought by both Syria and Iran.

Clearly, Putin was not the ever "aggressive Kremlin autocrat" unrelentingly portrayed by US mainstream media. Still a moderate in the Russian context, he again made a major decision by balancing conflicting groups and interests. In this instance, he accommodated longstanding hardliners ("hawks") in his own security establishment.

The result was yet another Cold War tripwire. With the S-300s installed in Syria, Putin could in effect impose a "no-fly-zone" over large areas of the country, which had been ravaged by war due, in no small part, to the combat presence of several foreign powers. (Russia and Iran were there legally; the United States and Israel were not.) If so, it meant a new "red line" that Washington and its ally Israel would have to decide whether or not to cross. Considering the mania in Washington and in the mainstream media, it was hard to be confident restraint would prevail.

All this unfolded around the third anniversary of Russia's military intervention in Syria in September 2015. At that time, Washington pundits denounced Putin's "adventure" and were sure it would fail. Three years later, "Putin's Kremlin" had destroyed the vicious Islamic State's grip on significant parts of Syria, for which it still got no credit in Washington; all but restored President Assad's control over most of the country; and made itself the ultimate arbiter of Syria's future. In keeping with his Russia policy, President Trump probably was inclined to join Moscow's peace process, though it was unlikely the mostly Democratic Russiagate party would permit him to do so. (For perspective, recall that, in 2016, presidential candidate Hillary Clinton called for a US no-fly zone over Syria to defy Russia.)

• As I finish this book, another Cold War front also became more fraught. The US-Russian proxy war in Ukraine acquired a new dimension. In addition to the civil war in Donbass, Moscow and Kiev began challenging the other's ships in the Sea of Azov, near the vital Ukrainian port of Mariupol. Trump was being pressured to supply Kiev with naval and other weapons to wage this evolving maritime war, yet another potential tripwire. Here too the president should instead have put his administration's weight behind the long-stalled Minsk peace accords. But that approach also seemed ruled out by Russiagate, which by October 2018 included yet another *Times* columnist, Frank Bruni, branding all such initiatives by Trump "pimping for Putin."[124]

After five years of extremism exemplified by these more recent examples of risking war with Russia, there remained, for the first time in decades of Cold War history, no countervailing forces in Washington—no pro-détente wing of the Democratic or Republican Party, no influential anti-Cold War opposition anywhere, no real public debate. There was only Trump, with all the loathing he inspired, and even he had not reminded the nation or his own party that the presidents who initiated major episodes of détente in the 20th century were also Republicans—Eisenhower, Nixon, Reagan. This too seemed to be an inadmissible "alternative fact."

And so the eternal question, not only for Russians: what is to be done? There was a ray of light, though scarcely more. In August 2018, Gallup asked Americans what kind of policy toward Russia they favored. Even amid the torrent of vilifying Russiagate allegations and Russophobia, 58 percent wanted "to improve relations with Russia" as opposed to 36 percent preferring "strong diplomatic and economic steps against Russia."[125]

This reminds us that the new Cold War, from NATO's eastward expansion and the Ukrainian crisis to Russiagate, has been an elite project. Why, after the end of the Soviet Union in 1991, US elites ultimately chose Cold War rather than partnership with Russia is a question beyond the limits of this book and perhaps my ability to answer. As for the role of US intelligence elites, what I have termed Intelgate, efforts are still under way to disclose it fully, and being thwarted.[126]

A full explanation of the Cold War choice would include the political-media establishment's needs—ideological, foreign-policy, budgetary, among others—for an "enemy."[127] Or, Cold War having prevailed for more than half of US-Russian relations during the century since 1917, maybe it was habitual. Substantial "meddling" in the 2016 election by Ukraine and Israel, to illustrate the point, did not become a political scandal.[128] In any event, once this approach to post-Soviet Russia began, promoting it was not hard. The legendary humorist Will Rogers quipped back in the 1930s, "Russia is a country that no matter what you say about it, it's true." Back then, before the 40-year Cold War and nuclear weapons, the quip was funny, but no longer.

Whatever the full explanation, many of the consequences I have analyzed along the way continue to unfold, not a few unintended and unfavorable to America's real national interests. Russia's turn away from the West, its "pivot to China," is now widely acknowledged and embraced by many Moscow policy thinkers.[129] Even European allies occasionally stand with Moscow against Washington.[130] The US-backed Kiev government still covers up who was really behind the 2014 Maidan "snipers' massacre" that brought it to power.[131] Mindless US sanctions have helped Putin to repatriate oligarchic assets abroad, an estimated $90 billion already in 2018.[132] Mainstream media persist in distorting Putin's foreign polices into something "that even the Soviet Union never dared to try."[133] And when an anonymous White House "insider" exposed in the *Times* "the president's amorality," the only actual policy he or she singled out was Russia policy.[134]

I have focused enough on the surreal demonizing of Putin—the *Post* even managed to characterize popular support for his substantial contribution to improving life in Moscow as "a deal with the devil"—but it is important to note that this "derangement" is far from world-wide.[135] Even a *Post* correspondent conceded that "the Putin brand has captivated anti-establishment and anti-American politicians all over the world."[136] A worldly British journalist confirmed that as a result "many countries in the world now look for a reinsurance policy with Russia."[137] And an American journalist living in Moscow reported that "ceaseless demonization of Putin personally has in fact sanctified him, turned him into the Patron Saint of Russia."[138]

Again, in light of all this, what can be done? Sentimentally, and with some historical precedents, we of democratic beliefs traditionally look to "the people," to voters, to bring about change. But foreign policy has long been the special prerogative of elites. In order to change Cold War policy fundamentally, leaders are needed. When the times beckon, they may emerge out of established, even deeply conservative, elites, as did unexpectedly Ronald Reagan and Mikhail Gorbachev in the mid-1980s. But given the looming danger of war with Russia, is there time? Is any leader visible on the American political landscape who will say to his or her elite and party, as Gorbachev did, "If not now, when? If not us, who?"

We also know that such leaders, though embedded in and insulated by their elites, hear and read other, non-conformist voices, other thinking. The once-venerated American journalist Walter Lippmann observed, "When all think alike, no one is thinking." This book is my modest attempt to inspire more thinking.

Endnotes

1. *Wall Street Journal*, May 11, 2018
2. Quoted in *Wall Street Journal*, October 14, 2014
3. Quoted in *New York Times*, March 5, 2014
4. *Washington Post*, March 14, 2014
5. *New York Times*, March 15, 2014
6. Fred Hiatt, July 15, 2013
7. *Times Literary Supplement*, June 22, 2018, p. 2
8. Keith Gessen, *New York Times*, June 18, 2018
9. Michael Wines, *New York Times*, February 20, 2000; and BBC News, June 16, 2001
10. *New York Times*, December 15, 2004
11. Bret Stephens, *Wall Street Journal*, November 28, 2006
12. Joel Goldberg, Fox Cable News, March 9, 2018
13. Robert Kagan, *wsj.com*, September 7, 2018
14. Blaine Harden, *New York Times*, September 24, 2017
15. Quoted by Carol Morello, et al., *Washington Post*, July 20, 2018
16. Anne Applebaum, *Washington Post*, July 8, 2018
17. Robert Legvold reviewing Chris Miller, *Putinomics*, in *Foreign Affairs*, May/June 2018, p. 201
18. Martin Gilman interviewed by Mark Whitehouse, *bloomberg.com*, July 9, 2018
19. *Times* editorial, July 17, 2018
20. Quoted by John McCormack and Jenna Lifts, *The Weekly Standard*, July 30, 2018, p. 16

21. David Leonhardt, September 19, 2018
22. Nadezhda Azhgikhina, *TheNation.com*, April 10, 2018
23. Marlene Laruelle, *Johnson's Russia List*, September 10, 2018
24. Kremlin.ru, May 7, 2018
25. See, for example, the Moscow *Times* report in *Johnson's Russia List*, September 7, 2018.
26. See, e.g., Susan B. Glasser, *politico.com*, December 22, 2017
27. Frank-Walter Steinmeier, quoted in *AFP*, June 18, 2016
28. For the former quote, see Patrick Armstrong and Steve Shabad, *Johnson's Russia List*, July 31, August 1, August 4, 2014.
29. For the latter, youtube.com/watch?v=TS17WJW8qE
30. Carlos Lozada, *Washington Post*, June 17, 2018
31. Joe Scarborough, *Washington Post*, August 13, 2018
32. Kremlin.ru, May 25, 2018
33. Kremlin.ru, March 8, 2018
34. Quoted by Andrew Kuchins, *Johnson's Russia List*, December 8, 2017
35. Timothy Heritage, *Reuters.com*, September 30, 2009
36. *New York Times*, November 12, 2017
37. *Washington Free Beacon*, July 26, 2017
38. Ivan Katchanovski, orientalreview.org/2015/09/11
39. For this episode, see my *Failed Crusade: America and the Tragedy of Post-Communist Russia*, exp. pb edition, 2001
40. cfr.org/report/contain-russia
41. *washingtonpost.com*, May 23, 2017
42. *nytimes.com*, May 24, 2017
43. the guardian.com/uk-news/2017/apr/13/british-spies-first-to-spot-trump-team-links-russia
44. theguardian.com/us-news/2018/jan/30/trump-russia-collusion-fbi-cody-shearer-memo
45. *washingtonpost.com*, February 13, 2018
46. *nytimes.com*, February 18, 2018
47. *nytimes.com*, February 18, 2018;
48. newyorker.com/news/news-desk/reading-the-mueller-indictment-a-russian-american-fraud
49. *Washington Post*, February 21, 2018
50. *nytimes.com*, February 19, 2018;
51. thedailybeast.com/msnbc-analyst-john-heilermann-suggests-devin-nunes-compromised-by-russia

52. opcw.org/news/article/opcw-marks-completion-of-destruction-of-russian-chemical-weapons-stockpile/
53. nbcnews.com, May 28, 2017
54. *reuters.com*, May 23, 2017
55. quoted in *New York Times*, June 9, 2017
56. Masha Gessen, *New York*, July 25-August 7, 2016, p. 45
57. Tim Dickinson, April 3, 2018
58. Jerry Brewer, February 24, 2018
59. Ross Douthat quoting Anne Applebaum, *New York Times*, March 23, 2014
60. Jill Dougherty, cnn.com, March 29, 2018
61. Eli Lake, *bloomberg.com*, March 9, 2018
62. Mark Galeotti, *guardian.com*, March 23, 2018
63. Thomas Graham, *Financial Times*, June 1, 2015
64. national interest.org/feature/america-russia-back-basics-21901
65. hoover.org/research/vladimir-putin-and-russian-soul
66. Michael Farquhar, *washingtonpost.com*, September 26, 2014
67. Gregory Feifer, *foreignpolicy.com*, June 22, 2015
68. *Washington Post*, January 5, 2018
69. *Washington Post*, August 13, 2018
70. *washingtonpost.com*, April 23, 2018
71. *washingtonpost.com*, April 20, 2018
72. *Washington Post*, July 8, 2018
73. nationalinterest.org/feature/stumbling-war-russia-25089
74. *bloomberg.com*, April 24, 2018
75. gordonhahn.com/2016/03/09
76. Shmuel Herzfeld, Haaretz.com, September 16, 2018
77. jta.org, January 28, 2018
78. alternet.org/grayzone-project/john-mccain-and-paul-ryan-hold-good-meeting-veteran-ukrainian-nazi-demagogue-andriy
79. amnesty.org/en/latest/news/2018/03/ukraine
80. *theintercept.com*, May 18, 2018
81. *New York Times*, May 16, 2018
82. *New York Times*, May 21, 2018
83. slate.com/articles./news-and-politics/cover-story/2016/07
84. yahoo.com/news/u-s-intel-officials-probe-ties-between-trump-adviserand-kremlin-175046002
85. motherjones.com/politics/2016/10
86. *New York Times*, August 5, 2016

87. *New York Times*, August 10, 2016
88. un.org, April 13, 2018
89. Eugene Rumer, carnegieendowment.org, April 17,2018
90. Quoted by Gerald F. Seib, *wsj.com*, April 16, 2018
91. nationalinterest.org, April 4, 2018
92. Max Bergmann quoted by C.J. Hopkins, counterpunch.com, July 10, 2018
93. Mark Landler, *New York Times*, June 29, 2018
94. Ann Gearan, *Washington Post*, June 30, 2018
95. *Times* of London, June 28, 2018
96. Jonathan Chait, *New York*, July 9-22, 2018
97. Lyle Goldstein, nationalinterest.org, July 14 2018
98. Quoted in *New York Times*, July 17, 2018
99. Quoted in thehill.com, July 26, 2018
100. Quoted in *New York Times*, July 17, 2018
101. See Burgess Everett and Elana Schhor, *politico.com*, July 16, 2018
102. Quoted in *New York Times*, July 17, 2018
103. Tweet, August 10, 2018
104. Neil MacFarquhar, *nytimes.com*, August 12, 2018
105. Quoted by Felicia Sonmez and Carol Morello, *washingtonpost.com*, August 19, 2018
106. Cited by Mattathias Schwartz, *New York Times Magazine*, June 27, 2018
107. *washingtonpost.com*, July 26, 2018
108. *washingtonpost.com*, August 12, 2018
109. Douglas Brinkley with Don Lemon, August 17, 2018
110. Matt Zapotosky and Devlin Barrett, *washingtonpost.com*, August 14, 2018
111. TASS, August 27, 2018
112. Victor Navasky and Katrina vanden Heuvel, eds., *The Best of The Nation*, New York, 2000, p. xvii
113. Reported by Felicia Sonmez, *washingtonpost.com*, October 2, 2018
114. Woodward, realclearpolitics, September 14, 2018
115. Kai Bird, *The Washington Post*, September 30. 2018
116. Jim Sciutto, Tweet, May 1, 2018
117. Nic Robertson, CNN.com, September 18, 2018
118. Jane Mayer, October 1, 2018, pp. 18-26
119. Kay Bailey Hutchison quoted by businessinsider.com, October 2
120. southfront.org, September 30
121. Michael Schwirtz, *nytimes.com*, September 17
122. Michael McFaul, *washingtonpost.com*, September 28, 2018
123. *Washington Post* editorial, September 9

124. *New York Times*, October 7
125. news.gallup.com/poll/241124
126. On September 22, 2018, the *Times* reported that Deputy Attorney General Rod Rosenstein had proposed secretly recording President Trump. Rosenstein denied the report, but the *Times* did not retract its story. On the same day, the *Times* also reported that intelligence agencies had dissuaded the president from declassifying documents directly related to Intelgate.
127. Two leading geopolitical thinkers have presented at least partial explanations. See John Mearsheimer, *Foreign Affairs*, September/October 2014; and Anatol Lieven, *Survival*, Vol. 60, issue 5, 2018
128. See, e.g., Kenneth P. Vogel and David Stern, *politico.com*, January 11, 2017; and Aaron Mate, *TheNation.com*, December 5, 2017
129. Sergei Karaganov, *Johnson's Russia List*, September 24, 2018
130. Andrew Rettman, euobserver.com, September 26, 2018
131. Ivan Katchanovski, *Johnson's Russia List*, September 17, 2018
132. Tyler Durden, ibid., September 24, 2018
133. Jackson Diehl, *Washington Post*, March 19, 2018
134. *New York Times* opinion page, September 6, 2018
135. Anton Troianovski, *Washington Post*, September 9, 2018
136. Anton Troianovski, *washingtonpost.com*, July 12, 2018
137. Patrick Cockburn, *Johnson's Russia List*, September 24, 2018
138. Jeffrey Tayler, *theatlantic.com*, March 18, 2018

Index

About the Author

Stephen F. Cohen passed away on September 18, 2020, at the age of 81. He was Professor Emeritus of Politics at Princeton University, where for many years he was also director of the Russian Studies Program, and Professor Emeritus of Russian Studies and History at New York University. He grew up in Owensboro, Kentucky, received his undergraduate and master's degrees at Indiana University, and his Ph.D. at Columbia University.

Cohen's other books include *Bukharin and the Bolshevik Revolution: A Political Biography*; *Rethinking the Soviet Experience: Politics and History Since 1917*; *Sovieticus: American Perceptions and Soviet Realities*; (with Katrina vanden Heuvel) *Voices of Glasnost: Interviews With Gorbachev's Reformers*; *Failed Crusade: America and the Tragedy of Post-Communist Russia*; *Soviet Fates and Lost Alternatives: From Stalinism to the New Cold War*; and *The Victims Return: Survivors of the Gulag After Stalin*.

For his scholarly work, Cohen received several honors, including two Guggenheim fellowships and a National Book Award nomination.

Over the years, he had also been a frequent contributor to newspapers, magazines, television, and radio. His "Sovieticus" column for *The Nation* won a 1985 Newspaper Guild Page One Award and for another *Nation* article the 1989 Olive Branch Award. For many years, Cohen was a consultant and on-air commentator on Russian affairs for CBS News. With the producer Rosemary Reed, he was also project adviser and correspondent for three PBS documentary films about Russia: *Conversations With Gorbachev*; *Russia Betrayed?*; and *Widow of the Revolution*.

Cohen visited and lived in Soviet and post-Soviet Russia regularly for more than forty years.

He lived in New York City with his wife, Katrina vanden Heuvel, who is editor and publisher of *The Nation*. They have a daughter, Nicola (Nika). Cohen also has two other children, Andrew and Alexandra.